Domesticating the Airwaves

Domesticating the Airwaves

Broadcasting, Domesticity and Femininity

Maggie Andrews

continuum

Continuum International Publishing Group

The Tower Building
11 York Road
London SE1 7NX

80 Maiden Lane
Suite 704
New York, NY 10038

www.continuumbooks.com

First published 2012

British Library Cataloguing-in-Publication Data
A catalogue record for this book is available from the British Library.

ISBN: HB: 978-1-4411-0571-4
PB: 978-1-4411-7272-3

Library of Congress Cataloging-in-Publication Data
A catalog record for this book is available from the Library of Congress.

Typeset by Fakenham Prepress Solutions, Fakenham, Norfolk NR21 8NN
Printed and bound in India

Contents

Illustrations

Acknowledgements

This book carries a special thank you to the very helpful staff at the BBC Written Archives, the British Film Institute and Mass Observation Archives, their assistance to researchers is invaluable. *Domesticating the Airwaves* has been a long while in the researching and writing and thanks are also therefore due to many friends, students and colleagues who have exchanged and shared ideas with me along the way. Special thanks also go to Lynda Jerrom for proofreading, to Andy Medhurst and Fan Carter for many conversations and much encouragement over the years.

Without the unerring practical and emotional support of my husband Neil this book would not have been written and no words can thank him enough. Finally this book is dedicated to the next generation – Lucia, Edu, Erin-Marie and Florence – whose consumption, pleasure and interest in broadcast media's association with domesticity is already being established by *Big Cook, Little Cook* (2003–) on CBeebies.

Introduction

Television is a domestic medium, not only consumed in the home but, along with other media, central to the home; as Silverstone has pointed out, television is 'part of home – part of its idealisation, part of its reality' (1994, p. 28). Furthermore a brief look at contemporary television programme schedules, or an intense day of channel hopping, provides plenty of evidence that television is preoccupied with domesticity. Drama, soaps and sit-coms are predominantly set in domestic spaces, interviews carried out on sofas in pseudo-domestic settings and a significant part of many schedules is given over to programmes about purchasing and improving homes or domestic skills such as cleaning, cooking, child-rearing, shopping and gardening. This book argues that an understanding of this phenomenon requires an historical analysis; for the roots of broadcasting's preoccupation with domesticity, lifestyle celebrities and domestic skills was firmly established with the introduction of radio into the 1920s and 1930s home, which was identified as a feminine sphere.

In the inter-war era, the perceived female listener and her concerns influenced the nature of broadcasting, dictating the tone and linguistic framework of inter-war broadcasters – 'domesticating the airwaves' and contributing to the low status of broadcast media in the ensuing years. The inter-relationship between the domestic setting of radio and the cultural associations of home and femininity have been explored in the influential work of Lacey on German Radio (1996) and Hilmes on USA radio (2006), and their work has framed the approach taken in this book in trying to analyse gender, broadcasting and domesticity in an integrated fashion and with detailed attention as to how this inter-relationship is played out in particular texts.

This book draws upon the historiographical approaches of social, women's and gender history (Roberts, 1984; Tebbutt, 1994; Summerfield, 1996; Abbott, 2003) which have explored women's domestic experience and the construction of separate spheres (Vickery, 1993) and Feminist Cultural History which has in recent years displayed a growing fascination with domesticity, in the work of Giles (2004), for example. Although Beetham's (1996) and Winship's (1987) texts have pointed to the role of women's magazines' in the construction of femininity and domesticity there has in historical work been a tendency to downplay the contribution of broadcasting to these areas. This book suggests that although cultural analysis of contemporary culture, such as Hollows (2008) have integrated an analysis of broadcasting with that of domesticity, historians have been slower to explore these areas and therefore attempts to encourage a wider engagement with broadcasting: a hitherto neglected area of feminist cultural history.

Traditional histories of broadcasting have tended to focus on broadcasting institutions and particularly the BBC and key figures such as Reith (Briggs, 1995. Crissell, 2002). Problematically, however, as Street (1996, p. 9) has pointed out, there is a tendency for the history of broadcasting to become the history of the BBC, while oral histories, newspapers and magazines suggest that in the past, as now, people listened to the radio, watched the TV, channel hopping as the mood took them. Other historical approaches have charted the development of radio and latter television genres (Kilborn, 2000; Wagg, 1998) or interrogated the role that broadcasting played in the development of citizenship and politics (Scannell and Cardiff, 1991). It will be suggested that a historical approach, which focuses upon the relationship between broadcasting and domesticity, will offer an alternative cultural history of the mediums. The work of Moores (2000) on radio and new media technologies, Spigel (1997) on television in the USA), and Silverstone (1994) and Morley (1986, 2000) on television in Britain do indeed explore the integration of broadcasting media into the domestic space, how it became integrated into tensions and power battles of that domestic space and comes to define domestic space. Silverstone, Hirsch and Morley argue that the media pose a range of problems for the regulation of the porous boundaries of domestic spaces, which 'are expressed generally in the regular cycle of moral panics around new media or media content, but on an everyday level, in individual households they are expressed through decisions to include and exclude media content and to regulate within the household' (1992, p. 20). As ground-breaking and influential as Silverstone, Hirsch and Morley's research is, it works within a paradigm that problematically lays emphasis on the significance of media's effects on the home, with less attention given to how the domestic space in which broadcasting was consumed shaped the nature of broadcasting itself. Alternatively, Douglas' work on radio in the USA challenged scholars to understand not merely how radio influenced the everyday lives of ordinary people, producing a new soundscape, but to see broadcasting not as a one-way medium but as structured and moulded by 'the imaginary listener with whom the broadcaster is always in dialogue' (2004, p. 18). To understand how the feminine domestic sphere of the home literally *domesticated the airwaves*, it is necessary to look closely at the actual broadcast media texts which were produced, the linguistic tone and visual style, the narrative focus or the preoccupations of these texts which points to a more complex cultural history.

Domesticity is also grounded in materiality. For the large number of rural women who had to carry all domestic water into their homes from external wells, taps or delivery points in the 1930s and 1940s, or the mother of small children coping in a tower block in the latter part of the twentieth century, domesticity is not merely a discursive construction, even if it is experienced and shaped by discourse. Consequently it is important to draw upon the changing social history of housing provision and consumer culture (Hartley, 1999) in the twentieth century to understand its inter-relationship with broadcasting. The inter-war period experienced significant private house building, particularly in the Midlands and the South; however the overall inadequacy of housing stock was to be exasperated by wartime bombing. The post-war period saw a growing expectation that the government and local authorities would, in the main, shoulder responsibility for the provision of housing for the working-class, a task they struggled to fulfil adequately. The ideological revolution of Thatcherism, however, undermined this and firmly established a link between idealizations of the domestic home and property ownership. A link that is integral to late twentieth and early twenty-first century lifestyle programming on television.

Domesticity and the home is not merely bricks and mortar, it is a site of complex and changing social relationships, power struggles and identity formation which have been caught up in wider shifts in social relationships in the twentieth and twenty-first centuries, such that Chaney points out that the 'home may well be a part of a larger gamut of living arrangements … one's family will be dispersed through several homes and households' (2002, p. 57). By the end of the twentieth century there was a greater emphasis on the individual and a transformation of intimacy (Giddens, 1992) leading to a greater diversity in households and families. No longer was domesticity perceived to be inhabited by white, middle-class, heterosexual couples with 2.4 children; instead, by the beginning of the twenty-first century, broadcasting represents, within the mainstream and prime-time viewing in both soap operas and lifestyle programming such as *Come Dine With Me* (2005), a greater diversity in terms of race, ethnicity, class, regionality and sexuality.

It is important however to see broadcasting, radio and television texts, not merely as a reflection of social change but also utilizing a constructionist perspective, as playing a role in constituting that change. In the 1920s and 1930s the entry of 'the wireless' into the domestic space of the home dramatically changed men and women's experience of domesticity, offering education and reducing isolation through a shared listening experience and a sense of belonging to wider imagined communities. But broadcasting did not merely change domestic leisure patterns, from its earliest incarnation it discursively intervened in constructing domesticity. Whatever the intentions of individual broadcasters, or indeed advertisers and governmental departments, this cannot be seen as a purely educative process or even a project of governance. Domesticity is itself a contested, fluid and shifting concept and idealzation; individuals, however, construct their views of domesticity through the languages, discourses and images that broadcasting offers to them (Hall, 1997).

The methodological approaches used in the research for this book have been eclectic: reflecting its multi-disciplinary approach. Textual analysis of a range of radio and television texts has been undertaken; although many of the radio programmes have been studied through the scripts which is all that remains of most 1930s and 1940s radio programmes. Popular newspapers and magazines, including daily newspapers and the *RadioTimes* and *Radio Pictorial*, have also been examined, to identify the discourses that surrounded both broadcasting in general and particular programmes. Files, memos and other printed materials at the BBC Written Archive (BBCWA) and the British Film Institute (BFI) have been used to shed light on some of the debates and tensions that surrounded the production of particular media texts and personalities. Finally, oral history interviews, Mass Observation (MO) Archive located at Sussex University and autobiographies have provided an alternative and more personal approach to the material.

This book is organized chronologically with a strong reliance on case studies; consequently the book is selective: there are gaps as well as inclusions as themes are developed. The first chapter is introductory, establishing the relationship between domesticity, broadcasting and femininity in the inter-war period, how the radio, entered the home, defined the home and moulded itself to fit into the home; how the domestic setting of its reception and the female viewer determined that domesticity would be a key preoccupation of broadcasting. The second chapter engages with competing discourses of domesticity in the BBC's *Household Talks*, listened to by numerous housewives each morning in the inter-war years. It provides an example of broadcasting's earliest engagements with an attempt to provide domestic education and information; arguing that the contested nature of the domestic discourses in this programming undermined the educative intentions of the BBC and the ability of radio to operate as a form of governance.

Chapter Three focuses on two early lifestyle celebrities – the restaurateur, Marcel Boulestin and the gardener Mr Middleton – whose place in the mainstream evening schedules of radio and television provided domestic-focused entertainment. It will be suggested that they provide a forerunner for the construction and popularity of lifestyle celebrities of the following years. The media personas they presented were polysemic; their appeal rested upon an ambivalence in relation to masculinity, sexuality and the exact class and geographical identities they both inhabited.

Chapter Four argues that in wartime – when domesticity was under fire, fractured and extended – the wireless played a role in linking both domesticity and the family to spaces, places and individuals displaced from 'the radio's hearth'. Wartime established radio and the BBC at the heart of the nation, however, as Chapter Five demonstrates, there were both changes and continuities in the post-war era. Although a range of popular radio programmes with a strong focus on domesticity were initiated, including *Woman' Hour* (1946–) *Mrs Dales Diary* (1948–69) and *The Archers* (1950–). By the of the 1960s, television, and more importantly commercial television, had become the main source of domestic entertainment. With the introduction of ITV in 1955 consumer-culture was more in evidence in a range of texts and domesticity became an over-the-top performance, particularly with the rising popularity of the television cook Fanny Craddock. This perfomivity of domesticity began to undermine the association between domesticity and femininity; for if domesticity was a performance that had to be learned perhaps it was not a natural or innate characteristic of women.

Chapter Six looks thematically at how in the 1960s and 1970s television broadened the range of domestic 'realities' it portrayed in soaps, docudrama and documentaries, placing working-class domesticities into the homes of the nation in text such as *Coronation Street* (1960), *Cathy Come Home* (1966) and *The Family* (1974). It will be argued that although this extended the domesticities which viewers witnessed, the challenge that this presented to middle-class viewers was undermined by the three tropes used to represent working-class domesticity: nostalgia, the working-class as victims of material circumstances (especially housing problems) and finally the working-class as sexually amoral or aberrant.

Chapters Seven and Eight look at the end of the twentieth and early twenty-first centuries. Chapter Seven argues that, in the wake of the social and legal change of the 1960s and 1970s, domesticity in both political discourse and a range of broadcast media texts is seen as in crisis, a focus for intervention from politicians and chat-show hosts. However, as political discourse turned its attention to domestic governance, both the boundary between domesticity and politics became blurred and its association with femininity loosened. Domestic concerns, issues and discourses increasingly became intertwined with news and political programming. Finally, in Chapter Eight it will be argued that with the increasing domestic turmoil portrayed in chat shows, soap operas, reality TV and drama the ideal of domesticity was both displaced into a striven for future or onto a nostalgic past. In everyday lives in contemporary culture television bears witness to more diverse and contested domesticities but also ones which are the subject of ethical debates.

Chapter One

Domesticating the airwaves

> To come home from work on a November evening, through the wet confusion of the city, the humid press of bus or train or tram, the rain dimmed streets that lead to the lights of your own home; to close the door behind you, the curtains drawn against the rain and the fire glowing on the hearth – that is one of the pleasures of life. And it is when you are settled by your own fireside with no inclination to stir from it until you get up to go to bed, that you most appreciate the entertainment broadcasting can bring.
>
> You can sit by the fireside and hear great music, rousing songs, talks on every subject under the sun: plays constructed to appeal to the ear alone; your favourite comedians and dance bands … The radio has brought to your fireside resources that can hardly be too highly prized on a typical November night. (*Radio Times*, Fireside number, 15 November 1935)

The BBC began broadcasting in Britain in November 1922; however radio's shift from the spectacular to the mundane occurred in the 1930s (Moores 2000) with 'nine million receivers under licence by 1939, and regular audiences significantly larger than this' (Crisell, 1997, p. 17). Initially the cost of the radio and its licence was detrimental for many so that purchase and consumption of wirelesses were restricted to: the middle-classes, the technically competent who made their own radios and those who listened at village clubs, in schools or the listening groups that were set up to encourage active engagement with the wireless and the educational talks provided in the evenings by the BBC. However, as Richard Lambert (1938), editor of the *Listener,* pointed out, 'the majority of listeners took no notice of group listening, they did not want to be educated by the radio at all' (1940). What listeners

RADIO TIMES November 18, 1938 Vol. 61 No. 790 Registered at the G.P.O. as a Newspaper 9

Radio Times Home Number

Broadcasting House does not really look quite so homely as Mervyn Wilson has made it in his drawing above, but it might well do. When all is said and done, broadcasting, with all its elaborate mechanism, is based on and aimed at the home.

That is the great difference between radio and other forms of entertainment, though it is not only entertainment that radio brings into the home. It is because their voices are heard in the home that so many talkers, announcers, teachers, and preachers have become real friends to many listeners who have never seen them.

Try to imagine what would have happened to broadcasting if wireless sets had not been simple enough and cheap enough to use at home—if we had had to do our listening in a crowd, as we go to the theatre and the cinema. Broadcasting would have become a mass entertainment, as theatre and cinema are. It might have been grander, more imposing, more sophisticated, but could it have been so intimate, so friendly? And how many homes would have still been lonely—how many 'shut-ins' would have missed the companionship that broadcasting brings!

But there is no need to labour the point. Every listener knows what broadcasting is to *his* home; and in his article over the page Mr. Elliott has some penetrating things to say about what it means to try to bring comfort to people in their own homes by means of the voice alone. In this number of the RADIO TIMES we have tried to give you some idea of what home means to the broadcasters themselves. You will read their own memories of their homes—the homes of their childhood, or the homes to which they return after their broadcasts.

There are homes on both sides of the microphone, and broadcasting is the connecting link between them, even if there is not as yet a wistaria-covered porch in front of Broadcasting House!

Mervyn Wilson's cartoon of Broadcasting House, the home of the BBC, with wisteria growing up the building and the washing hanging on the line. From the Home Number of the *Radio Times*, November 1938 wanted was to be entertained by the wireless in their own homes, a new form of domestic leisure, and by the 1930s radio was established as a mass domestic medium, widely available for all classes and primarily listened to in the intimate space of the home.

This popularity of radio as a new form of mass domestic leisure was facilitated in the 1930s by the mass production of easy-to-use sets, which in the words of an advertising slogan of the period spelled a, 'Good-bye to knob twiddling' and an end to the era when wireless was the domain of technically confident men engaged in solitary listening on home-made crystal sets with headphones. One explanation for the initial unpopularity of the radio was 'the way the technology was gendered' (Bailey, 2009, p. 53) and 'one East End woman was so indignant that her husband preferred fiddling with his new wireless to coming to bed she hurled a book at him' (Bourke, 1994, p. 77). This gradually changed, although even in 1938 the *Radio Pictorial* had an article on 'Tuning-in without tears' (15 April 1938) featuring a young woman in a flowery dress accompanied by the caption 'See how easy it is?' which simultaneously acknowledged both how problematic early radio tuning had been and the significance of women in the 1930s domestic radio audience.

As domestic space was, in the inter-war period, emotionally and symbolically constructed as a feminine sphere – a place of mundane belonging for women – a perception developed among many in the 1930s that, as radio was listened to in this feminine domestic sphere, women would have more listening hours available to them and would become radio's key audience. Advertising by radio manufactures such as HMV and imagery in the *Radio Times* and *Radio Pictorial* magazines frequently portrayed women listening to the radio – the very image of domestic contentment. Such contentment was not shared by discourses that circulated around radio's entry into the home; anxieties surrounded the domestic associations of radio, the domestication of the medium itself and its focus and mode of address. Anxieties which were not entirely allayed even as the radio began to be seen as a tool to combat domestic loneliness, intrinsic to the idealization of home and as a medium for the education of housewives.

RADIO AND THE DOMESTIC: A SOURCE OF ANXIETY IN THE 1930S

The domestic reception of the medium, and the consequent assumption of a high proportion of woman listeners, evoked much anxiety and debate in the inter-war period and beyond, epitomized in a contribution by A. A. Thomas to one of the annual Women's Issues of *Radio Times* under the title 'March of the Women' (1 November 1934, p. 18). In what he described as a 'nightmare', Broadcasting House (by then the home of the BBC) was taken-over by women who announced; 'henceforth we are going to run the whole show, it is our duty to expel the entire male staff'. Given the very limited number of women who worked within the BBC and who, as Curran and Seaton point out 'were never announcers, rarely presenters' (2003, p. 123) and that in the inter-war period 'the proportion of women in administrative and creative posts declined' (2003, p. 123) Thomas' nightmare was unfounded. Nevertheless, towards the end of the narrative he describes his plight: 'I am the only unhappy male left in the building … They are coming for me now. Beautiful (but inexplicable) hands are seizing me. I am being carried, microphone and all to the top floor. The lift – well yawns. They are about to throw me down the lift well' (*Radio Times*, 1 November 1934, p. 38).

Even if the potential Freudian readings of this extract are set aside, it expresses anxieties worthy of consideration. Less than 10 years after women are finally enfranchised on the same terms as men, this was the nightmare; that a public institution – the BBC – might be overrun by women. A nightmare that started, I would suggest, not within the institutional working practices but with the female listeners and the anxieties about domestic and feminine associations that surrounded the wireless in the 1930s and that continue to pervade popular discourses that surround broadcasting today. Indeed Carey (1992) has described how many intellectuals despised the wireless as having supposedly middle-brow, suburban and emasculating associations and Broddy (1994) refers to the 'emasculinisation of broadcasting' as on a parallel with the emasculinisation of men through the depression when unemployment forced them into the domestic sphere. The gendered domestic associations of radio have arguably discursively structured broadcasting's low status ever since. Spigel charts similar anxieties expressed about radio in the USA as late as the 1940s and 1950s when Philip Wylie's book entitled *Generation of Vipers* suggested that 'women had somehow gained control of the airwaves' and made 'radio listening into a passive activity that threatened manhood, and in fact civilization', adding: 'The radio is mom's final tool, for it stamps everyone who listens to it with the matriarchal brand' (Wylie, 1955, quoted in Spigel, 2003, p. 333).

Certainly 'Radio brought revolutionary changes to the lives of millions of women' as the MP Margaret Bondfield pointed out when praising 'the company of sound' and 'what radio could do for women' in the *Radio Times* (12 November 1937). She went on to suggest that 'the greatest change of all is the fact that the slender wire brings the world and its affairs into the tiny kitchen and living rooms which hitherto had isolated so many housekeepers in the performance of their duties'. Thus the entry of the wireless into the home dramatically changed men and women's experience of domesticity, offering entertainment and education while reducing isolation as Mrs Mackay, who lived in the wilds of Colleden Moor, explained to the *Radio Times*, 'You cannot understand what the wireless means to us up here … ' (24 March 1939, p. iv). The domestic space into which radio was broadcast and in which listeners, such as Mrs Mackay, enjoyed listening, was and remains as much a discursively as a physically constructed space: the focus of fantasies, which operate both in the imagination and the mundane minutiae of everyday life. The discourses, such as those that construct domestic space and domesticity, are subject to challenge, unpicking, reworking and negotiation, ultimately unstable and contradictory; as Hall points out 'ultimately meaning begins to slip and slide ... to drift, or be wrenched, or inflected in new directions. New meanings are grafted onto old ones' (1997, p. 270).

Furthermore the 'domestic' is, as Silverstone (1994, pp. 25–51) points out, a relational concept, which partially explains its fluid and shifting nature: the private world of the domestic space relies upon an ostensible 'otherness' of the public world. Symbolically domesticity is constructed as a place of mundane belonging, discursively linked to women and femininity. Its supposed 'other 'is the public world of commercialism, politics and municipality, where a sense of belonging for women is often tentative, uncertain and conditional. Giles (2004) argues that:

> the feminine has frequently been represented as a refuge from the repressions and alienations of modernity, a symbolic space of redemption, nature and authenticity in which the injuries of modern living can be healed. In this version, the apparently timeless feminine values of intimacy and authenticity are set against the masculine experience of alienation and dehumanisation that constitute modern history. (p. 9)

The wireless, a symbol of modernity, crossed the boundaries between public and private, masculine and feminine spheres; as a 1935 documentary on the BBC pointed out: 'the microphone provided a new means for distributing opinion and knowledge to millions of listeners'. Into the domestic space of 'authenticity and intimacy' the radio brought politicians or, as they were described in this documentary, 'opinion leaders ... Ramsay MacDonald, Stanley Baldwin, George Lansbury' entered into the home via the airwaves. Thus women listeners found themselves engaging with politics, gaining a familiarity with and experiencing the public world, from the 'safety' of their homes. There was thus a blurring of the boundaries of public and private. Grenville Robbins, writing in the *Radio Times*, exclaimed that 'It suddenly struck me how much my home resembles a wireless set'. He went on to explain that different rooms offered different atmospheres as different programmes and stations also did (31 March 1933, p. 20). Anxieties about broadcasting's capacity to enable public worlds to enter the private domain of the home, to threaten the idealized status of the domestic space as a safe retreat from the world, have informed and continue to inform discursive debates that surround broadcasting. What is suitable, acceptable, desirable or tasteful to 'enter' the home has taxed and continues to tax the great, the good and the chattering classes. However, the wireless did not merely penetrate the home (to use the BBC's terminology from the inter-war period); just as importantly the home and the domestic seeped into the public space of broadcasting. The reception of the wireless in the home, the perceived listeners and their concerns influenced the nature of broadcasting – *domesticating the airwaves*.

THE DOMESTICATION OF THE MEDIUM: HOMES BOTH SIDES OF THE MICROPHONE

The BBC was, technically speaking, set up as a monopoly broadcaster and became a Public Corporation in the turbulent economic crisis of the 1920s – a status which, as Curran and Seaton point out, rested upon its 'rejection of both market forces and politics in favour of efficiency and planned growth controlled by experts' (2003, p. 112). Under the leadership of its Director General John Reith the BBC developed the ethos of Public Service Broadcasting (PSB), which entered the homes of the listening public with the avowed aim of 'Educating, Informing and Entertaining' them. The relationship between the experts who ran this national station and the domestic listeners it addressed was, in this era, complex, fluid and contested. There was thus not only a rejection of market forces – and the model of commercial radio espoused in the USA – but also a cultural commitment to become an institution of national significance, which was recognized when the GPO

'The Radio Home as some famous artists might have seen it.' An indication of the multiplicity of ways in which the idea of the radio home could be interpreted. From *Radio Times*, November 1935

films unit made a documentary about the BBC in 1935 entitled: *BBC Voice of a Nation*. In this documentary the BBC, uncertain of its status as a new technological medium – a cuckoo in the nest of many homes – frequently presented itself and its broadcasters via language and metaphors related to domesticity. The documentary emphasized the significance of Broadcasting House as a 'house' and home and explained 'you who pay your 10/- a year to own this house'. Likewise the *Radio Times* introduced listeners to Alexandra Palace to their listeners as 'The Home of Television' (23 October 1935).

Mervyn Wilson's cartoon in a special Home Number of the *Radio Times* in 1938 visually endorses the domestication of Broadcasting House – it is portrayed festooned with a washing line, with climbing plants growing up it. Furthermore, the editor of that issue explained, 'there are homes both sides of the microphone and broadcasting is the link between them even if there is not as yet a wisteria–covered porch in front of Broadcasting House!' (14 November 1938, p. 2). Interestingly this imagery, with wisteria around the door, is not easily seen as a symbol of modernity; rather like the political rhetoric of Baldwin at the time, it draws upon an association with the rural and the idealization of the rural home and cottage which, as Howkins (1987) has argued, was central to notions of Englishness in the inter-war era. A fascinating fluidity between the urban and the rural was seen in the same year when the BBC instigated a new comedy serial, *Bandwagon*, starring Arthur Askey. The fictional setting of the programme was a flat at the top of Broadcasting House in which the residents kept a goat. Thus the domestication of Broadcasting House was taken one stage further when the significance and centrality of the domesticity to constructions of national consciousness were linked to this new national institution – the BBC smoothing the entry of 'the wireless' into the domestic space of the home but also fluidifying the boundaries of public and private spheres, with analogies going both ways. The general public was consequently fascinated with the personal and intimate details of those who worked in both Broadcasting House and Alexandra Palace. The popular press and everyday gossip avidly followed, for example, the dismissal of the BBC's Chief Engineer – Peter Erskley – when he was cited in a divorce case in 1929. For those who worked at the BBC this was perhaps an unexpected and more problematic consequence of the domestication of the airwaves.

There is perhaps in the history of broadcasting a tendency to focus upon institutions: predominantly the BBC. However, people then, as now, were active discerning listeners, searching for programmes that appealed to their taste, apt to respond back to, snipe at, ignore, make fun of and finally switch off radio broadcasts that had no appeal. Broadcast programming included: talks, news, variety and panel programmes, quizzes, plays, documentaries, and a range of music and concerts. Radio listening in the 1930s involved channel hopping – between the BBC's regional services, their national programme known as the 'Home Service' and foreign commercial stations such as Radio Normandie from 1931 or Radio Luxemburg from 1933, as Street (2006) has documented. My own research with oral interviewees, in autobiographies and at Mass Observation Archives (MOA) provides evidence to support this. Indeed elderly interviewees remember with affection every word of The Ovaltineys' theme song from Radio Luxemburg, although they often struggle to remember many BBC programmes. 'The Ovaltiney's jingle was infectious. It still comes uninvited to my mind at times … I am sure no high court judge would have dared feign ignorance of it' (Street, 2006, p. 273). Signature tunes and jingles were an intrinsic element of commercial broadcasting's advertising and sponsored programmes principally directed at the domestic consumer with household products such as, Cadbury's, Bird's Custard, Force Breakfast cereal jostling for the housewives' attention alongside Kraft Cheese, Stork margarine, Brooke Bond Tea, Andrews Liver Salts, Macleans toothpaste, Ovaltine and Horlicks which announced. 'you will be happy, healthy and wealthy, If you start with Horlicks each day … (Street, 2006, p. 273) Through advertising, domesticity was also a central focus of commercial broadcasting.

Radio Luxembourg was particularly popular on Sundays, when a Variety Listening Barometer indicated that nearly half of all listeners tuned in (BBC Written Archives [BBCWA], R9/9/1); a consequence of the BBC schedule's tendency to 'improve listeners rather than provide the sort of programme they wanted … what people felt especially in need of was output that was light-hearted and relaxing. What Reith decreed they should get – were programmes which did not begin until 12:30 and consisted entirely of religious services, serious talks and classical music' (Crissell, 1997, p. 46). If the BBC tended to ignore the taste of their audience on a Sunday, they did attempt to conform to a growing awareness of all broadcasters of their domestic audience, listening at home by the fire, which necessitated developing a 'conversational' rather than 'declamatory' tone: 'intimate rather than intimidating' (Cardiff, 1986, p. 230) 'which attempted to emulate the language of domestic interior within the public or near public sphere '(Sparkes, 2004, p. 6). Indeed, as Lacey points out, 'As radio matured, it became more familiar in address, …. the prevailing atmosphere of a public meetings was gradually replaced by the consciously studied informality befitting the familiar setting' (1996, p. 193). The domesticity of the listener 'was celebrated in numerous articles in *Radio Times* and in its occasional "Home" and "Fireside" issues' (Cardiff, 1986, p. 229) and there was a growing expectation that the ideal broadcaster, as Eckersley pointed out, needed 'to approach the microphone with the idea of sitting down in the best armchair and talking interestingly' (*Daily Mail*, 2 March 1932). The development of a private rather than public lexicon of speech for broadcasting's domestic audience was emphasized by Hilda Matheson, one time BBC Talks Director, who pointed out that 'Early experiments with broadcast talks showed that it was useless to address the microphone as if it were a public meeting … the person sitting at the other end expected the speaker to address him personally

(1933, p. 75). Radio required a linguistic framework involving the use of 'we' and 'our', imaginary dialogues and questions, as if the broadcaster was chatting to the listener at their fireside; the airwaves needed to be domesticated not merely in topic or focus but in tone, as Basil Maine explained, 'because radio is enjoyed in the house and by families gathered around the fire, they must be addressed and entertained as if the broadcaster were one of their company ... they are right to expect as much' (1939, p. 42). The importance of the personal address to the domestic listener and the 'shared pleasures of the hearth' (Frith, 1983) was also noted by Tom Harrison who, following a discussion with Roy Speer, a BBC variety producer, recorded that 'He and James Dyrenforth (author of *Adolph in Blunderland*, etc.) think that radio should not be aimed at a studio audience but at a home audience, and that the studio audience breaks up the intimacy' (MOA, TC 74 /4/A).

By the end of the 1930s, across all stations and countries, broadcasting increasingly attempted to develop a more informal and domestic mode of address, although the BBC, self-consciously aware of its role as a public institution, found this more tortuous than its commercial competitors who also appealed to their listeners by offering 'glamour and escapism' (Nicholas, 1996, p. 4) alongside celebrity news and soap operas. Relatively speaking, the gossipy style of commercial broadcasting mirrored the 'politics of everyday living ... supportive style in female speech' which was, as Tebbutt (1995) points out, one of the main forms of entertainment in working-class areas and which, as Coates (1986) states, is utilized by women to maintain social relationships and friendships. It is perhaps then not surprising that women 'began to make up an increased portion of the audience of the offshore commercial stations Radio Luxemburg and Radio Normandie in the late 1930s' (Hilmes, 2006, p. 12). Arguably, any sense of intimacy was more significantly undermined by all BBC broadcasts – even discussions or question-and-answer sessions – being scripted. The scripts were altered and approved well in advance of the broadcast; the tension between the intimacy of domestic listening and the formality of the scripting process was compounded by the middle-class background of those who worked at the BBC, explaining why one interviewee described the BBC as 'a bit toffee nosed you know' (Mrs Jones, 6 April 2002). Indeed, in 1936 the MP Ellen Wilkinson in her local newspaper complained:

> The BBC is much too respectful of its bigwigs and far too impersonal for women to get really fond of the wireless, as they are in America ... I think there would be a lot to be said for trying the experiment of having a woman introduce the talks and not merely with 'Mr – is here to talk to you about –' but words of greeting, the kindly neighbour who has just dropped in for a words and a few casual remarks at the close. If the same voice gave the talk it would help establish the personal link. (*Sunday Sun*, 26 April 1936)

The domestication of broadcasting also involved Radio Aunties and Uncles on the BBC's Children's Hour lightening the tasks of many mothers preparing the evening meal by amusing the children at 5:00 p.m. each day, giving the technological and public medium of radio a domestic role in the home. (They did this so successfully that a BBC audience survey of television viewers carried out in 1939 resulted in the almost unanimous suggestion for the provision of a television children's hour.) Increasingly, evening plays, dramas and documentaries also carried a heavy focus on domesticity – with portrayals of domestic life in a range of different areas and historical eras so that one writer in the *Radio Times* noted: 'we never fail to enjoy these microphone glimpses into other people's lives and we are gradually acquiring a series of mental pictures of other parts of Great Britain in which we never actually lived; in some instances we wished we lived there; in others we confess we don't' (*Radio Times*, 26 April 1934 p. v).

These glimpses into other people's lives also included a range of fictional families and households, as early soaps and comedy serials broadcast on radio gained enthusiastic audiences. *Radio Pictorial* encouraged listeners to 'tune into Number Seven

Happiness Lane' – to meet the inhabitants of a 'theatrical boarding house' on Radio Luxemburg at 10:15 a.m. on Sundays (17 June 1938, p. 10). Alternatively the Buggins family – Mrs Buggins, the three children, father and grandma – were first introduced to BBC listeners in 1925 and then broadcast regularly from 1928, going on to provide rationing advice during World War II. The star of the show, Mabel Constanduros, was frequently the focus of *Radio Times'* articles on her private domestic life away from the microphone. The pseudo intimacy and personalization suggested in such features was extended by a range of radio celebrities who, as Hilda Matheson observed, provided an:

> intimate touch between humans who might otherwise never come within hail of each other; it enhances the factors of personality. This is true of broadcasters and for listeners ... the listeners often feels he has made friends with those who speak to him not in a merely sentimental way, but through a real communication of thought and feeling. (1933, p. 241)

Thus *Radio Times* in the inter-war era carried articles on, for example, 'A Day in the Life of Harry Hall' and introduced readers to the leader of the BBC Dance Orchestra in his pyjamas cleaning his teeth, while features such as 'Stars in their Firesides' (18 November 1938) enlightened readers on the details of the colour schemes, carpets and fireplaces of a number of radio celebrities including Sir Henry Wood, instigator of the BBC proms. In so doing the *Radio Times* acted as a forerunner of contemporary gossip magazines such as Hello and *OK*, and radio celebrities became part of listeners' or fans' 'extended family' (Hermes, 1995).

LONELY LISTENERS AND CROONERS

Many broadcasting histories tend to take domesticity as static, known and understood broadcasting's technologies and discourses having been adapted to the 'domestic' sphere. Drawing upon a range of sources, including oral history, Moores emphasizes the place of broadcasting in everyday life and sees the domestication of radio bringing about changes in the style and operation of radio sets and broadcasting schedules which were adapted to fit into the perceived routines of family life. He explores the significance of the geography of the home, emphasizing how radios were placed within the 'living room' – leading off the kitchen at the back of the house – and in so doing prescribed a particular version of domesticity and radio use. The placement and control of the radio and later television in the home needs to be seen as part of the contestation that takes place over the meaning and practices of domesticity and private lives.

Domesticity was then, as now, multifaceted and hugely varied, differently interpreted in urban, rural and suburban situations, between classes and within individual households (as radio purchase was in the 1930s). There was a significant number of multiple occupancy households: almost all middle-class homes had domestic servants, for example, and many radio listeners lived in bedsits or 'rooms'. Discussion of the incorporation of the wireless into the domestic spaces of the home in the inter-war era was not confined to families but instead the wireless was offered as a substitute for the family: a range of alternative friends and relations with whom to socialize. The *Radio Pictorial* heralded the 'Radio as the Bachelor woman's answer to loneliness' as 'with the switch of a button', her own room is filled with unseen friends who have much to give and tell, 'thus magically loneliness is converted into leisure' (6 October 1938, p. 23). One interviewee, an assistant gardener on a large estate in Surrey in the 1930s, whose job required him to live in, described the enormous pleasure his first radio provided, enabling him to listen to a range of entertainment in the evenings, offering leisure and 'comfort and company' amidst the working world of domestic service. (Mr Edwards, 8 April 2002). Such lonely, deserving and discerning listeners were heralded by the *Radio Times*, for example in the following poem:

Into her lonely cottage every night
Comes music, played a hundred miles away;
And now each dumb and solitary day
Melts into music with the dying light:

And as she hearkens, unto her it seems
That she is one with the vast listening throng
Held rapt together by the strains of song,
Made one in music dreaming the same dreams:

And her old heart, not lonely anymore,
Sweeps in ethereal melodies afar
Through aerial regions, and a singing star,
Among the singing stars she seems to soar.

It is significant that the widow in the poem was listening to music in her cottage; what sort of music the lonely listener consumed was another cause for concern and anxiety. Despite the BBC's Reithian Public Service Broadcasting project a women listener explained in the *Radio Times* 'light music is among the pleasures that weave themselves into our daily routine more and more often and more and more closely' (29 October 1937, p. 9). Mass Observation day diaries, writers of the era and my own oral history interviews indicate that listening patterns were varied; listeners active and discerning; feedback from the Publicity File of the 'Women's Interests Section' reported that what people really wanted was music and popular music, meaning dance bands and crooners. If this was not available on the BBC listeners turned to the European commercial radio stations which selected their musical content on popularity. Street has pointed out that 'the huge enthusiasm amongst the young for dancing fed the emergent record and gramophone industry, which in turn was to significantly fuel the public appetite for popular music radio as home-centred entertainment grew' (2006, p. 69).

The BBC devoted a significant amount of airtime to music – having its own celebrity band leaders such as Harry Hall – but

" Imagine her . . . . sitting by the little open fire on which she cooks her meals, with the receiver over her ears, her eyes closed for rest."

'Granny by the fireside': the ideal solitary listener for whom the wireless brought companionship. From *Radio Times*, September 1924

became anxious about the suitability of the supposedly sexual and intimate singing of crooners being broadcast into the private sphere of the home. Crooning, described by the *Sunday Sun Newcastle Weekly* 'as sugary whispering' (2 April 1940, p. 194) or by Alan Jenkins as 'Intimate Personality Singing', who also pointed out in the *Radio Times,* they were 'mercilessly abused as an effeminate monstrosity' (21 May 1937). They were seen by some as low-brow and inappropriate for the ordinary and apparently all too easily influenced lonely female listeners. Their intimate quiet style required the singer to be very close to the microphone and, almost by implication, the vulnerable audience of housewives in their homes. Broadcasting had already begun to be perceived as entering not only domestic space but also the consciousness of individuals, the private interiority of the mind. On one hand this was seen as a positive antidote to loneliness, as the following extract from the *Radio Times* suggests:

> We often hear of the blessings that radio has brought the lonely countryman or the unvisited sufferer in hospital. The entertainment is generally urged as being the chief amongst these blessings, but radio attacks loneliness in an even more intimate way. There are thoughts and images passing through all our minds all the time and in loneliness these assume an exaggerated importance so that they haunt and finally obsess us. Here it is that radio is so invaluable, for it provides other voices, which drive out the melancholy ghosts with laughter and music. (12 April 1937, p. 10)

However, the intimacy and femininity of radio listening contributed to crooning being perceived as threatening to the BBC's sense of itself as a national institution and its role as guardian of the quality and taste of the cultural input broadcast into homes. As Andreas Huyssen points out: 'critiques of taste are often linked to feminisation' (1986, p. 47) and this perhaps framed the comments of a writer in the *Radio Times* who suggested: 'crooning is inseparable in meaning from lullabies and Negro mothers ... Indeed this element in crooning seems calculated to lavish maternal instinct upon all who listen. It is not improbable that male listeners find female crooning protective and seductive' (21 May 1937); crooning's sensuality, intimacy and association with black music and of course mass culture created further anxieties; consequently memos specified exactly how close singers could be to the microphone and virtually banned crooning.

The wireless' attack on loneliness was not merely about providing a new domestic soundscape or a distraction for the deserving, lonely and possibly housebound listener – it was also seen as connecting listeners to each other and to each other's homes; thus Lance Sieveking in 1934 wondered 'How many listeners, if any, are subconsciously aware of simultaneously sharing with thousands of millions of other people the thing to which they are listening?' (p. 37). Broadcasters and critics, for example writing in the *Radio Times,* seemed acutely aware that domestic listeners shared their listening experience with numerous others in isolated domestic spaces; they were thus symbolically linked to and potentially gained a sense of belonging to wider 'imagined communities' (Anderson, 2006). Jennings and Gill argued 'the fact that millions are all listening to the same programme gives them a sensation of being part of the nation in a way that was rarely experienced in the past' (1939, p. 12), while *Radio Times* enthused to listeners 'we are at one with the homes scattered around the world where women are busy keeping the home fires burning' (17 December 1937, p. 80). Although listening usually took place in private and was often focused upon domestic topics, it was simultaneously a public activity, an activity participated in with others across the nation, or across international boundaries following the establishment of the Empire Service in 1932, leading Margaret Bondfield, for example, to describe the radio as the 'medium through which countries talk to each other' (*Radio Times,* 12 November 1933, p. 81).

Thus when Moores argues that, by the 1930s radio had moved from the status of 'unruly guest' to become, symbolically at least, a 'good companion in the home' (Moores, 2000, p. 42) the wide range of 'homes' and listening practices that this refers to needs to be understood. The good companion that the radio was perceived to be combated loneliness, breaching the walls which surrounded, structured and confined domestic spaces that were sites of isolation for the blind, housebound, the ill and even some of those in rural areas – where the radio, it was suggested, helped to keep rural farmers and their lonely wives on the land. One writer in *The Times*, enthusing on the socially positive effects of broadcasting, reported: 'One of the few farmers who admit to making money was heard to say … that his livelihood had been threatened because his wife refused to stay another winter in the country, [and] that he bought a wireless, and with that the solution to the problem' (14 August 1934, p. iv)

RADIO DEFINES THE HOME

The multifaceted pleasures offered by radio listening rested in part on its symbolic association with fantasies of home, for, as Giles points out, the domestic is 'an arena in which women experience and live out … fantasises; the nature of these fantasises and the understanding of "home" in producing and articulating our profoundest wishes has varied across time and across cultures' (Giles, 2004, p. 3). In the inter-war era, fantasies of home began to include a wireless which as HMV radio adverts suggested could 'bring glamour' into the mundane, everyday world of the home; the sociability, the companionship, the style and modernity of a radio entered imaginings of the domestic and the 'what ifs' that were the fantasies of home.

Indeed at times the radio served to define the home – as a feature in the *Radio Times* under the title 'It's Still Home!' indicated:

> In these days wherever there is a home there is a radio set. Also wherever there is a radio set there is something very reminiscent of a home, even though it could be the loneliest output in the Empire. These two unusual 'home' pictures show appreciative listeners to the BBC's Empire programmes. The one above was taken in Nyasaland East Africa; the other shows a group of Dinkas listening in the Southern Sudan to the chimes of Big Ben. (18 November 1938, p. 17)

Here, within problematic discourses of race and colonialism, listening to the radio invested a location with the experience of

It's still Home!

In these days wherever there is a home there is a radio set. Also, wherever there is a radio set there is something very reminiscent of home, even though it be in the loneliest outpost of the Empire.

These two unusual 'home' pictures show appreciative listeners to the BBC's Empire programmes. The one above was taken in Nyasaland, East Africa; the other shows a group of Dinkas listening in the Southern Sudan to the chimes of Big Ben.

'It's Still Home!' The radio begins to define the home in this extract. From *Radio Times*, November 1935

domesticity, which operated at the emotional and symbolic level – fluid and shifting – the object of fantasies and dreams. Although the spatial frames the domestic, it is through discourse that domesticity is invested with meaning. Here radio became central to the discourse of domesticity and served to provide a sense of domestic cosiness and belonging to spaces in the empire.

Exhibitions such as Radio Olympia, imagery and advertising in the *Radio Times* and the *Radio Pictorial* suggested that wireless played a central role in fantasies of domestic bliss facilitating intimacy, cosiness and a sense belonging through shared radio listening. As Bailey (2009) points out 'broadcasting became an ideal medium for organizing domestic life and bringing the family together around the radio hearth' (p. 54). Many adverts used the visual iconography of radio to connote an idea of domestic modernity which was expandable to friends who were sometimes portrayed as being invited to a radio party, In this version of domesticity, the fireplace or the kitchen table of 'old' is either accompanied by or replaced by the wireless – a forerunner of the role of the television which in the post-war era symbolically became the 'heart of the home'. Indeed the term 'radio-home' became part of the *Radio Times* rhetoric in the 1930s, with guidance on how to wire up houses so that the radio could be heard in all rooms and inhabitants' listening was not interrupted as they went from room to room. Alternatively, other articles explained how to enable the domestic servants to listen to different radio channels, when their tastes differed from the homeowners (*Radio Times*, 18 December 1936).

Some idealized representations of radio listening visually structured white middle-class men in positions of power, as providers and owners of the new technology of radio, a perspective supported by one interviewee who claimed that her father always controlled the choice of programme on the radio (Mrs Lordington, 10 June 2003). Alternatively the radio was portrayed as contributing to the creation of 'companionate marriages' and peaceful domesticity; a Hailglass lampshades advert in the 1928 BBC handbook addressed 'To the Women of Britain' advised them that 'the radio has undoubtedly helped you to keep your husbands and boys away from the club and kept them at home where they thus experience the benefits of your gentle charm and influence'. Oral history interviews undertaken by Moores indicate that 'for some families radio listening in the home was seen as a continuation of Edwardian and Victorian home entertainment and less morally dangerous than public places' (Moores, 1998, cited in Street, 2006, p. 68). For others the value of a wireless to domestic contentment lay in providing domestic distraction for men, as one of my interviewees explained: 'My sister had five children in three and half years – I said to her you must get a radio' (Rose Lynch, 1 August 2002).

The 1935 documentary *The BBC – The Voice of Britain* suggested that radio, had become for many, symbolically at least, an intrinsic element of the 'domestic comfort' of the home, embracing ideals of peace, tranquillity and respite from the world through which fantasies of the home were discursively constructed. Images of domestic listening portrayed in the documentary included a couple who listened to the radio by the fire, the husband reading his paper while the wife did her knitting; listeners of Britain enjoying a music radio broadcast, one man sat in chair, wearing a suit, reading with his feet up on the fireplace; a women in a chair by a table lamp listening intently; the camera then cut to a vicar sitting doing his crossword puzzle, his bookshelves behind him, finally a labourer with a pick and shovel is shown walking home from work to the welcoming sounds of his radio. Importantly the pleasures of the radio were seen as democratic, accessible to all; Priestley suggested 'the very modern things, like films and wireless and sixpenny stories, are absolutely democratic, making no distinction whatever between patrons' (1977, p. 376), while a *Radio Times* writer reported overhearing someone on the bus explaining 'Get this into your noddle, Broadcasting is the people's entertainment. Well-to-do people don't give a trap for it, they've got plenty of pleasures' (*Radio Times* supplement 24 March 1939, p. v11). Indeed by 1938 Rowntree Social Surveys on the *Condition of People* included 6d a week for the wireless (to cover the cost of battery club and saving towards the licence fee) alongside a daily newspaper, travelling to work for wage earners and foodstuffs, all as essential expenditure to maintain national efficiency; although with evidence of the effects of the great depression in many areas, the survey simultaneously accepted that 40 per cent of adult males did not earn enough to cover these expenditures (1938, p. 9).

Mass Observation Day Diaries from August and September 1937 indicate that radio was indeed well ensconced in everyday domestic life, listened to during mealtimes, sitting by the fire or undertaking domestic chores such as letter writing, embroidery, cooking and ironing. For example one diarist recorded:

> 10 a.m. 'went downstairs to listen to Sally Sam on the wireless. While I listened helped mother to cut beans, Father had now gone to work at the Railway Station. Then helped with the washing up.' 1:45 p.m. I returned home late. My parents were at dinner and mine was in the oven. It was roast beef and baked potatoes and cabbage and beans followed by apple pie. We listened to the Ovaltine programme while we ate. (MO, 12 August 1937 DS 13).

This respondent continues to record a range of activities to which radio provided a soundscape; an approach to radio listening which was not wholeheartedly approved of by many of the correspondents in the *Radio Times* who discussed 'the ideal listener'. There was strong condemnation for those who listened indiscriminately to the radio, using it merely as a background to other activities. Such listening merely incorporated the 'public' sphere of broadcasting into the mundane domestic world without an attempt to delineate its 'difference'. As *Radio Times* explained: 'the good listener listens. He does not combine listening with conversation, coughing, sneezing, French knitting and switching over to a different wavelength at half minute intervals. These occupations may well be delightful in themselves but I prefer my listening neat' (*Radio Times*, 10 January 1936, p. 11). Neat listening emphasizes the boundaries of public and private with a specific, focused reverential mode of behaviour for listening. MP Margaret Bondfield was not alone in being disconcerted, by 'young people who automatically tune.in as soon as they are within reach of a set' and felt that 'It is surely a matter of concern if any proportion of the population find it difficult to study unless surrounded by noise' instead she and others encouraged people to listen with 'discrimination and self-control' (*Radio Times*, 12 November 1937, p. 23). The concerns endlessly expressed, about whether listening was discerning and discriminating, signify an attempt to control the boundaries between public and private and to maintain an investment in the ideal of the domestic space as an escape from the public sphere.

Radio was thus able to be both a soundscape to domestic life and become a signifier of domestic tranquillity, entwined in fantasies of home for listeners who experienced the domestic simultaneously at a symbolic, imaginary and mundane level. However, evidence also suggests that, for many, the lived experience of radio listening fell short of the fantasy of domestic contentment. An article in the *Lancet* in 1938, which described suburban neurosis and focused on a composite 'Mrs Everyman' who finds suburban domesticity tedious to such a degree that it threatens her health and complains: 'the wireless was always the same old stuff' (quoted in Gardiner, 2010, p. 309). Alternatively, for others, the wireless became a new weapon in the often gendered and frequently personal battlefield that domesticity could become. In the evenings, in particular, power over the radio and the choice of stations was a weapon of subtle and not so subtle domestic tension over who controlled leisure and domestic space. Jennings and Gill's 1939 survey indicated that 'fathers' most frequently chose the programmes – but also points to more complex decision-making processes. Mothers and housewives already had an established and culturally expected role policing the boundaries of the domestic sphere and some utilized the opportunity of studying the programmes during the day to plan out the evening's listening. One man said in connection to this: 'The mother has come into her own. One comes in and she gets tea for him, and at last she'll say – Now clear the cloth there's a good play coming on. She's got it all arranged, you see, all thought out' (Jenning and Gill, 1939, p. 42).

Broadcasters targeted the 'family audience – either as the household group as a whole or in particular scheduled slots at selected family members' (Moores, 1988, reprinted in Mitchell,

2000, p. 124), distributing children's programming, plays, music and talks to provide a rhythm for domestic life practices (Lacey, 1996) so that Moores argues radio was involved in the 'domestication of standard national time' (Moores, 1988, p. 38). All the same, one young woman described the impossibility of individual listening as 'one of the petty tyrannies of family life' (Jennings and Gill, 1939, p. 22). The solution to such tensions by the 1930s lay in the continued decrease in the price of wireless sets and the emergence of multiple-listening households (p. 24).

EDUCATING FEMALE LISTENERS IN THEIR HOMES

For many housewives, such as the wife of a gamekeeper living in an isolated cottage on the edge of woods who enjoyed listening to the Buggins family and Vauderville (*Radio Times*, 31 March 1933), the value of a radio was indeed to combat loneliness. For others it lifted the spirits and broadened their outlook and in the 1930s radio was seen as an important medium for education both by the BBC and many women themselves as the response of one Mass Observation diarist, who described herself as a housewife in Cricklewood, confirms. This listener had two children, a daughter of 11 who had passed the scholarship exam and obtained free secondary education and a younger child of five. She described herself and her motor mechanic husband as working class, with a modern labour-saving home within which she listened to radio talks; for, as she explained: 'The radio is my inspiration and relaxation. Talks inspire me to deeper thinking and reading, while I often do a tiresome job of sewing while listening, Music makes me caper about madly if I am alone and have excess energy and to switch on when I am tired and hear something familiar like Hangles Largo is heaven itself' (MOA – DS 81, 7 July 1937).

Mothers and housekeepers it was hoped would discriminate in their listening and recognize and utilize radio's educative and improving functions. Filson Young, writing in the *Radio Times*, perceived women as 'by far the best listeners – the most receptive, the most attentive' (16 November1934, p. 546) and went on to suggest:

> The broadcaster is a publicist on a very large scale and his function is generative and creative; the function of the listener is receptive and cultural. The broadcaster sews the seed; it is only the listener that can germinate and produce anything. It is by the nature of broadcasting that much of the seed is wasted and falls on barren land ...
>
> And here in my opinion is the particular importance of women to broadcasting. In my opinion they are the best listeners – the most receptive, the most attentive, the most appreciative and in the best sense the most critical. (*Radio Times*, 16 November 1934, p. 546)

After an early edition of *Women's Hour*, which started in 1923, was abandoned a year later on the recommendation of the Women's Advisory committee (not to return until the post-war era), from 1924 the BBC's commitment to programming for women in the 1930s took the form of *Household Talks* broadcasts between 10:45 and 11:00 every weekday morning aimed at 'ordinary' housewives who, as Moores suggests, were seen 'as the feminine monitors of domestic life' (2000, p. 47). The seeds Filson Wilson was anxious to have sewn, covered a variety of topics; there were talks on travel, the law, religious broadcasts and in the era of women's progression towards full enfranchisement political education was provided by MPs such as Eleanor Rathbone, Megan Lloyd George and Ellen Wilkinson. The radio provided women, confined to the home by their domestic responsibilities, with access to public events and experiences. As Hilda Matheson Talks Director from 1927–32 explained:

> Women listeners stand to gain from the whole range of programmes – concerts and plays to which they could not ordinarily go, public ceremonies which bring them in touch with people and events

> of the day, news and topical talks, sporting events and entertainments. But broadcasting can give them also, as it were, a preparatory course to help them catch up; to feel less at a disadvantage to keep abreast of wider interests. (1933, p. 37)

That broadcasting had educational potential seems to have been a view that was not just held within the confines of the BBC in the 1920s and 1930s; one working-class, lifelong member of the Labour Party, I interviewed, described radio as 'providing a university education' for those without the benefit of the 1944 Education Act (Mrs Lynch, 9 May 2002). Similarly, Mrs Florence Knightly, a cleaner from St Pancras, London, who declared herself an 'enthusiastic listener' for a *Radio Times* in an interview in 1939, pointed out that:

> I think radio is a proper education. People can go to the pictures and dance halls for fun, but it's not all of us got the time or energy to go out to study. Wireless makes listening easy. The people might be talking in the same room. Twenty years ago a woman like me wouldn't know anything about politics, but thanks to the radio I can hold my own quite well. (*Radio Times*, 24 March 1939, p. v)

Nerina Shute, in an article entitled 'Radio Happiness' in *Radio Pictorial*, suggested that the radio was a way to broaden the mind, 'forget yourself' and 'stop minding your own business all the time and get interested in the outside world' (29 November 1935). Nevertheless a perception quickly developed, that 'to catch a women's interest' broadcasting must focus upon 'the intimate unseen details of her daily life' (*The Times*, 1934, p. iii) and the BBC's *Household Talks* were primarily focused upon domesticity, and a pattern established whereby Friday's talks were on some aspect of childcare: weaning, health education, careers, nutrition, behaviour, etc, Tuesday was often utilized for cookery talks and Thursday from 1934 became the regular slot for *At Home Today*, a magazine-style programme on domestic topics; other days were more varied with, for example, Daisy Pain in 1937 instructed women on the weekly wash, carefully explaining to the listeners with respect to men's underpants and vests that 'these must be kept comfortable or they can make a really cheerful man quite grumpy or irritable' (9 November 1934).

Bailey has argued that these radio broadcasts acted as a form of governance 'as one of many domestic technologies whose intended use was, in part, to regulate and direct women's behaviour and conduct for patriarchal reasons of state' (2009, p. 63) suggesting 'the family was no longer an autonomous social institution composed of independent individuals. Rather, a whole series of values and privileges emerged the family into a an agent for maximising social economy and social order' (2009, p. 63). However, Bailey's arguments do not contextualize domestic education on the wireless and ignore the contradictory and complex nature of texts and listeners engagement with them. Thus when in their 1939 survey of broadcasting Jennings and Gill stated, 'The whole attitude to housekeeping and motherhood is undergoing modification in the direction of increased knowledge, control and dignity, here again broadcasting is not the sole agency at work but it is one of the most effective' (1939, p. 74), they were overstating the case. Not least because, as will be explored in the next chapter, there was a plurality of contradictory discourses on domesticity broadcast by the BBC in the 1930s. Furthermore it needs to be noted that the domestic focus of the BBC's educational and talks programming was not always directed at women or restricted to daytime programming; there was a range of talks on gardening for weekend and evening audiences, and talks for schools on domestic topics in the afternoons. These programmes produced some of the first celebrities of lifestyle programming, including Marcel Boulestin and Mr Middleton who will be the focus of Chapter Three. What is clear is that in the inter-war years broadcasting encountered and altered domesticity, and that in turn a domestic mode of address and a pre-occupation with the domestic was established in broadcasting – a preoccupation that was there to stay.

Chapter Two

Early domestic goddesses: competing discourses of domestic expertise

DOMESTIC GURUS

This chapter explores the competing ideas about domesticity articulated by a range of experts in the BBC's *Household Talks*, broadcast every morning at 10:45 from 1929. Broadcasting's domestic goddesses are by no means a new phenomenon; rather such experts are an intrinsic element of mass media aimed at women as domestic consumers. Consequently experts have offered instruction on domestic skills, cookery and how to organize a home through lifestyle-focused media texts (TV, radio, websites and magazines) for over 200 years. Mrs Beeton, whose *Beeton's Book of Household Management* was first published as a complete volume in1861, is still a household name. The weighty volume was based upon Isabella Beeton and her husband's publication of the *English Woman's Domestic Magazine* described by some as Britain's first successful women's magazine (Beetham, 1996). In the inter-war period, the growing anxiety about domesticity among the middle-classes, linked to the decline of domestic servants and their own subsequently increasing involvement in domestic tasks (Humble, 2004), combined with the emergence of radio as a popular medium to provide a new outlet for domestic gurus. Furthermore, concerns about 'national efficiency' and the demand that motherhood and housework be considered 'as important to the survival of the nation as advances in war technology or industrial production' (Giles, 2004, p. 117) had emerged at the beginning of the twentieth century during the Boer War and gained significance during World War 1 (Davin, 1978). The economic crisis of the inter-war period in which unemployment reached 3 million, an estimated 20 per cent of the working population, by 1931 (Laybourne, 1999, p. 105) increased unease about health and welfare, and made working-class domesticity a focus for the informal education of women in both the media and a range of women's organizations, including the Women's Cooperative Guild and Women's Institutes. Indeed the BBC used to contact Women's Institutes and Townswomen's Guilds to promote up and coming *Household Talks* series, and to sell the accompanying recipe leaflets they produced (BBCWA, R44/619).

Similarly, the class-differentiated market for women's magazines, established in the previous century, continued to grow and offered a range of domestic advice to housewives. *Good Housekeeping* appeared in 1922 followed by *Women's Own* (1932), *Women's Illustrated* (1936) and *Women* (1937) which by 1939 was selling three-quarters of a million copies a week (Winship, 1987; Gardiner, 2010). Such magazines pronounced their views on what was correct in terms of domesticity; however careful analysis suggests that rather more reader engagement and rather less discursive inconsistency than some previous analysis has indicated (Warde, 1997). Furthermore, discourses of domesticity should not be seen as necessarily having reflected 'reality' but rather served to construct and give meaning to the lived experience of domesticity for urban, suburban and rural women in the era. Both 'Women's Magazines and the advertising that financed them were however a visual experience' they offered a fantasy experience to the reader who was able to selectively flick through the images and commentary on offer (Giles, 2004, p. 119).

Broadcasting was aural; it relied upon the voice, tone, style, skill and personality of the broadcaster to communicate, connect and engage with the ordinary listener – it was consequently an arena into which a veritable army of lifestyle gurus quickly scuttled. The written and broadcast media were not divorced from one another, recipes from radio broadcasts were often published in *Radio Times* and occasionally in the *Listener*, and many broadcasters who made a name for themselves on radio cashed in on this by writing for the press. Mrs Webb, a prolific radio broadcaster, was Cookery Editor for *Farmer's Weekly* in the 1930s. Indeed, in the contestation over domesticity in the inter-war period, anxiety about the dire state of British cooking and the demise of the supposedly feminine domestic skills, particularly in the urban and suburban areas, was often countered by a nostalgic and idealized version of the rural domestic home, which was symbolically and ideologically often perceived to be the heart of the nation, given ruralism's centrality to notions of Englishness (Howkins, 1987). For the BBC, striving since its inception to become 'the voice of the nation' and acutely aware of the significance of the role it was perceived to be playing in terms of contributing to forging a sense of nationhood, not least to ensure the continuance of its charter and licence to broadcast, rural domesticity was appealing. Yet the corporation found itself in an increasingly problematic position, although in the inter-war years domesticity was predominantly perceived as 'naturally' associated with women, intrinsic to their femininity, simultaneously a range of competing and overlapping discourses circulated seeing the domestic role of women as something either 'skilled' or 'scientific' which needed to be both analysed and learned. The BBC provided a platform for a range of experts who articulated what they considered housewives needed to be taught and produced a range of competing knowledge that jostled to be heard by women. The basis of authority from which these experts – who in the Foucaudian sense produced knowledge – 'through language and practices' made it meaningful was varied. Ideas of science and scientific management jostled with rural domesticity, while perceptions of women as empowered consumers were undermined by the pressures that women faced as 'household managers'. Importantly, domesticity was then, and continues to be, shaped by economic circumstances and class. Working-class women's knowledge and skill developed from their lived experience was also included in the *Household Talks*, something listeners valued. Consequently the gambit of advice provided by the BBC, and other media, to housewives in the 1920s and 1930s did not offer a monolithic discourse of domesticity and, given that many of the views expressed by experts contradicted one another, the media operated as space for contestation (Hall, 1981) over domesticity rather than a site of governance.

HOUSEWIVES AS CONSUMERS AND MANGERS

Radio – both the commercial stations and the BBC – addressed domestically oriented women, 'monitors of domestic life' (Moores, 2000), as consumers, shoppers and managers of the household budget, the subjects of attempts at governance (as they were responsible for domestic life and the health and welfare of the nation). Women were both consumers of radio (which was in itself a new domestic consumer item) and were also seen as consumers of many of the products advertised on commercial radio. The BBC was by no means divorced from consumer culture, 'even in the anti commercial programming of the BBC – by contributing to the familiarization of a leisure and commodity – orientated way of life' (Lacey, 2002, p. 23). Housewives were often encouraged in the purchase of modern equipment and provided with guidance in its use. For example, in the series *How to Use an Electric Cooker* (1930) Miss Vaughen finished a programme by suggesting 'do let me urge you to save electricity by having a self-contained electric kettle and an electric iron' (14 October 1930), while in 1937 the *Radio Times* announced 'We are a nation of shoppers' (1 January 1937), a headline taken from the title of a new Tuesday-evening series of talks initiated by Helen Simpson who explained: 'We are all shoppers the questions to be dealt with, are how we shop; and when; and why and what ways could we do it better?' (*Radio Times*, 5 January 1937, p. 76).

This emphasis on a consumerism can be identified from the 1880s onwards, but it was accelerated in the 1930s. Although many were unemployed, for those in work the falling cost of living and rise in real income provided the means for a new consumerism. The removal of the pound from the gold standard in 1931 and the subsequent fall in interest rates during the 1930s brought home ownership within the grasp of many of the middle-classes, who moved to new developments in the suburbs that sprung up around London and a number of cities in the South and Midlands (Gardiner, 2010). The modern well-equipped houses with electricity enabled their occupants to benefit from the fall in the cost of the living to enjoy consumer cultures, made more accessible through chain stores such as Marks and Spencer and Woolworths. A sense of the modern as being closely linked to getting and spending was also aligned to visions of the 'good life and time to enjoy this' (Giles, 2004, p. 21). The new homes provided markets for domestic products which were sold in stores, advertised on commercial radio, in newspapers, women's magazines and in cinema films. 'New technology and consumer markets for domestic products, debates about how homes could and should be run, the decline in domestic service and the growing emphasis on housing, household finances, family hygiene and nutrition, evidenced in government surveys and political debate, created a cultural space in which the materiality and efficient running of homes was fore grounded' (Giles, 2004, p. 122): a cultural space that the BBC was keen to fill.

Women's expectations of and experience of domesticity in the inter-war period was contradictory and varied, subject to significant regional and class variations. The majority of housewives did not work outside the home – although some working-class women earned money in part-time jobs and running shops, others took in washing, sewing and lodgers, or undertook child-minding. In 1931, although approximately five and a half to six million women were in the workforce, in white-collar jobs, the new expanding light industries and of course domestic service, the vast majority of working women were single. 'There were exceptions – middle class married women did not work outside the home, even before they had children, and the assumption, (if not the practice) held true for working class women too'

(Gardiner, 2010, p. 553). Many historians, as Bourke has pointed out, have 'proved unwilling to believe the decision of working-class women to be full-time housewives' was voluntary' (1994, p. 15). Bourke challenges this, arguing instead that domesticity appealed to working-class women and their menfolk (1994, p. 63). A view which is supported not only by oral history but also by analysis of many of the post-suffrage organizations which were arguing for women to undertake one job rather than two, and for a re-appraisal of the status of domestic labour (Andrews, 1997).

While a large number of middle-class women had servants, maids and labour-saving devices such as vacuum cleaners, working-class women's experience of domesticity was framed by material circumstances. If the 1930s saw an improvement in standards of living for some areas of the UK, in others such as Jarrow, Stockton and South Shields, where unemployment in traditional industries such as shipbuilding and steel was high, it was quite another story. Although infant mortality was falling, maternal mortality was rising as women 'struggled to balance their budgets and feed their families in the face of overwhelming odds' Roberts, 1984, p. 161), with varied housing conditions, patchy or limited access to water, electricity and reliable cooking facilities (Webster, 1998). Despite this, Roberts argues that, since the end of the nineteenth century, 'Working class women were heavily criticised for their lack of ability as household managers, and most especially for their lack of cooking skills, in selection of food' (1984, p. 151). Roberts may be presenting anxiety, concern and criticism as more uniform that it really was; certainly, since the late nineteenth century, a number of social commentators, intelligentsia and politicians had voiced concern about the health and welfare of the nation and in particular that of the working class. The inter-war economic crisis exaggerated these concerns but awareness of problems was not matched by any agreement on policy or remedies. While Boyd Orr's study of Food, Health and Income (1937) emphasized the link between children's growth and nutrition and recommended an increase in young children's milk consumption, others campaigned for housing reform and slum clearance, while eugenics gained currency with a number of those who advocated social reform and Birth Control such as H. G. Wells and Marie Stopes.

Given the BBC's public service ethos and the context of these wider debates, in a period of economic crisis, it is perhaps not surprising that there was a more frequent concern with consumer choice in relation to budgeting rather than presenting consumerism as a liberating sphere of creativity and autonomy. Memos retained at the BBC archives indicate that the *Household Talks* were primarily targeted at working-class women, intended to provide informal domestic education for 'housewives on whom the burden of domestic survival fell' (Tebbutt, 1995, p.11). Indeed, within working-class culture, the housewife, who was 'discursively constructed as a manager of home and all importantly the budget', found her skills were needed as both a 'financial manager and moral guide' (Roberts, 1984, p. 125) and these skills in many respects defined working-class housewives. While such skills could be empowering and offer status, for many managing was highly stressful as the family's economic survival, security and future rested upon it. 'The good wife was to a large degree equated with the good manager ... the threat of violence for many lay behind failure to manage. Financial difficulties could ... be blamed on her poor skills and neglect of duties' (Ayers and Lamberts, 1986, p. 197). Such an ethos ignores the uncertainty of men's wages, which meant that for some women managing became easier with the regularity and predictability of unemployment benefits. Consequently the BBC produced a series devoted to budgeting, with titles such as *The Ideal Budget* (6 January 1931), *New Pennies, Old Purse* (1933); and *The Frugal Housewife* (1935), and in so doing could be seen to be addressing a need which was often welcomed. Thus Miss Petty explained in *Ideal Budget*, 'In working out an ideal budget – which simply means portioning out the income to the best advantage – the first consideration is food for the family. Health is, as everyone knows, the most important thing in life and if the income is small, the amount apportioned for food must come first' (BBCWA, Ref Petty T402). How money should be apportioned however, and the basis on which Miss Petty and other domestic experts felt able to instruct the working-class housewife was open to debate and liable to be fiercely contested.

THE APPLIANCE OF SCIENCE TO DOMESTICITY

Initially the BBC drew upon high-profile women or women's organizations for domestic expertise, with the Women's Institute, playing upon the symbolic association between the rural and the nation, quickly took up a role in shaping the new medium. The National Federation of Women's Institutes (NFWI) chair-women Lady Denman, who was on the BBC Women's Committee in the early 192s, gave the first talk of the 1930s the series *The Countrywoman's Day*. Lady Denman's role as NFWI chair gave her authority, legitimating her expertise; many less well-known women who broadcast in the inter-war era rested their authority instead upon the twin axis of experience and common sense. Many had already built up a reputation as a 'domestic expert'; such as Miss Florence Petty (known as the Pudding Lady), who was one of more popular broadcasters of the 1930s, and had a homely, economical and pragmatic approach to cooking and budgeting. She had been heavily involved in the St Pancras School for Mothers, founded in 1907 in Somers Town (a poor district of London near Easton Station) (Ross, 2007, p. 192). She had been a Ministry of Agriculture lecturer to working class audiences in World War I before becoming a broadcaster for the *Household Talks*. Her advice, which included the benefits to the temperament of drinking cabbage water, would not always have stood up to scientific scrutiny.

Alternatively, the morning slot provided an opportunity for the predominantly male experts of the world of science, medicine and nutrition, infant health and welfare to enter the housewife's kitchen via the new technological medium of radio. Professor Allen Ferguson 'described' what science has done for the home in the series *Inside and Out* (*Radio Times*, 12 March 1935, p. 900), while Professor Mottram, a dietician from the King's College of Household and Social Science, University of London, focused upon the 'new science of nutrition' which had 'led to an increasing emphasis on the role of vitamins and minerals in the diet' (Beardsworth and Keil, 1997, p. 83). Radio doctors also reinforced the developing knowledge about childhood illness and health. Such ideas were not always articulated upon gender lines; Elizabeth Craig, writing in the *Radio Times* in 1934, argued, for example: 'If you want to raise the reputation of the British Kitchen which has been under a cloud for as long as I can remember, the reformation must begin at home (*Radio Times*, 14 May 1934, p. 698). She then went on to suggest that it 'needs to be well grounded in domestic science'. Domestic science in this period, although not always well received, was not only informed by nutrition but also by ideas of scientific management.

The publication of Fredrick Taylor's *The Principles of Scientific Management* in 1911, which put forward a system for managing industrial production, suggested that optimum organization, rationalization and simplification of tasks could increase productivity. It was not long before these ideas began to be applied to housework and within a year Mrs Christine Frederick published a series of articles applying these principles to housekeeping in the *Ladies Home Journal*, a popular American women's magazine, and later a book entitled *Scientific Management in the Home: Household Engineering* (1920). She explained that 'the purpose of scientific management was to save time and effort and to make things run more smoothly' (1920, p. 8). After a brief introduction describing the previously sorry state of her domestic life which included 'a continuous conflict to do justice to all the household tasks and yet find enough time for the children … do justice to herself … and being generally too spiritless, to enjoy listening to his [her husband's] story of the day's work' (1920, p. 7), she adopted a set of 12 guiding principles which included: ideals, common sense, competent counsel, standardized operations, standardized conditions, standard practice, despatching, scheduling, reliable records, discipline, fair deal, efficiency and reward. She then expanded on each of these principles in greater detail and explained that 'Homemakers like other managers must know what they are striving for' (1920, pp. 10–11). It is, however, worth noting that many of the categories described and the ideas espoused were polysemic, open to multiple interpretations and applications, and consequently the label of scientific was able to be applied, almost randomly, to a wide range of domestic practices.

The ideas of scientific management quickly spread to Europe, as Lacey points out with respect of German radio in the inter-war period: 'The overriding message was that there was no part of women's experience that could not benefit from rationalisation whether it be domestic technology or the results of science laboratories or the rationalization of housework' (Lacey, 1996, p. 154). While on the BBC *Household Talks* on the organization, cleaning, design and decoration of the home, along with principles of scientific management, shaped the 1929 series *Common Sense in Household Work* and an article in the *Radio Times* which explained: 'The woman who practices method in her housekeeping, the woman who has a place for everything and insists on everything being put in its place as soon as finished with, who puts a full stop to one job, when this is possible before tackling another, will never be in a muddle' (*Radio Times*, 27 April 1935, p. 264). Interestingly it seems to suggest the replacement of feminine multi-tasking with masculine rationalization. Nevertheless, Jennings and Gill soon suggested that the benefit of listening to talks about housewives in other lands was that it enabled 'Drudgery to become a problem to be tackled scientifically' (1939, p. 12).

For the middle-class housewife, scientific management represented a move from disciplining servants to self-discipline; it was also intrinsically interwoven with consumer culture (Rutherford, 2000). Rationalization went hand-in-hand with the purchase of labour-saving technology, much of which was adopted by 'Women's striving, to be freed from the thraldom of domestic duties carried out in archaic and inefficient ways' (Ryan, 1995, p. XX). Indeed, Mass Observation reports indicate that 'the majority of complaints about housework came from middle class women' (Giles, 2004, p.114). For middle-class housewives, as Nolan argues, 'Household rationalization was both alienating and appealing. It provided one way to be modern even if that meant the modern management of the traditionally defined home and family. It enabled them to be a new woman, even if the rationalized housewife conveyed little of the glamour usually associated with the term' (1990, p. 573). For working-class housewives, with poor housing conditions and little hope of purchasing new technology such as electric cookers, it must have seemed irrelevant.

PROFESSOR MOTTRAM

Tension and struggles between different versions of domesticity, domestic expertise, knowledge and authority soon surfaced, despite the BBC's attempts to take an eclectic view; for example in three series of talks on *Fruit and Vegetable Preserving, Meals in Summer* and *Meals for Special Occasions* each of the four talks in each series was given by a different speaker, including Miss Petty and Professor Mottram and his wife. Similarly, the 1931 series of talks – *Family Budgets* – was initially introduced by Mrs Petty and then featured ordinary housewives in subsequent weeks – including a miner's wife, policeman's wife, tailor's wife and a countrywoman – explaining their budgets, with Professor Mottram concluding the series. It was an ambitious project, given that memos were written the previous year by BBC personnel complaining about Mottram saying:

> had to listen patiently to somewhat lengthy diatribe on the subject of unscientific domestic talks. I really sympathise with his keenness, which is highly complementary to the BBC. His

> contention is that the newspapers are past praying for but the BBC has a reputation for scientific accuracy ... I was careful to point out that it was not my 'pigeon'. (Memo from Miss Matheson, subject: Miss Petty's Talk, 19 September 1930)

Mottram sought to vet everyone else's scripts and wrote a number of letters expressing rather disparaging views on the 'unscientific' advice given by women broadcasters. Miss Petty at times was singled out for criticism; much of his anxiety about the *Family Budgets* related to the proportion of the budgets spent on food. In an attempt to soften Mottram's approach it was suggested by the BBC that 'as the science is still so very much in its infancy, ... there is room for considerable divergence of opinion' (PT/EIS, 6 March 1931). This plea went unheeded in June that year, when Mottram explained to listeners in a programme on *Meals in the Summer* (3 June 1931) 'You will say – and quite rightly – that I haven't given you much practical advice or that what advice I have given you is very expensive' (BBCWA Mort/Mull T350). Indeed many listeners wrote in and did just that, as he continued to undermine the ordinary listener's instinct and practices, which he often presented as misguided or just plain wrong.

Other broadcasters were aware that there was always an underlying tension between nutrition and economy; for example Miss Petty, informed no doubt by her work with working-class women in London, broadcast on how to feed a family of four for 12 shillings a week. She recommended a number of filling foods: dumplings, bread and jam, sheep's head, and mock goose and savoury pudding (both made with minced liver). Alternatively Mottram's inability to understand the economic constraints which governed working-class women's' food selection arguably lay behind his attack on porridge in 1935, which led to a vitriolic exchange of letters with a Scottish nurse. Mottram displayed his prejudices when he wrote 'oatmeal without milk and sugar is a fool of a food and any but the Scots would have found it out long ago' (23 July 1935) and went on to say 'When the lady explained in her concluding remarks that she was a trained nurse I understood why she was getting my hackles up. I equate trained nurse with opinionated. I also equate Scot with opinionated. A Scottish trained nurse must be opinionated squared' (23 July 1935). Nevertheless he continued to broadcast, despite criticism and falling out with Lord Woolton, the Minister of Food, over winter salads during World War II. It was finally suggested that he might, at the age of 74, be somewhat out of touch in 1956 (BBCWA, Professor Mottram File).

MRS WEBB – A RURAL DOMESTIC GODDESS

Arguably, with scope for such controversy, Mrs Webb was a persuasive legitimating source of authority on domestic matters throughout the 1930s, who the BBC frequently relied upon it its choice of experts because of her association with rural domesticity. This is reflected in her career; she who had been a speaker for Hampshire and Surrey WIs. She, and others, broadcast on fruit and vegetable preservation, British honey and poultry during 1931, for example. She drew upon her radio fame to have a number of books successfully published during the 1930s, covering topic such as: preserving, economical cookery, farmhouse cookery and wartime cookery. Throughout the 1930s Mrs Webb bombarded the BBC with suggestions for programmes, and occasionally gave BBC personnel the products of her garden and kitchen in the hope that these would smooth the way to further radio appearances. She was rewarded with a large number of cooking series on all manner of subjects, including 'dealing with bumper apple crops', pot roasts, tasty ways with bacon and potato surprises, continuing to broadcast through World War II and post-war period. Her broadcasts were considered popular, her accompanying leaflets sold well and in 1935 she began a series entitled *Farmhouse Cookery* on Tuesday 2 April, having made, at the BBC expense, a tour of farmhouses in various counties collecting recipes.

Mrs Webb's *Farmhouse Cookery* made repeated reference to rural architecture, privileged the 'old fashioned' and discursively set the scene for the 'natural' even 'innate' skills of farmers' wives to be foregrounded. In one programme she recalled:

> As I stepped over the threshold with its sandied stones and past the old grey walls of the farmhouse I knew that behind me lay the real spirit of adventure in cookery. Fearlessness based on skill and knowledge, a flair for producing the right effects, the perfect flavours, judgement and tradition asking no help from Modern appliances ...
>
> ... once a week, bread and such bread – plain, spiced, currant, wholemeal, Yorkshire teacakes, pies, cheese cakes, tarts, and great big useful fruit cakes, by magic from the work of that pair of capable and utterly efficient hands ...
>
> I looked at the fireplace, watched the flames travelling under the oven, 'How do you manage to keep the heat going, you usually burn coal of course?' 'Oh no', the answer came swiftly. 'Oh dear no, I never trust coal, or anything else than wood for my baking. I understand wood better, and know exactly what heat it will give.'
>
> 'Do you have failures?'
>
> 'Failures? Of course not, I know exactly what I want to make and make it.'
>
> 'Well how do you manage to arrive at such delicious pies as these/Do you weigh the ingredients?'
>
> 'Never. I could not spare the time. I just know how much the flour butter, lard, milk, water and eggs will make.' (2 April 1935)

This exchange constructed in a script written some time, I suspect, after the interview, which articulated, through the absence of even weights and measures, the anti-thesis of a scientific approach to domesticity. Here common sense and experience prevailed, although it must be acknowledged that 'common-sense' and 'experience' are themselves constructed and contested discourses.

Alternatively other series within the *Household Talks* remit clearly carved out spaces for 'experts' to be brought to task and questioned on their actions by a representative of the 'ordinary housewife': a position the 'rural expert' Mrs Webb happily took up. In 1934 she questioned a range of officials on the operation of the newly established marketing boards (for example the Milk Marketing Board). A series entitled *The House that Jack Built* (1936) was predicated upon the assumption that Jill would certainly have built a rather different one. In each programme a male representative of the public world of house building – a planner, an architect, a builder and so on – had first to explain his job and then answer criticism from a much more privatized 'common sense' domestic approach to housing – articulated by the broadcaster Mrs Thorpe. This mode of the interviewer mediating 'between expert speaker and the lay public' had been established early in 1933 to ensure experts were comprehensible to inexpert listeners (Cardiff, 1986, p. 237). Thus while Professor Mottram broadcast personae was as an expert instructing the ordinary housewife, both Mrs Thorpe and Mrs Webb were constructed – as on the boundary between 'ordinary housewife' and 'extra-ordinary' broadcaster – as they adopted a discursive position of 'a friend at the fireside'.

Interestingly the BBC Talks director appears to have considered that cookery talks came better from a woman (letter to Mottram, 27 January 1931). Control of food, diets and cooking 'are regarded by many as a means of controlling the impact of the external world on the interiority of the body so that the relationship between food and the body is about control' (Foster, 2004, p. 253). Arguably many working-class women felt this area of their control was threatened or undermined by scientific experts. It is in considering the wider cultural significance of diet, its interrelationship with the axis of gender and class power relations that the controversy around different discourses of domestic expertise seen in *Household Talks* can best be understood.

Household Talks, like all broadcasting, offered listeners a sense of belonging, and encouraged them to actively participate. Their effectivness was defended by Miss Wace of the BBC Talk department who explained: 'I do not feel the talks broadcast in the morning are thrown away. The fact is that in the last two years we have sold 370,506 pamphlets issued in connection with the Morning Talks proves I think that we are reaching a very vast public here. The pamphlets after all have to be obtained at some degree of trouble, for 3d in stamps has to be sent' (BBC file on Mottram). The listeners sending for a pamphlet responded actively to an invitation to join an imagined community made up from other listeners, which offered a synthetic interaction based on a shared listening with other housewives in their homes. As Shingler and Weiringa point out, by participating in such a community, audiences may feel pressured to conform in some ways to the consensual 'common sense' of the community (1998, p. 129), which consequently may exert governance. Given the diversity of opinion and expertise on domesticity in inter-war broadcasting, what lay within parameters of common sense is significant. It is with this in mind that I want to suggest that the inclusion of 'listeners' and working-class women's expertise is very important for the representation of private individuals and their expertise in the public domain and created 'new communicative entitlements for previously excluded social groups' (Lacey, 2002, p. 88; see also Scannell, 1980).

Family Budgets, already mentioned, and Mrs Webb's *Farmhouse Cookery* (1935) were examples of the inclusion of the ordinary women's experience which began to blur the distinction between broadcaster and listener. Helen Simpson's series, *What Will You Make?* (1933), set listeners household problems – usually involving making a meal out of a limited list of leftovers – and included listeners' solutions to these problems in the following week's broadcast, in so doing she elevated the housewives' ability to 'manage' limited resources to national significance. The 1934 series *How I Keep House* took this one stage further and handed over the whole broadcast series to working-class women without them being framed by introductory and concluding comments from supposed 'experts'.

HOW I KEEP HOUSE

The series *How I Keep House* was introduced in *Radio Times* in the following terms:

> Different housekeepers from town and country will give an account of how they manage their day's work, explaining why they find their houses easy or difficult to run, how they spend their money, how they plan to fit in with the irregular hours that are kept by many wage-earners or with particular claims of young children. It is hoped that many useful tips in the art of homecraft will be passed to listeners. (4 September 1934)

Although there were some 'tips' for listeners, *How I keep House* tended to be straightforward accounts of numerous small actions women undertook to maintain their families economic survival – for example never letting the children have the extravagance of spreading their own teatime bread with jam. In this they were unlike expert's advice programmes, which offered fantasies of improvement and progress by the appliance of science; these narratives were rather about the struggle to prevent regression into debt and, worse, poverty – they were about managing. All women explained how they divided up their housekeeping, how they shopped and what they cooked or bought. The women's authority and expertise was initially based upon trade union recommendation. In a BBC letter to the Amalgamated Union of Building Trade Workers asking them to recommend a suitable housewife, it was explained: 'We have only chosen housewives who do all their own work, of course, and who manage on small sums. We have also tried to include only those who have a reputation of being good housekeepers. Again, we feel we should have speakers who have the care of young children.' Women's reputation as good housewives rested upon the women being known to have skills as managers of the household budgets. Although the BBC extended their choice of women beyond the union movement – all women's authority was based upon their status as the wife of a working man and this is how they were listed in the *Radio Times*, e.g. 'Wife of a Norfolk farm Labourer'. Geographical location or regionality and their husband's work were seen as key elements structuring these women's domesticity and their legitimate expertise. The smallholders wife's experienced is summarized by the *Radio Times* in the following way:

> How I keep House by smallholder's wife
> – her and husband Londoners –
> She will describe how they lost their money on poultry and had to mortgage their property in order to carry on. A hard life. No fixed wage coming in. All the work entailed in summer visitors to eke things out. Stock to feed, no modern conveniences, it says much for the country that, in spite of all, she has no wish to live in town again. (30 October 1934)

The broadcast scripts were constructed in response to two pages of guidelines and questions provided by the BBC, they were then edited prior to rehearsal and live broadcast. The format produced by this process ensured uniformity between the scripts, which had a style something like an imaginary conversation with a silent interviewer. This invited the audience to place themselves as the interviewer having their questions answered.

In a broadcast that was a far cry from idealized images of rural domesticity in *Farmhouse Cookery*, Mrs Betts, the wife of an agricultural labourer, offered a different form of knowledge about rural life, explaining how she made a hot dinner every day with a pudding to save on the purchase of bread and because her 'husband doesn't feel he's had a dinner without a pudding'. Picking blackberries and crab apples to make into jam for the winter, sewing her children's clothes and the limited use of her oil stove were vital strategies she employed to ensure her family's survival, alongside her husband's bee-keeping and their allotment. She further described how her Sunday joint lasted four days and was followed by 'suet puddings flavoured with the gravy set aside from the meat', a thrifty practise which along with reheating meat Professor Mottram was known to criticize. It was firmly rooted within a working-class discourse of domesticity as a 'struggle to manage' rather than the scientific discourse of some experts.

Momentarily at least, a series like *How I Keep House* placed working-class women and their ability to cope with the daily crisis of hand-to-mouth existence ... 'greatly prized' in working-class women's culture (Tebbutt, 1995, p. 11), centrally as the 'experts' on working class domesticity as opposed to the objects of others expertise. To talk on the BBC in the 1930s gave these women and the women they represented a voice of national importance, momentarily, at least, their minutiae, experience and 'common sense', their everyday domesticity became the defining ones. Thus when Mrs Betts went on to explain on national radio that:

> It's a nuisance with children having an outside lavatory. They (the children that is) often make the excuse to get into the garden but it means I have to come too. We have to carry all our drinking water a distance of 60 yards but my husband does that for me and we catch our washing water in a tank outside the back door. All dirty water has to be carried out on to the garden a distance of 20 yards, a bother on a wet washing day. (11 September 1934)

She was shifting the boundaries of public and private, alongside definitions of women's place, status and expertise and, in tandem with extra-parliamentary women's organizations in the post-suffrage era, she was putting housing reform and the campaign for improved rural water supplies, so vital for the lived experience of rural women, into the public sphere (Andrews, 1997; Thane, 2010). The significance of housing was also emphasized by a Scottish miner's wife who explained that 'I find my work is much more difficult than it might be, especially since I have been in one of the modern 3-apartment houses built by the Country Council ... but had to give it up when my husband was recovering from injuries received in the course of his work' (25 September 1934). For this working-class housewife modernity and rationalization were financially unsustainable.

Letters indicated that women listeners appreciated the series, although the Grocer's Federation complained about the almost weekly references to the importance of the Co-op for women's budgeting, and only the policeman's wife expenditure came up to Professor Mottram's exacting standards: an indication perhaps of his distance from the lived experience of working women. It was pointed out to him in a letter from the BBC that the policeman's family had a higher than average income and that perhaps the series had shown that the BBC speakers were over-estimating the size of working-class budgets (BBC WA -PT/MHW, 29 October 1934). How the majority of housewives reacted to the series is, because of the paucity of sources, very hard to grasp, as indeed it was at the time. Nevertheless, the new weekly wireless magazine, *Radio Pictorial*, heralded Margery Wace responsible for Women's Talks as the 'Housewives' Friend' (*Radio Pictorial*, 9 September 1934). Listener figures do not exist for stations or programmes; the potential audience may not have turned their radio or their concentration on; some of them at least may well have been listening to another BBC regional or a foreign station. Some enthusiastic letters have been kept: one is from a listener who wrote to thank the BBC for the talk by the wife of a Liverpool clerk and suggested that it 'might be rebroadcast during the evening so that young people away during the day may hear it'. Another described the series as 'an interesting and educative broadcast' going on to add 'Although I have had a home for nearly 19 years now, it is true that one is never too old to learn and I will say I gathered many useful hints from your talk' (BBWA, R5 240). The format was reworked with a more diverse and challenging group of women and men in a later series entitled *How I Manage* in 1937. The title foregrounded the working-class discourse of domesticity as a 'struggle to manage', as did the testimony of one week's speaker, a widow with four children under nine years of age, living on 24 shillings a week, who after describing the minutiae of her weekly budget explained, 'I was unable to pay the baker, so I must let the rent go one more week in arrears this week, so that he gets paid this week and I shall be able to pay the two shillings that are outstanding on the repairs of the boy's boots' (18 May 1937).

Respectability and appearance were key to working-class culture and involved the 'subsequent hiding of financial hardships and pressures' (Tebbut, 1995, p. 84). In this series not only the anxiety and constraint but also skill and resourcefulness of housewives, buying things on tick or using pawn shops (Roberts, 1984) is shifted from behind individual closed doors and shared with other women listening to the radio behind their closed doors. Cardiff has suggests that the presentation of everyman … including working people … added a democratic twist' to the BBC which evoked some controversy and was rare before 1935. (The controversy, he argues, is because of the emphasis on character rather than the experience that documentary interviewers tended to emphasize (Cardiff, 1986, p. 24).) However this is not so in these series, which focused on ordinary women as 'experts', which is perhaps an indication of the growing priority of the ordinary listener, despite the BBC's often perceived paternalism and aloofness in the 1930s. The production of discourse involves power and inter-war radio gave some power to the audience, to the ordinary housewife as listener and broadcaster. What these talks indicate is that the BBC was not such a monolithic and top-down organization, controlled by Reith, as popular history suggests. In any large organization, employees are apt to find spaces and places of autonomy and independence, and the consequences can be surprisingly radical.

WOMEN'S CONFERENCE 1936

Household Talks was not merely ahead of its time in the inclusion of working-class women as experts, it was at the forefront of audience research. In November 1935, through the *Radio Times*, Miss Mace, of the BBC Talks department, asked housewives for suggestions on improvements to the morning talks, in advance of the setting up of the BBC's controversial Audience Research Department. The following year, on 24 April 1936, nearly 400 women from a range of organizations, including the WI, Six Points Group, Women's Committee against War, Women's Labour Party, Council of Midwives, Women's Farm and Garden Association and Suffragette Fellowship, attended a conference held by the BBC at Queen's Hall, London, on the *Household Talks*. Mrs Mary Agnes Hamilton (a governor of the BBC) opened the first discussion and spoke of 'the importance of women's work in the home and the high degree of skill it called for', and went on to suggest 'part of the object of the broadcast morning talks was to throw scientific light on the home problems of food, cooking and health with which working women were faced under conditions of the greatest difficulty' (BBCWA, R 44/86/1).

It is hard to gauge the impact of the conference on BBC programming, the BBC Director-General John Reith apparently sat with his head in his hands much of the time. Discussion on the timing of the talks – introduced by Mrs Webb – explored whether the talks should be earlier, later or in the afternoon, and a domestic servant and secretary of Ewhurst WI explained how she took the stair rods into the kitchen to clean so that she could hear the *Household Talks* each morning. Another discussion on the topic of 'Are cookery and child welfare talks of value?' concluded that 'talks should be given by people who know what they are talking about', although it was not clear which of the regular broadcasters they excluded from this category, 'the most popular speaker was a woman who said that men should be taught by the radio to help in the home' (*Daily Mirror*, 25 April 1936, p. 2).

The conference was reported in the national, and the local press, the *Manchester Guardian*, claimed: 'One got a complete view of the harassed housewife, getting her children off to school, running out to the shop, preparing the mid-day meal, interrupted by calls from tradesmen and worrying all the time lest she should not be able to sit down and listen to the talk' (25 April 1936). It is thus hardly surprising that *The Scotsman* reported that the answer to the question 'what do women want from their radio programmes?' had 'many, many answers' (27 April 1936). The *Daily Express* gave those women listeners not invited, a chance to air their views by sending letters to the paper. Summarizing them they suggested that women 'in the main support the BBC Talks policy, finding them instructive and helpful, although a Mrs Airey pointed out: 'The housewife does not turn on the wireless to be taught her job. She wants something to take her mind out of the kitchen. Why should women always be instructed rather than entertained' (*Express*, 24 April 1936, p. 19). Although in discussing German radio Lacey argues that 'It was the labour of housework that was most widely addressed by and accompanied by the form and content of daytime radio' (1996, p. 160). In Britain multiple listening possibilities provided by European channels challenged this and pushed the BBC to a greater awareness of audience views and opinions. Arguably it was the awareness that many women wanted to be entertained which lay behind the conference and *Household Talks* sensitivity to their audience for whom, after all, there was a temptation to remain with other stations which began broadcasting in the morning before the BBC. The letter from a listener, who announced 'as a housewife I would like to say that I find your domestic talks helpful and entertaining' (*Radio Times*, 1 December 1937, p. 15) must have been very welcome at the BBC.

The *Daily Herald* described the Women's Conference as significant and in October was pleased to announce, with an indication that they too felt scientific discourses had been overplayed: 'For the first time in its history the BBC will allow talks about children to be made of the human stuff mothers like to hear. Instead of talking endlessly of child psychology and isms speakers are to be allowed to talk about pretty children, curly hair, fine limbs and bright eyes' (12 October 1936). Significantly, the following year, the BBC again privileged rural women's domesticity with a new broadcaster at teatime between 3:45 and 4:00 p.m., Margaret McCook Weir, a mother of four boys from Suffolk, described herself as 'living a peasant's life in isolated East Anglia' (on a 100-acre farm) and explained that 'the 'fields must come first' and 'you learn to look on the fields as your home and the house as a cave to shelter in' (29 September 1937). Again, from the many competing discourses of domesticity in the era, the BBC drew upon a form of expertise which carried credibility – rural domesticity, despite the reference to agricultural work these broadcasts focused on domesticity. She explained, 'Having four babies I feel I've been washing napkins all my life, and I can scarcely imagine a morning without washing, drying, airing and adjusting, pining or inspecting napkins' (BBCWA, T310).

Weir espoused simultaneously the childrearing practices of Truby King and her own rather more personal and bohemian approach to child care which allowed her four boys to spend their summers running naked and free on the farm and a rather take-it-or-leave-it approach to schooling for the under sevens. Like the women in *How I Keep House*, her broadcasts avoided an idealized domesticity. Her knowledge of domesticity was framed by financial limitations making-do with second-hand and collapsing prams and – in an abandonment of any semblance of scientific management – endless unfinished tasks, particularly when it came to cleaning. She still lapsed into idealized versions of the domestic with reference to 'laborious slow housekeeping' and suggesting the 'secret of country contentment … is … all one's pleasures being in the home'. However, her discourse were not so idealized or instructional as many of the earlier broadcasters; referring to her children she admits, 'Sometimes in fact I loathe them and their ever pressing demands threaten to overwhelm me' (BBCWA, T310). Significantly the radio again acted as a democratizing medium by giving a voice to women who sometimes loathed their children's demands. Working-class women as experts were also given airtime when Olive Shapley, who worked for the BBC in the Manchester region, created *Miners' Wives* in 1939. After spending a week living with the Emmersons, a mining family in County Durham, Shapley then travelled with Mrs Emmerson to spend a week with a mining family in France. The resulting programme involved Mrs Emmerson discussing 'her impressions of the way of life in two mining villages' (Shapley, 1996, quoted in Mitchell, 2001).

Bailey has argued that 'broadcasting represented a paradoxical challenge to the patriarchal authority of the head of the house. What father now said had to be reconciled with what "Auntie" said. And for the most part, wireless was saying that in household matters at least, mum knows best. In this sense *Household Talks* were potentially empowering for women, in so much as they were invested with a "natural" authority' (2009, p. 58). Arguably, the process was more complex than this, lifestyle media such as the BBC's household talks, which focused on domesticity, emphasized the gendered performance of housewifery and domestic labour, for if domestic labour was a 'natural' feminine skill it would not need to be learned – thus at one level such programmes always caused 'gender trouble' (Butler, 1990) Furthermore, careful examination of the competing discourses of domesticity in these talks and within inter-war culture suggests that the wireless operated as a space in which the competing discourses of science, scientific management, consumer culture, managing and rural expertise competed for legitimacy. Arguably, programmes such as *How I Manage* gave a public recognition and legitimacy to working-class women's 'managing' of budgets and households. They brought into the public sphere the experiences of women who at times loathed their children, avoided paying the rent and used gravy to make suet pudding to eke out their meager budgets. However, as Bourke points out, as housework became more skilled and specialized 'progressively excluding male members of the family and enhancing the bargaining position of women ... It was an exclusion based also on the need of women to insure their eminence within the household' (1994, p. 70). What it led to was a shift in the areas of domesticity that men participated in – the next chapter looks at some areas of male expertise and participation, and how gardening became one area of significance.

Chapter Three

The gardener and the chef: broadcasting celebrities – 1930s style

INTRODUCING TWO AMBIVALENT BROADCASTING CELEBRITIES

On 12 July 1937 the privileged few, who were both wealthy enough to afford a television set and lived close enough to Alexandra Palace to get a signal, were treated to a television programme involving two of the most famous lifestyle broadcasting celebrities of the inter-war period. A BBC memo in preparation for the press release announced:

> Two well-known Television artists met before the camera tonight. They are M. Marcel Boulestin, who has led viewers up paths to culinary heights during the last winter, and Mr C. H. Middleton, whose garden in the Palace grounds we hope will be a source of much horticultural enlightenment. They have a topic in common, Salads – making salads and salad growing. M. Boulestin will prepare some of his favourite salads, and Mr Middleton will tell viewers how to grow or where to get their ingredients. (BBCWA, memo from Mrs Mary Adams, 12 July 1937)

The first regular high-definition television service had begun transmitting from Alexandra Palace, North London, on 2 November 1936; its signal was picked up on approximately 400 sets within a radius of 40–100 miles for 2 hours a day. As television sets cost between £35 and £150, at a time when a new Model T Ford car cost £150, they entered the living rooms of only the wealthy. The desirability of the medium grew, with the assistance of advertising, demonstrations at exhibitions and the televising of the coronation procession of George VI in May 1937, so that by 1938 about 5,000 TV sets had been sold (Crissell, 1997). Marcel Boulestin and Mr Middleton moved onto this new medium, with individual and then a joint appearance, having already established themselves as successful lifestyle broadcasters on radio. Their subject matter – cooking and gardening – and their celebrity personalities were reassuringly familiar to an audience engaging with a new medium. By the mid-1930s both men were established and popular radio broadcasters – not in the underpaid and less prestigious daytime schedules aimed at housewives but in evening and weekend prime-time slots. Boulestin had an already established celebrity status as a restaurateur, writer and food critic, and moved comfortably into radio, educational films and then television, while Middleton's appeal as a celebrity persona was as an 'ordinary', informal, self-deprecating gardener who had been 'discovered' by the BBC and who, like many contemporary broadcasting celebrities, was constructed as a 'friend' of the viewers. Both their careers provide evidence of the growing centrality of broadcast media to 1930s domestic culture, and serve as a case study of broadcasting's populism, intimacy, growing informality and preoccupation with domesticity which have precipitated anxieties about the medium ever since.

Furthermore and just as importantly, in setting a precedent for the popularity of lifestyle programming, there was in both Boulestin and Middleton's celebrity personae a degree of ambivalence in relation to masculinity, sexuality, and the exact class and geographical identities they inhabited. Broadcasting's celebrity identities or personae are established through 'long term continuity in time' … 'accomplished through talk' and 'routinization' which makes their performance of personality familiar to the audience (Brand and Scannell, 1991, p. 111). However, the celebrity personae emphasize the constructed nature of identity and the idea of 'the self as a presentation or performance designed to be appropriate to the circumstances and setting in which it is produced' (Goffman, 1960, p. 39). Furthermore, as Butler (1990) has argued, gendered identity exists only through performance.

As domesticity was associated with the feminine, Boulestin and Middleton as lifestyle celebrities drew attention to the gendered nature of their performances by their focus upon the domestic; particularly as they both made reference to the rural, the peasant and the feminine in their broadcasts, and rejected the use of science or rationality – familiar tropes for men to affirm their masculinity.

They and their broadcasts were polysemic, open to different readings and interpretations, and offered multiple points of recognition, identification and communality for their varied and diffuse audiences, which radio needed in order to establish significant listener numbers. Their ambivalent identity performances gave their audiences permission to play with, subvert and rework the possibilities of their own identity positions – to be who they wanted to be, at least in their imagination (Jackson *et al.*, 2001). Thus radio culture operated to offer 'symbolic repertoire' far earlier than the post-modern turn in the latter part of the twentieth century. For many men, in a time of economic crisis and uncertainty, what they may have imagined and aspired to be was home-centred and ordinary and they were able to enjoy the pleasures of taste and food that the domestic sphere could offer. Indeed, Ravetz (1995) suggests that social ambitions were focused on the desire for privacy and a home; in this, the inter-war years and marked a cultural revolution in aspirations (Meller, 2002). For many in the industrial heartlands, it may have seemed an aspiration with only a remote chance of fulfilment; nevertheless they tuned into these broadcasters in their thousands.

BOULESTIN AS RESTAURATEUR AND WRITER OF GASTRONOMIC LITERATURE

Boulestin's established celebrity reputation went beyond his expertise on food and rested to a significant degree on his exotic French 'otherness'. In the *Times* obituary after his death, Boulestin was described as: 'a music critic, novelist, actor, a caricaturist, designer and decorator, broadcaster and restaurateur' (*Times*, 23

October 1943, p. 6). His early career included time spent in the Paris bohemian milieu of Collette and her first husband Henry Gauthier Villars (known as Willy) for whom he was a secretary and ghost writer. He also served in the French Infantry during World War I and ran a less than successful interior design shop. Boulestin came to the attention of the general British public with the publication of his first cookery book in 1923 – *Simple French Cooking for English Homes* – which sold for 5/- (25p), and was reprinted the same year as well as in 1925, 1928, 1930 and 1933. A subsequent book, *Second Helpings*, also came out in 1925 and also had a cover designed by the artist Labourer. The food writer and critic Elizabeth David later endorsed the significance of these books pointing out:

> It was uncommon in those days ... for publishers to commission artists of such quality to illustrate cookery books, a little of the success of Boulestin's early books must be acknowledged to his publishers who ... produced them in so appropriate form in large type on thick paper: chunky, easy little books to handle, attractively bound. (David, 1965)

Other books followed and while his food journalism extended to the *Daily Express*, the *Morning Post*, the *Daily Telegraph*, *Country Life*, *Harpers Bazaar*, the *Manchester Guardian* and the *Spectator*, and from 1923–9 he produced a 'Finer Cooking' series for *Vogue* and also ran a School of French Cookery – simple and advanced – at 76 George Street, Portman Square, London. His writing for the *Evening Standard* led to the *Evening Standard Book of Menus* in 1935. Boulestin's autobiography described his meeting with Robin Adair as 'the turning point' of his life and referred to 'the charm of a beautiful friendship, which opened like a beautiful flower, generously offering its perfume' (Adair, 1948, p. 42). There seems little doubt that they became not only collaborators in first a catering business and then the opening of restaurant in Leicester Square in 1925, but were also lifetime companions and lovers. It was the opening of Restaurant Boulestin in Convent Garden, close to the Opera House, in October 1927, that placed Boulestin at the centre of London's social elite. His clientele included MPs such as Harold Nicolson, film stars including Douglas Fairbanks Junior, aristocrats such as Lady Diana Cooper and Baron Schroeder, and King Edward VIII and Mrs Simpson prior to the abdication. Such clientele did not ensure the profitability of the restaurant – his insistence on finest quality ingredients was expensive – but they provided Boulestin with glamour by association and he thus became an 'aspirational and inspirational' celebrity for his fans and followers (Stacey, 1994).

Mennell has suggested that food writing can be categorized as either gastronomic literature or cook books (Mennell, 1996) with the latter more often associated with female domestic cooking. Certainly Boulestin's cookery writing contained a literary bent; it is not simply a series of instructions to be followed, but arguably it proposed a philosophy of food which, like Boulestin himself, played upon the margins of these distinct categories and bore the mark of his bohemian youth in Paris. The Victorian upper-middle-classes had increasingly seen a taste for French food as a mark of 'distinction' (Ashley *et al.*, 2004) and Boulestin's celebrity restaurant catered for the urbane, British elite, serving French food only, but he promoted not hotel food but French peasant food, the rural and the feminine cooking of the housewife, a style of cooking which he suggested in his first radio broadcast, on 26 April 1927 (entitled *Wastage in the Kitchen*), avoided the waste found in many British kitchens (BBCWA, Boo-BOU T48). Waste, he suggested, was a consequence of cultural assumptions about what can and cannot be eaten. As he pointed out in one of his broadcasts: the French dictionary describes a dandelion as 'a wild plant usually eaten in salad', while in the English dictionary it was 'a common plant with a yellow flower' (BBCWA, *Kitchen Sense*, 28 June 1935).

His concern about waste could perhaps be seen as an engagement with the economic constraints of the era, but Boulestin's argument that cooking is an art was more complex and had an echo of William Morris and the Arts and Crafts Movement of the late nineteenth century, which had suggested that everyday practices and feminine crafts could be elevated to 'art' (Callen, 1979). As an 'art', food was to be seen as important; in a British Gas Association film (1936), Boulestin explained 'Food is an extremely important thing in life. We have several meals a day. These meals must be good ... it means the happiness of the individual.' He also extolled the kitchen and food as the very heart of the home, something women should take pride in despite the struggles that poverty and financial hardship created. As he explained in a broadcast talk entitled *Kitchen Sense*:

> To the woman who looks after her own small house. It is specifically to her that I preach interest in her house ... to use everything, to do her upmost; and that she may not do it with resignation, for that is the wrong attitude in life; she must take pleasure in her fight and in the same way personal satisfaction in the performance of domestic duties ... I can imagine no more charming picture than that of the wife seeing to the perfection of the evening meal and the husband on his way home from work looking forward to it. Happiness sits smiling at their table. (BBCWA, 28 June 1935)

It is a heterosexual idyll which Boulestin did not participate in; broadcast in the evening, he was talking to both a male and female audience and his words were open to multiple interpretations. It was at one level a reappraisal of the significance and importance of cooking, a re-evaluation of domestic labour and the centrality of food to domesticity, and importantly there was s strong hint that pleasure was important. A Bakhtinian analysis of food suggests that, like sex, it brings into focus the uncertain boundaries of the body, while excess in eating highlights the physical degradation of potentially uncontrollability of lusts (1984). As Schaffer points out, at the beginning of the twentieth century 'taste was seen as a vulgarly body based desire' (2010, p. 113). Boulestin remarked upon the English unwillingness to discuss food and suggested that greediness and, by implication, uncontrolled desire should be practised. He complained: 'They talk about scientific knowledge and teaching dietetics yet all that is wanted is more greediness and a little more common sense for there is no doubt about it cooking is more common sense than science' (BBCWA, Scripts, 21 June 1935). A message he maintained when in December 1937 he was the after-dinner speaker for the New Health Club's third annual dinner at the Cafe Royal, arguing: 'Science has done nothing for good food but spoil it' (*Times*, 8 December 1937, p. 21). No doubt it was Boulestin that Professor Mottram of King's College has in mind when he ranted in a letter to the BBC: 'What I'm against is this infernal talk in England that people ought to be taught cooking and to produce the sort of cooking we hear is practised by all French housewives' (BBWA, Mottram File). For the evening listeners, relaxing by their fireside, Boulestin's broadcasts enabled them to flirt with ideas of London glamour, physical pleasures, sexual ambiguity and greediness, and thus provided enjoyable entertainment.

BOULESTIN AS BROADCASTING CHEF

Developing his radio personality in 1935, Boulestin took part in five episodes of a 45-minute weekly variety programme entitled *The Bungalow Club*. It was set in an imaginary domestic space – a bungalow – and language confusion and cultural stereotypes were the butt of much of the humour. Jokes relied upon mixing up 'Morris' and 'Maurice', 'cockles' and 'cockroaches', etc. Boulestin's persona in the text rested upon the twin axis of his Frenchness and his gastronomic knowledge. He also continued to broadcast on radio in 1937, when he made a programme on 'dishes with milk' when the Ministry of Health advocated increased milk consumption and made programmes on 'Polite Wine Drinking', but it was on television that he really came into his own.

'Bringing New Glamour into the Home.' A sketch produced for an HMV advertising campaign in 1937, the glamour of the technology was replicated by the glamour attached to the broadcasts of restaurateur Marcel Boulestin. (Image reproduced by courtesy of the History of Advertising Trust Archive http://www.hatads.org.uk)

When a viewer survey of television was carried out in 1937, disapproval concentrated on the demonstrations of cooking, washing and ironing that the BBC had shown, which were condemned as of little interest to those who could afford television sets (BBCWA, R 9/9/1). Indeed *Suggestions for Dishes to be Prepared and Cooked in 15 Minutes,* which Moira Meighn demonstrated using a single heated ring, must have seemed incongruous to the average television viewer. Although in May 1939 both the BBC and manufacturers invested more than £4,000 each in a big advertising campaign to promote television purchase, and the London Department store, Selfridges, provided a large display to promote sales, the cheapest sets were 21 guineas. Consequently, when Boulestin appeared in the first really successful television cookery series, it was entitled *Cook's Night Out,* the, no doubt correct, assumption was that those who could afford a television could also afford a cook and would only venture into the kitchen if cook was out for the evening. Indeed the scenario of cook having a night off was borrowed from Boulestin's film for the Gas Board entitled *Scratch Meal* (1935), in which Boulestin and friends were apparently marooned in a country house by bad weather. He responded to the situation by rolling up his sleeves and cooking a three-course meal – including soup and pilaf – from odds and ends found in the pantry. He was accompanied and assisted only by a tall be-spectacled man, presumably his 'companion' Robin Adair. His accessible tone, the slightly camp perfomativity of his pepper grinding and parsley decoration, all earmarked him out as a potential tele-visual performer and BBC memos indicate that it was his performance in gas films which convinced BBC personnel of his suitability for television.

In the first episode of *Cook's Night Out,* on Thursday evening at 9, Marcel Boulestin demonstrated how to cook an omelette (21 January 1937), in so doing he was able to showcase the simple skill of the French peasant tradition for which he was by then well known. Indeed the Omelette Boulestin was one of the signature dishes available at his Covent Garden restaurant;

it thus associated the glamorous public space of the restaurant with the private domestic sphere – a phenomenon that TV chefs of the 1990s such as Gary Rhodes and Jamie Oliver were later to evoke. The French theme was continued the following week with Fillet of Sole Murat, followed by Escalope of Veau Choisy, Salade and finally Crêpes Flambé. With a series of five programmes, each week was supposed to teach viewers one dish, which all together would produce a five-course meal. The French focus furthermore affirms the middle-class tastes of his audience, who 'rich in what Bourdieu terms cultural capital' were then as now seen as 'maintaining distinctiveness by cultivating tastes in exotic and foreign foods' (Beardsworth and Keil, 1997, p. 88; see also Bourdieu, 1984).

The programmes went out live but were repeated – with much washing-up undertaken by Boulestin's secretary/assistant, Robin Adair, in between performances, and indeed negotiations which preceded the programmes included the provision of a dressing room with a washbasin to make this possible. The circumstances in which the programmes were produced were challenging, as Boulestin describes in his autobiography, edited by Robin Adair after his death:

> While genuinely cooking my dish or sauce, I had to improvise a commentary of clear and precise directions, to finish on the stroke of a pre-arranged second, and to hurry unobtrusively if necessary. I kept a watch on the table, out of the camera's range and also received a signal one minute before the end.
>
> There was a very restrictive space for working, containing a table, a stove and myself, moving about as little as possible, so as not to upset the focus of the cameras. All this in the terrific heat of the blinding lights above and around me, added to which was the heat of my stove. (Adair, 1948, p. 119)

Boulestin's autobiography and the correspondence that surrounded his first television series and other BBC broadcasts indicate Boulestin's careful management of his image and fees; for example, he did not want to be referred to as a chef as he is a restaurateur. This is an indication of his playing the ambivalence of his class associations – chefs are labourers, restaurateurs are capitalists – and yet Boulestin was employed to do physical labour and cook what he promoted as peasant food. He also insisted that the eight dinner plates required for presenting the food had to be dark, as his food would not show up sufficiently on white plates. He was paid £15 guineas for each broadcast and the BBC files certainly carry a significant amount of correspondence on his fees. Careful image management is also demonstrated in another part of the autobiography when Boulestin indicated he was aware that direct involvement with advertising and consumerism carried risks to the celebrity persona that he had created and marketed:

> I was quite willing, for example, to make films and brochures for the gas company. I did not refer to the advantages of gas, but demonstrated them in the value of our cooking which was indirect publicity for them; but I always refused, even for quite considerable sums, to boost synthetic preparations while I was spending my time in preaching that everything should be made by the cook in the kitchen. I could not agree such a contradiction. One must have some principles other than that of earning a lot of money by any sort of means, and my reputation or integrity could only gain by this policy. In the end it was the more adroit; otherwise I would soon have ceased to be taken seriously. (Adair, 1948, p. 115)

Boulestin's involvement with the gas company was by no means unique; gas and electricity companies from the 1920s until the 1980s used home economists, television cooks and chefs to assist them in carving out a market for their products (Goldstein, 1997). At some points the BBC considered this compromised their non-commercial status, but in the 1930s they were more concerned about cost-cutting, and correspondence indicates that the British Gas Association loaned the BBC the cooker for Boulestin to use during his broadcasts free of charge, facilitating an astute piece of early product placement. Although the gas company had to determinedly pursue the BBC to ensure that the cooker was eventually returned, Boulestin continued to broadcast one-off demonstrations in magazine programmes or in his own series alone, and at times with Mr Middleton, through the early years of television. Arguably Boulestin's programmes always erred on the side of gastronomic advice rather than cooking instruction; for example he appeared in *Gourmet's Christmas* presented by A. Miller Jones and aired on 23 December, which was rather late to influence anyone's shopping and planning over the festive season.

MIDDLETON – THE PALLY OLD FRIEND ON THE RADIO

If Boulestin brought his celebrity status to broadcasting, Mr Middleton – as he was known throughout the country – by contrast, had his celebrity status created by radio, a medium for which he was eminently suited in tone, style and manner. His mediated radio persona emphasized his ambivalence and social mobility in terms of class and geographical identity and belonging. His subject matter – gardening and often by implication the suburban garden – created a 'sympathetic familiarity' which many listeners identified if not as a familiar experience then as a familiar aspiration; he was thus able to be seen as representing their interests (Marshall, 1997).

Born in 1897 in the Northamptonshire village of Weston by Weedon, where his father had been a gardener on a large estate, C. H. Middleton moved south in his teens, entered the nursery trade and market gardening, gaining knowledge with the assistance of evening classes. He was engaged in food production work during World War I and also spent time working at Kew Gardens for the Ministry of Agriculture and the Royal Horticultural Society. Having been an instructor in horticulture for Surrey County Council and given lectures to allotment societies and Women's Institutes, he began broadcasting fortnightly on *The*

Week in the Garden in May 1931. This was followed by a weekly series entitled *The Weekend in the Garden* in 1932 and *The Garden* in 1933, and he was 'given free rein to arrange the gardening talks' in 1934 (*Radio Times*, 8 November 1935, p. 15). In doing so he focused on the home garden, referring frequently to his own back garden rather than the institutional or corporate gardens that he had experience of in his working life. He continued to broadcast talks on the radio most weeks until 1945; he also produced a number of schools programmes on gardening from 1933 until 1937, when he set up the BBC garden at Alexandra Palace which was the basis for weekly afternoon programmes on early television.

Gardening programmes can be seen as entirely consistent with the BBC's public service remit; the idea of encouraging gardening as a morally improving pastime for the working classes had begun to gain credence at the end of the nineteenth century when, as Constantine points out, it was thought 'the working class gardener would cultivate a concern for domestic life and a respect for property, and this should lead to social harmony' (1981, p. 391). Indeed Neville Chamberlain suggested in 1920 that 'every spadeful of manure dug in, every fruit tree planted converted a potential revolutionary into a citizen' (Feiling, 1966, p. 86, quoted in Constantine, 1981, p. 391). A new garden was seen as leading to a new gardener; although working-class gardeners did not always see their activities as leisure or recreation. For many the appeal was economic, as a garden or allotment could provide cheap food; some estimates suggest that prior to World War I as much as 25 per cent of a working-class families' food could be home-grown if they had access to gardens or allotments (Bourke, 1994; Constantine, 1981, pp. 396–7). Thus, a woman Bourke interviewed explained: 'my husband does the garden, Mind you he doesn't like doing it – he does it to get the benefit of it – with the vegetables' (1994, p. 90).

However the perceived spread of 'gardening naiveté' led the National Allotments Society to be formed in the early twentieth century with a number of branches in working-class areas

'Entertain … and be Entertained.' An HMV advertising campaign in 1937; Mr Middleton's broadcasts always maintained an emphasis on broadcasting's key role in providing domestic entertainment. (Image reproduced by courtesy of the History of Advertising Trust Archive http://www.hatads.org.uk)

(Bourke, 1994, p. 88). In the 1920s Mrs Marion Crane began giving gardening talks on the radio, but it was Mr Middleton who made them truly popular.

Broadcast talk is two-way talk (Scannell and Brand, 1991; Montgomery, 1986); it is not that the audience overhear broadcast talk – rather it is spoken with a strong sense of the domestic audience in mind, even though it is spoken into a microphone in a broadcasting studio; the interactivity is, however, performed, although no immediate response is provided. It is a one-way communication parading as two-way communication. In order for this to work effectively, a skilled and carefully structured performance is required. Mr Middleton was one of the first masters of such performances and hence became a celebrity. Arguably the domestic focus of his subject material facilitated this – he spoke to an audience in their home while conjuring up images of the home – or at least the garden of a home. His conversational voice, slightly rural regional accent, rolling tone and easy accessible manner gave him the air of someone who had just popped in for an informal chat by the fireside; more than most he either understood or instinctively produced a scripted informality that was comfortably listened to within the domestic space of the home. One script begins with, 'As I was sitting here waiting for the red light to twinkle I was trying to recollect a poem I used to know about the month of May' (4 May 1934). His gardening programme did not use Latin names for plants or attempt to appeal to the cultural capital of middle-classes; significantly he was un-reverential in his approach to established gardening maxims. Thus when listeners wrote in to ask when to plant evergreens or how late to mow lawns, for example, he suggested 'Some say you should never cut grass after October, but I've cut mine at Christmas and it didn't seem to mind' (26 October 1934). His scripts meandered through topics, with diversions and asides, structured as conversation, occasionally asking his listeners a question – such as to whether they had lost particular plants or trees in recent weather. There were no commands issued or injunctions, only suggestions and musing – statements carried proviso's and tags or were qualified as he began sentences with phrases such as: 'well now', 'very well', 'suppose instead', 'that's as may be' and 'perhaps I can explain that in another way'. His relationship with his listeners relied upon a pseudo personalization in his mode of address, and an impression created in his self-deprecating narratives that placed him on a par with his audience. When he interviewed a range of visiting specialists in his broadcasts, Middleton positioned himself as the representative of the ordinary gardener; during one programme, while he was discussing vegetable growing and digging with one of his guests, he interjected:

> Thanks very much, it all sounds a back breaking business, doesn't it? But as Mr James says deep digging is the basis of cultivation so it is no use trying to dodge it. It isn't such terribly hard work if you do a little at a time. Personally I find the best method is to get someone else to do it, easier that way. (11 October 1934)

In an interesting turn of phrase on a subsequent occasion, he welcomed the audience saying 'Good evening. I haven't brought a specialist along tonight so you'll have to put up with the family practitioner for once' (19 October 1934). His use of the term 'family' suggested his role as a radio broadcaster within the domestic household, while the medical metaphor of specialist as opposed to practitioner was a reference to the numerous problems listeners wrote in to him about, which covered areas as diverse as borrowing lawnmowers from neighbours and squirrels eating crocuses. He arguably used a more feminine linguistic code – with the high number of provisos and tags on sentences – intended to establish a relationship rather than command action. This is picked up on in a *Radio Times* article which explained: 'Listeners write to him from everywhere – amateur and professional gardeners alike. They appreciate his "human pally sort of talks" and tell him he is "like an old friend" and he finds the same friendliness in them' (*Radio Times*, 8 November 1935, p. 15). The correspondence from listeners – which Middleton frequently referred to in his broadcasts – built up the relationship between the celebrity and his audience, for example:

> Well I have a bundle of letters here and I hardly know which to look at first. But first I should like to thank all those of you who have sent such nice personal letters, I am sorry I don't answer many of them to you direct – but even if I don't answer you I should like you to know I appreciate them very much and I'm afraid I must apologise to all those who don't get answers (8 February 1935)

His gardening style was gentle nurturing – he warned against over-pruning, 'There is far more damage done by over rather than under pruning' and pointed out that 'when moved roses become surgical cases which take time to recover' (16 November 1934). Although vegetable gardening could be seen to emphasize the masculine role of provider or become an area of competition and public affirmation in vegetable shows, for example, arguably he opened up a feminized space of nurturing for men within the domestic sphere. Domesticity was predominantly perceived as a female sphere of influence; however gardening offered men scope for creativity and influence, which was not seen as emasculating unlike some domestic tasks such as cooking or washing (Bourke, 1994, p. 91). Bourke's study of working-class autobiographies indicated that men were definately involved in doing housework, but this was not necessarily childcare or cooking, from the end of the nineteenth century to the middle of the twentieth century there was an increase in a range of other activities related to the household – many of which, for example 'do-it-yourself repairs, redecorating, gardening required a certain level of economic security' (Bourke, 1994, p. 82) and increasing levels of home ownership, something which was opened up for some with lower interest rates and house building in the 1930s.

Masculine domesticity may have been as much a space in the imagination as a physical reality or something which necessarily required action. Gardening offered men a series of 'what ifs' and opened up different ways of being within the domestic sphere. Middleton's broadcasts acknowledged the importance of the fantasies and 'what ifs', for example when he discusses the pleasures of seed catalogues, musing:

> One of my favourite jobs for January is to sit in a cosy armchair with the new seed and plant catalogue and build floral castles in the air. I like catalogues especially the descriptions and eulogies of the new varieties. They always make me wish I had bags of money and a large garden so that I could fill up one of these order forms form beginning to end. Still it's wonderful what you can do with a few shillings if you go the right way to work. (4 January 1934)

The relationship between the broadcaster and the listener was built up here with reference to the cosy armchair in which many of the listeners were indeed listening to his talk, while there was also a an acknowledgement of the consumerism of lifestyle broadcasting and the necessary negotiation between fantasies and the financial constraints in everyday life. That there may be little relationship between the 'what if' and lived experience is highlighted in a *Punch* cartoon in 1937, with two women chatting over the garden fence and remarking 'My husband is very keen on gardening, he never misses a single talk on the wireless', while behind her lies a neglected garden (*Punch*, 24 September 1937, quoted in Briggs, 1981, p. 126).

Whether due to economic necessity, as a leisure activity or form of masculine domesticity, the popularity of gardening endorsed by Mr Middleton's broadcasts, grew in the inter-war period. A survey conducted in Birmingham just prior to World War II indicated an overwhelming enthusiasm for the newly acquired gardens of suburban developments and a Mass Observation survey conducted in wartime on housing indicated that the vast majority of respondents wanted homes with gardens (quoted in Constantine, 1981). Thus on 1 June 1939 *The Nurseryman and Seedsman* announced: 'We have been called a nation of shopkeepers we might with equal satisfaction be called a nation of gardeners' (quoted in Constantine, 1981, p. 399). Certainly the reduction in working hours, with the growing adherence of an 8-hour day, provided more time to be spent in the garden, even if 'urban conditions denied most people the opportunity for gardening' (Constantine, 1981, p. 393) restricting them to tubs, window boxes and rear yards.

Importantly, the perceived nation of gardeners offered a plethora of potential commercial opportunities for a lifestyle celebrity such as Mr Middleton and concerned BBC memos noted that he had turned down an offer of £1,200 a year from Radio Luxemburg to do a weekly 5-minute broadcast preceded by an hour's rehearsal. Radio Luxembourg's approach to Middleton is both an indication of the populist tone he adopted and the growing market for DIY products and gardening materials, which they envisaged could be advertised around his broadcast. His recommendation of particular plant varieties had already led to listeners rushing to make purchases and subsequent shortages. Street has questioned the dominance of the BBC in the inter-war period giving 'commercial radio a more significant role in the development of broadcasting than has previously been suggested' (2006, p. 211) and points to a number of crucial areas where developments were a result of the pressures from commercial broadcasting. Sundays were the day when the BBC lost audiences most significantly to commercial broadcasting. Mr Middleton's programme at 2 p.m. on Sunday was a key element of the BBC's populism in the midst of this – he had the audience appeal of popular music without upsetting the BBC's sensibilities about what was appropriate to be broadcast into the home on a Sunday as Mr R. J. Fry, who painted white lines on the road, explained: 'I don't listen much to talks except Sundays – and I always likes Middleton' (*Radio Times*, 24 March 1939 supplement, p. v11).

Broadcast gardening advice offered men relaxation after Sunday lunch while many women were occupied with the washing up, which resulted in calls for Mr Middleton to appear at other times in the schedule, and in 1937 an early attempt at audience research asked listeners whether they preferred his talks to be on Friday at 7:10 or Sunday at 2 p.m. He invited listeners to write in and let him know their preference and explained:

> There does not seem a better way of finding out what your wishes are whether you regard me as stimulation for the weekend's gardening or to send you off to sleep after Sunday lunch. The BBC wants to please you and I am quite prepared to do what I'm told as far as I can and give you what you want. (25 June 1937)

The closeness of the resulting plebiscite in favour of Friday evening indicated that the idea of being inspired by Middleton's talks into action was marginally more appealing than listening to the talks at a point when the possibility of action was over for another week. Despite the vote, Mr Middleton's gardening programme was almost always on Sunday afternoon. Once again lifestyle broadcasting was developed alongside print media, and other commercial possibilities had opened up with the increase in gardening magazines such as *Homes and Gardens*, *Amateur Gardening* and *Home Gardening* or in gardening journalism in the inter-war period (Constantine, 1981, p. 397). Middleton by the mid-1930s earned £1,000 a year for his weekly column in the *Express* newspaper and published a number of articles on gardening and vegetable growing books both in conjunction with the *Daily Express* and independently.

MR MIDDLETON: A MEDIATED BROADCASTING PERSONA

As with all modern media celebrities, the audience's relationship with Mr Middleton rested upon a broad range of inter-textual references, including interviews, pictures and articles in the *Radio*

Times, appearances on other radio shows and Christmas broadcasts. The BBC Talks department guarded its management of Middleton's persona jealously. The Talks department was anxious he might become stale from over-exposure. Memos shunted to and fro within the BBC departments about when and where he could be used, and they resisted him contributing to the morning *Household Talks* and removed him from schools' broadcasting to prevent over-exposure in 1937, although he was allowed to return again in 1939. The Talks department was less than pleased when in 1938 he was used as a voiceover for a drama by West Region and pointed out: 'It is very important that Mr Middleton's authority as a horticulturalist should be maintained' (BBCWA, Middleton Files). Nevertheless he was used as a speaker and BBC representative all over the place – at the Radio Exhibition at Olympia, the Ideal Home Exhibition and Southport Flower Show in 1938, for example, and then in Belfast. Sometimes he was required to give lectures to audiences of two or three thousand people, although his views did not always seem to be consulted before bookings were made. By the late 1930s he was a cultural reference point and on the radio sit-com *Bandwagon*, fictionally set in a flat at the top of broadcasting house, one character noted that 'Mr Middleton hadn't been to prune the window box' and variety artiste Nelson Keys impersonated Mr Middleton in one of the first variety acts on television.

Then as now, print media was a vital component in the construction of the broadcasting celebrity and for the BBC the *Radio Times* and the *Listener*, in which Middleton's talks were sometimes reproduced and for whom he wrote, were important element in this. The *Radio Times*, like the celebrity magazines of today, suggested that it gave readers insight into the private lives of broadcasting personalities; a feature in 1935 entitled 'People you Hear: The Gardener' included an image of Middleton in spectacles, a suit and spotted bowtie, and described him as 'the best known gardener in England'. He was invariably presented in a smart suit connoting an urban middle-classness, even though he was engaged in physical labour and was described and defined as 'country born and bred' (*Radio Times*, 18 November 1938). This *Radio Times* feature intermingled information about his gardening, broadcasting and publishing careers with information about his three brothers and sisters. It begins in a nostalgic dream-like world where his enthusiasm for horticulture – flowers and vegetables – was inspired by his father taking him to a greenhouse where he picked a rose. It ended on a heavily sentimental note:

> Every summer he spends a week with his parents, who celebrated their golden wedding four years ago, and he takes them for drives around the villages. There is no trace of that Victorian greenhouse in which as a boy he picked up a fine fat rose. But it lingers in their memories. Neither man nor boy, among the camellias and roses and cherry-pie could have seen what the future would bring. (*Radio Times*, 8 November 1935, p. 15)

Middleton's rural roots are emphasized here, as they are in a number of his Christmas broadcasts and yet in his home garden, which was an imaginary physical reference point in many of his broadcasts, he was placed within suburbia. A *Radio Times* article, entitled 'The Stars at their Firesides', gave this added credibility when it discussed a visit to Mr Middleton at his home and 'finding him collecting rubbish and piling it onto his bonfire in his garden near London' (*Radio Times*, 18 November 1938). His house in Surbiton was a late 1920s or early 1930s new build, and he pointed out to listeners that where cows once grazed there were now shops. He broadcast, however, from the very heart of London – in Broadcasting House, thus his regional identity and belonging was ambivalent – rural, suburban and urban, and yet none of them. To Silverstone (1997), the inter-war period saw a rise in the popularity of inhabiting a 'third space' an area that he describes as suburbia and identified as both urban and rural and yet as not either. Arguably the idea of suburbia was not so much a clearly identifiable imaginary space as a mingling of different but distinctive imaginary spaces in which the rural idyll was still significant: 'To me the word Home always conjures up a mental picture of a cottage with a white washed porch over the door. So does the scent of jasmine because the same cottage was nearly covered with it', Mr Middleton explained to *Radio Times* readers in an article entitled 'Memories of Home' (8 April 1938). In this Middleton operated as a celebrity, personifying something of his time which resonated with audiences (Dyer, 1998) as the fluidity of his class identity also did.

Mr Middleton's working-class roots were frequently referred to, but his earnings (from the BBC, publishing and gardening journalism) defined him as middle-class. For the aspiring new suburban middle-classes and respectable working-class he embodied social mobility. However, in the economic upheaval of the 1930s social mobility was not always upwards, and he also had, perhaps for the middle-classes, a particularly comfortable authenticity, a reassurance in being thought ordinary at a time of accelerated social change (Savage, 1990). The earnings and lifestyles of the lower working-class and respectable working-class were less identifiably differentiated from each other or other social groups than they had been in the nineteenth century. When the newspaper the *Star* demanded more gardening programmes in 1932, it suggested gardening was a defining characteristic of Englishness (9 January 1932) and Mr Middleton's popularity suggests that straddling class distinctions with a certain degree of ambivalence may have been successfully reworked as a version of 'ordinariness' that resonated reassuringly with his listeners.

Mr Middleton's Christmas broadcasts – usually on Christmas day but occasionally on Boxing Day, as in 1937, were seen as key to BBC's Christmas scheduling. So central was Middleton to the tone of Christmas broadcasting that the BBC arranged a car to bring him to the studio – a practice that they at times had to repeat when he was expected to appear on both radio and television within a limited timeframe. He did not discuss gardening for, as he pointed out: 'I'm sure the last thing you want to do today is work, so suppose we give it a miss for once and have a chat about the old days. I don't know why it is but Christmas time always make me think of the days when I was young and irresponsible and therefore happy' (26 December 1937). His tone was intimate, cosy and positioned in the nostalgic and rural, as if he was a guest at the listeners' own Christmas celebrations. In 1938 this was stressed when he began:

> A Merry Christmas and all that. I hope the pudding turned out well. You certainly look happy round the table with your paper hats on, especially granddad with his sun bonnet and ribbons. As for me I seem to be the only living thing in Broadcasting House at the moment. There was a rather sad looking announcer but he's faded away and left me all alone, and I haven't even got a mince pie or mistletoe to look at. Well now I'm sure you don't want gardening all mixed up with Christmas dinner so let's talk about Christmas and some of the pleasant memories associated with it (25 December 1938).

In presenting himself as alone, isolated in Broadcasting House, his presence in the family celebration of Christmas is less intrusive, while he simultaneously conjures up an image of a Christmas family party for those who, on their own, looked to the radio for company. The nostalgia of this material is open to different interpretations – for nostalgia, as Wheeler (1994) has pointed out, is a rejection of the status quo and so like ambivalence can be subversive. His Christmas broadcast in 1937 was nostalgic for skilled craftsmen of the past who 'hadn't an ounce of scientific knowledge but could produce good crops' (26 December 1937). A nostalgia for skilled craftsmen and against scientific rationalism at a time of unemployment and deprivation in many industries, including agriculture, opened up the possibility for audiences to take a critical stance towards the social milieu in which they lived. What is perhaps interesting to note is that although Taylor has argued that gardening experts in the 1990s 'marked a new sense of openness, legitimation, tolerance, towards a set of previously marginalised voices in mainstream programming' (2008, p. 97). Mr Middleton's career suggests that such voices were already in existence in the 1930s and the democratizing potential of the medium of radio can be identified in Middleton's broadcasts.

WARTIME – CELEBRITY AND POLITICS/CAMPAIGNS

The performed presentation of the early broadcasting personalities of Boulestin and Mr Middleton occurred through a number of ways: their audible accent and tone, their use of language, performance and clothes when they appeared on television, and of course through the selected narratives of their lives that were circulated through their broadcasts, in their publicity material, the popular press and the *Radio Times*. Wartime offered scope to harness such personalities for national campaigns; however, Boulestin's Frenchness was to find itself out of step with the national mood. In the summer of 1939, on the eve of the outbreak of war, Boulestin offered his services to both the British Ministry of Food and to the Army Quartermaster General but was rejected by both. Uncertain what to do, he lingered at his holiday home in Landes, France with Robin Adair, who was too ill to flee when France entered the war, and who consequently spent the war between hospital and German internment camps. Boulestin remained in France, living in occupied Paris visiting Robin and finally died in 1943. Adair returned to Britain, translated Boulestin's autobiography and broadcast on food for *Women's Hour* at various times in the 1950s.

Alternatively, Mr Middleton's very ordinariness was in step with 'The People's War' and he continued to broadcast on the radio, write for the *Radio Times* and the *Listener* during the war and his talks acquired a national significance as they encouraged food production – even in small spaces and the avoidance of waste. In so doing they became less meandering and more instructional in tone. The short Ministry of Information films he took part in were also instructing the public how to increase their garden's food production (which also involved a new tone) an indication of the role now played in their production by the Ministry of Information as well as the BBC. In September 1939, Mr Middleton's celebrity status was harnessed by the 'Dig for Victory' campaign, intended to increase wartime food supplies, although its success is hard to assess. It was one of 16 campaigns run during the phoney war and there are indications that the public suffered 'campaign fatigue' (Nicolas, 1996, p. 70). Vera Hodson (born 1901), when interviewed, noted that she 'also listens to Mr Middleton. Not that I have any intention of growing the things he talks about, but I like his personality and the ways he says pertaters' (cited in Abbott, 2003, p. 61). Interestingly, in 1940, when the Listener Research Unit circulated a policy document describing its image of 'the average listener', the description matched the persona created for Middleton: 'fond of his bit of garden and he likes his pint' (quoted in Nicolas, 1996, p. 63). An estimated 1.5 million allotment holders produced 10 per cent of the nation's food by the end of the war, with approximately half of all manual workers having an allotment or garden (Gardiner, 2004, p. 166), some of this uptake should be attributed to Mr Middleton leading the campaign and providing an important celebrity endorsement.

Bentley suggests that in the USA, 'Although women were deemed an important part of the victory gardening, the activity took on distinct elements of masculinity as the battleground imagery became infused into the act of planting a victory garden – in part perhaps the result of the media's substituting gardening for combat' (Bentley, 1998, p. 115). Middleton's wartime broadcasts also turned the garden into a combat zone, the enemy being defined in turn as bugs and slugs and potato blight. Certainly, in a broadcast with Eunice Kidd on 'Poultry in the garden' written up in the *Listener,* Middleton concluded: 'War on the slugs – and a good use for much of the garden waste. And after all that the prospects of a nice fat boiling hen to have with my leeks and greens next year. Yes I think we can all agree it's a good idea' (20 June 1940, p. 1170). Not everyone however found it an easy task to follow Middleton's good ideas; Natalie Tanner, living in rural countryside near Leeds, found that her battles against bindweed and rubbish to plant crops were thwarted by the activities of cattle and sheep which got to her crops before she did (Purcell, 2010, p. 43).

Taylor suggests that although 'class pervades both the garden as a site and gardening as a set of symbolic aesthetic practices' (2008, p. 128) there is a necessity to seek a more complex reading of Bourdieu and to recognize not just distinction but communality and solidarity in people's leisure, lifestyle and consumption practices (Savage and Longhurst, 1996, p. 288). Wartime campaigns certainly attempted to emphasize communalities across class boundaries, even if everyday life did not always reflect this. Mr Middleton, who in the 1930s had already established a community of listeners, across ambivalent class and geographical boundaries was consequently an ideal figurehead for the 'Dig for Victory' campaign; he was not, of course, the only radio personality to become involved in the war efforts, as the next chapter will explore.

Chapter Four

Domesticity under fire: fractured and extended

> I bought a little radio and it went right through the war. Saturday I used to go to bed early, cos Saturday night they used to have these plays 8–10. (Mrs Selsey, 27 July 2002)

World War II disrupted domesticity in ways not seen before or since. The everyday practices and routines of families were fractured by the conscription of men and, from 1941, of women into the armed forces and war-work, evacuation, billeting and the new patterns of both paid and voluntary work. Homes, the aspiration of so many in the inter-war years, were destroyed by bombing; the materials to replace or repair domestic accommodation remained unavailable for many years. At the same time, home, family and the domestic space was elevated as an ideal to be fought for and protected. Civilians were encouraged to 'keep the home fires burning', although for many their domestic life was increasingly unstable. The progress of the war became a shared national broadcast serial which linked different elements of fractured families who listened to radio news. The wireless developed and expanded its varied roles: it maintained a sense of home, linked those separated by war, provided domestic education and propaganda, and was a means of distraction and escape for many listeners. Predictably perhaps in fulfilling its many roles, the radio came to articulate many of the contradictions, inconsistencies and tensions in its discursive construction of domesticity in wartime.

Television production ceased on the outbreak of war and did not start again until 1946; most popular foreign commercial stations stopped broadcasting as France and Luxembourg were occupied by Germany and thus in wartime the BBC became more dominant and hence in many respects the 'voice of the nation'. Such a term should not be taken to imply that the listeners were necessarily listening intently to the words of the BBC broadcasts or revered the organization. Although the comments observed by one Mass Observation in Lawrie's Café, Bradshawgate, are not necessarily representative, it is interesting that they included a critique of the BBC: 'nearly everyone there is a pervert of some kind or another. And they're the people who hand out our culture' (MO, TC 49 Box 4/G). Arguably it was the reassurance, familiarity and domesticity of the 'voice of the nation' which offered comfort. One woman, when asked by a Mass Observation interviewer if she listened to radio serials, explained that she did not listen to them but she had them on as: 'It gives a nice friendly sort of feeling, but I don't listen to what they say' (MO, TC 74/1/E). Radio can be seen as having provided 'ontological security' for its listeners. Silverstone, with reference to television, has suggested that this is something which is always available, providing a dependable rhythm to life it provides reassurance and become an emotional prop to listeners just as a teddy bear or blanket provides security for a child separated from its parents (1994). Such a pattern of media consumption was arguably established in wartime when radio listening provided just such a security blanket for listeners separated from family, friends and familiar routines and lifestyles. The 'friendly feeling', the security and reassurance provided by radio, led to it being left constantly on in many homes, as one respondent explained to a Mass Observation interviewer when asked if she had the radio on a lot:

> Oh yes, we have it on all day. As soon as I come in I switch it on, and it's never switched off not until ever so late. Like tonight, when I get in, I'll go straight up to the wireless, and switch on, and then go upstairs and change, and you can't hear the wireless from upstairs, it's silly really but that's what I always do. (MO Radio Survey, 21 May 1940, MO, TC 74/1/E)

The reassurance that radio offered was recognized and it was hoped that the radio would combat 'panic hysteria and neurosis amongst the general population' which a committee of psychiatrists had suggested would break out in the first six months of the war (Nicholas, 1996). Interviewees remembered listening to the radio as being particularly significant to women on their own, who were unwilling to leave the house because of the blackout. One woman recalled 'We didn't do anything else except listen to the wireless and knitting, we were always knitting' (Mrs Lordington, 10 June 2002). Alternatively, adverts for Murphy Wireless sets described radio as 'Munitions for the Home Front' and suggested that it was patriotic to buy a radio if your home was badly equipped in terms of wirelesses.

Historical work on radio in wartime suggest that in the interests of reaching wide audiences with propaganda messages often intended to boost moral, it became more populist. However, with a diffuse audience in terms of age, gender, class and region, not to speak of temperamental inclination, to be popular was not easy. Some complained that radio was too sombre and focused upon the war; others objected to being 'coaxed into good humour' and one that the BBC appeared to 'think we are mentally deficient children'. Thus one Mass Observation observer summed up the situation astutely:

> There were relatively few people who were altogether satisfied with the programmes, but, as the figures indicate, most people found something they liked to listen to. Women were more critical than men, and more really disliked the programmes, perhaps because they listen to them more.' (MO, TC 74/3/A)

On 7 January 1940 the BBC introduced the Forces Service, a more populist and light-hearted channel, whereby 'programmes were planned to be appropriate to the conditions in which servicemen listened, i.e., in groups, and for the most part as background noise' (Nicholas, 1996, p. 51). Its mixture of variety, sport, advice and short news talks appealed to both listeners and critics. 'By 1942 Mass Observation found the Forces Programme had established itself as constantly more popular than the Home Service, especially among the working class women. It provides a sort of tap listening, available all day. Tom Harrison claimed it might as well be renamed "the Housewives Programme" … by 1942 90 per cent of listeners aged 16–20 preferred the FP' (Nicholas, 1996, p. 52). The light-hearted reassuring 'tap listening' was not merely enjoyed in the home. The setting up of the Forces Service acknowledged that radio was increasingly significant in public spaces. For those in unfamiliar surroundings, insecure or under threat, the presence of the radio and its association with domestic space both symbolized home, and provided familiarity, comfort and reassurance. For those billeted in hostels, for children and their mothers evacuated in unfamiliar surroundings or for those on army bases, the familiar sound of radio made their location more homely. For those newly involved in war work in factories, the familiar domesticated tones of the radio provided reassurance and a distraction when engaged in monotonous war work in alien or threatening public spaces. Nevertheless, Mass Observation reported some complaints about the endless playing of the 'National Anthem' and 'Land of Hope and Glory', their observer in Stepney also noted:

> A good many East End factories, big and small, have the wireless on all day … the workers say that it 'relieves the monotony … and livens things up', whilst one small factory owner explained: 'There's so little entertainment in wartime, and everyone's nerves are on edge – you have to have something to take their minds off. (MO, TC 74/1/D, NM Wireless in Factories, 10 August 1940)

Programmes such as *Music While You Work,* which broadcast for half an hour twice a day from June 1940, acknowledged the growing factory audience. Factories with equipment installed for transmitting music and radio broadcasts rose from 400 at the outbreak of the war to approximately 7,000, employing 4 million workers by June 1943 (Nicholas, 1996, p. 137). Although group wireless listening had been unpopular during the inter-war period, in wartime it seemed at times as if there was a communality in listening to the radio. Radio emphasized the linkage between the nation and the home, between public and domestic worlds, wherever people listened.

MAINTAINING A HOME

The protection of home and the 'British way of life' was central to the ideals that the war was perceived to have been fought for. The ideal of home and homemaker was not only crucial to the rationality of war, but was also gendered: the home that was being fought for contained and was created by women and in wartime was protected by men in the armed forces. As Nicholas pointed out, the home was 'idealised even more in wartime than usual'. A special 'Woman's number' of the *Radio Times* in November 1939 typically affirmed that 'In women's hands lie the tools of civilization. For it is from these homes that men draw inspiration to serve and work' (Nicolas, 1996, p. 115). Yet women's work was needed also, at first voluntarily, but from 1941 women too faced conscription. Strong but contradictory discursive regimes surrounded housewifery, and systems of financial support for servicemen's wives encouraged fidelity, yet the entry of women into factories and the services threatened to undermine this. Women served in the forces, however they were not active in fighting; hence, although initially utilized on anti-aircraft guns, this soon ceased as it was perceived as likely to undermine men's morale. Men were encouraged to fight to protect women and children in the home and not surprisingly, as Sokoloff has demonstrated, 'strong gendered ideologies of domestic and work structures survived intact amongst servicemen's wives and their communities in cities such as Birmingham and Coventry' in wartime (1999, p. 27).

The maintenance of everyday domestic life was seen as a part of the war effort and important to the morale of many of those who were in the armed forces, billeted or evacuated, and the BBC saw itself as playing a part in assisting this. But in trying to do so the BBC was involved in struggling with a series of contradictory and problematic messages – for the domestic home was not as it had been before the war; it was fractured and threatened; its make-up and occupants changed. The domestic as a lived experience was unstable, as an ideal it was also leaky, porous and stretchable. This instability was taken for granted when in 1940 the Listener Research Unit circulated a policy document which described their image of 'the average listener' and explained: 'His wife goes to the pictures once a week ... His wife works a sixteen hour day in the home and lost her looks when she was twenty-five. She uses "the wireless" even more than he does. If he is young enough he will be conscripted and his wife will go and live with her mother' (quoted in Nicholas, 1996, p. 63). The domestic unit is here both conceived as the average listener and his wife together and also as the average listener in the forces while his wife and her mother remain at home.

In the early years of the war, the magazine-style programme, broadcast each morning at 9:30, entitled *At Home Today*, demonstrated both the challenges of the instability of domesticity and of contradictory government discourses in relation to housewives. Broadcast weekly on the Home Service, at one level it could be seen as having reworked many of the traditions of *Household Talks* of the inter-war period. However, the series attempted to embrace a far wider range of domesticities than were represented in the pre-war period. A community who lived in caravans was discussed in one programme and it was suggested that, for evacuees from the cities, caravans might offer 'a castle of safety'. The use of the term castle is interesting, connoting the old, the secure and a sense of nationhood. Furthermore the word 'castle' is metaphorically linked to the phrase 'an Englishman's home is his castle' and signified the home as a space defended in wartime. Continuing the emphasis on classic ideological associations of home, there is reference to the 'warmth' and 'cosiness' of caravan homes and the sustainability of the rural life was pointed out when one caravaner was quoted as saying 'with a patch of potatoes and a goat my wife and I feel we could defy any blockade that this country could conceivably suffer' (22 November 1939).

The fractured nature of the homes was acknowledged when in the same week a speaker admitted: 'Our homes like thousands of others, were broken up and families scattered into Khaki and Navy Blue ... we have lost all the things we had no time to appreciate. Particularly that possession the companionship of those with whom we live.' Her talk, under the theme of 'the art of living together' – a plea for greater tolerance and consideration of others – is at one level about the future when families are reunited, but the structuring absence not articulated is that many families are having to get along and find companionship with friends, relations or evacuees and the servicemen billeted on them. Traditional homes were not destroyed, just in abeyance, and could be replaced by ties of emotional engagement, humour and relationships which were more significant than shared physical place (15 November 1939). Early in 1940, with an awareness of the number of men now in the services, there was a talk on 'Home without Father' by a widow who had been working and bringing up two young boys on her own for several years. She emphasized the importance of keeping the absent father's presence in the children's lives and advised listeners to:

> Let the children know that you, too, are missing Daddy very much and that you've got to help and cheer one another while he's away. For the woman who can look forward to her man returning has this blessed hope with her in trying moments. There are all sorts of little things about the house and garden that Daddy would like to see done; goodnight chats bring daddy into the home circle again; there are letters to write to him; grand preparations to be made for his return (7 February 1940).

In a problematic aside that positioned the speaker's class status and distanced her from the majority of her audience, she acknowledged that she had some domestic help in the house each day.

Another example of the stretchable nature of domesticity involved encouragement to housewives to extend domestic comforts to those away from home in the armed forces. Mrs Violet Campbell, from Aberdeen, described how her presumably large and emphatically middle-class home was opened up to a number of soldiers who came for a welcome, a wash, a supper of soup and suet pudding, and the dubious joys of wearing brightly coloured woollen slippers rather than army boots for the evening, all which served to provide 'a home from home for soldiers' billeted or camped in the area (25 September 1942).

Many of the *At Home Today* scripts reveal that the BBC articulated government policy that contained a shifting sense of what women could do, and the roles women should play in wartime. There was discussion of women running farms, working in factories and indeed a sense that if they were 'at home today' maybe they should get out of the home and do something to contribute to the war effort tomorrow. There was anxiety during 1941, particularly about limited recruitment of women to the armed services and and explorations of ways that the BBC could provide propaganda to assist this (BBWA, R 34/727/1). *At Home Today* programmes frequently focused on women in the services or in war work and arguably acclimatized women to conscription. Even when conscription was introduced, married women did not flock into the workforce; those with children under 14 were not compelled to work, nor those over 50. Medical problems as a result of childrearing on limited budgets with inadequate medical care meant that many women could not work. Thus 'only 41 per cent of wives without children or with children over 14 years did paid war work during the war' (Sokolooff, 1999, p. 30). Despite the popular mythology, there was not a significant shift in women's roles during the war or after it – the opportunities for social change that were offered to women during the war were not taken up by many or were taken up with limited enthusiasm and high absenteeism (Hinton, 2010; Summerfield, 1986). *At Home Today* and other programmes in the schedule which addressed the government's need for more women workers, did so by using women workers themselves, facilitating the continued expansion of ordinary voices on the BBC. For example, Mrs Lunn, a Yorkshire housewife was allowed to abandon her script 'to say what was in her heart; her sincerity', which, according to BBC producer Shapley, 'was ample compensation for her hesitant rather stumbling words' as she was one of nine women who talked about their lives and work in a series entitled *Women in Wartime*, part of a series on the Home Front (Shapley, 1996, p. 69).

The BBC also contributed to what Calder (1991) has described as the 'myth of the blitz', the idea that the indomitable British with good humour, stoicism, pluck and improvisation muddled through the horrors of war invincibly carrying on. Examples of woman doing just this from other countries were broadcast on the Home Service in *Women in the Front Line* (6 August 1940) and scripts were also reproduced in the *Listener* (15 August 1940, p. 250). Women of Finland and France were attributed with spreading contagious calm during bombing raids as they looked after each other in their homes. The BBC was able to provide its own example of maintaining the home, when Broadcasting House was itself hit by a 5,000lb bomb in October 1940 and transmission continued unabated. Likewise Margery Scott – discussing her war work for a local council – described on *At Home Today* how she had re-housed a family of 14 – including eight children, three lodgers, two dogs, a cat and her kittens, and 'Eddie from next door', who had all been bombed out of their home one Sunday morning before the next night's sirens sounded. The 'spirit of the blitz' was affirmed when the social worker triumphantly claimed that 'mother was able to get them all supper, wash their clothes and get them ready for work next day' (22 July 1942). An almost iconic representation of stoical civilians was provided by Tom

Harrison who described children playing in the remains of their bombed house with the words: 'The whole of the upstairs floor had been completely wrecked and the downstairs part was like a rubbish pit. But to these children it was still home' (17 July 1940 in MOA TC 74/3/A).

Despite the rhetoric, research (Calder, 1969) and my own oral interviews indicate that for many women maintaining a home was extremely arduous and stressful, little wonder that, as a discussion on the Home Service in 1945 pointed out, there was a falling birth rate. Many contributors ascribed this to poor housing, lack of money, men away too long abroad and concerns that men will stray and be unfaithful (4 January 1945). Little wonder also that for many their aspirations remained of a home and domesticity, as they had in the inter-war period. As war progressed, ideas shifted from maintaining a home to post-war planning and homes of the future moved up the programming agenda. In 1944 the *Radio Times* announced that the BBC would be running a series of eight programmes entitled *Homes for All*, which would explore the housing problems and encourage people to consider radical solutions to the housing crisis caused by both bombing and lack of house building during the war. One discussion focused upon the suggestions of both a Russian Economist and an American expert to deal with the 800,000 houses damaged by the war in southern England; another looked at the government legislation. *Radio Times* provided a background to debates the programmes aimed to stimulate and acknowledged that 'soldier or civilian setting his mind towards his post-war home will automatically conjure up a vision of a cottage' but suggested that prefabricated houses and flats may be a more realistic solution and illustrated the article with an ultra-modernist block of flats under the title 'new homes for old' (14 April 1944, p. 29). In post-war Britain many would find the visions they had conjured up would remain unfulfilled for some time.

WISE HOUSEKEEPING AND *THE KITCHEN FRONT*

From the summer of 1940, when the Blitz got under way, the war on the Home Front, involved increasing privations: air raids, the blackout, nights for some in air-raid shelters and endless queuing. Maintaining the domestic home became increasingly challenging in a framework of rationing and make-do-and-mend; domesticity faced an unparalleled level of government regulation and management; the radio was perceived as able to play a key role in acclimatising the general public to this while also boosting morale and providing information in programmes such as *Wise Housekeeping* and *The Kitchen Front*, with some overlap and to-ing and fro-ing in content between them.

At the outbreak of war, Britain was heavily dependent on imported food: 70 per cent of wheat was imported as well as significant amounts of meat, sugar and dairy products. As shipping lanes closed, British farmers could not respond quickly to demands for increased production, as the government had failed to stockpile vital fertilizers also imported from abroad (Howkins, 2003). Despite government reorganization of agriculture, the efforts of the Women's Land Army, Prisoners of War, garden owners and allotment holders, the food shortages were for many a structuring framework for domesticity during World War II. Despite the *Daily Express* campaign against rationing, it was introduced in January 1940 and, along with food subsidies, price controls and propaganda, made up the government's campaign to match eating habits to food supply. Given the already established relationship between broadcasting and domesticity – and that so much of the focus of the household talks in the inter-war period had been on domestic topics and food production – it is not surprising that the radio was seen as an obvious medium for propaganda on food, alongside women's magazines, posters, leaflets, public information films, and an army of educators and lecturers often working with women's organizations. Butter, sugar, bacon and ham were the first foods to be rationed; meat (although not offal) followed and cheese in 1941 along with preserves (jam and marmalade, syrup, treacle), and in 1942 margarine and tea. Bread was not rationed until after the war; there were foodstuffs such as eggs and milk for which individuals received a set allowance and dried eggs were introduced as a supplement for cooking. There were, however, shortages of some foodstuffs such as oranges and bananas, and other foods were subject to seasonal variations, all of which led to queuing to buy food. In many respects the nutritional value of the diet of many of the working classes improved during the war, particularly as children were provided with subsided milk. Food is not however merely about the provision of nutrients or appeasing hunger, food consumption is about identity and appearance and, as Bourdieu demonstrated, about class and cultural distinction (1984).

Wise Housekeeping covered a wide variety of topics: oil stoves, the points system on winter fuel, laundry for beginners, cake making for beginners, first aid for stockings, new and old ways for pink salmon. Despite continued concern that she would be called up, Ruth Drew in 1942–3 gave weekly bulletins on points of interest to housewives and then introduced an expert to give a more specialized talk, which at times included Mr Middleton, who discussed how to grow salads for town dwellers in window boxes or on flat roofs (R51/639). Work and the domestic front appeared in different parts of the schedule as the war progressed, with *Women's War* in 1942 having a member of the Women's Voluntary Service (WVS) discussing 'Improvised Cooking Facilities' and Dora Clarke who explored 'Our changed home life in Wartime' (R 47/852/1). Housewives' domestic role in fruit preservation was expanded to include food preservation centres and the *Radio Times* announced a programme on 'Fruit preservation and what you can do about it' in the following way: 'Speakers from the town and country describe the work of preservation centres and explain how you can help them and they can help you, If you have your own fruit and nowhere to send it – they suggest some of the ways you can preserve it yourself' (*Radio Times*, 28 August 1942, p. 10).

Kitchen Front was broadcast every morning at 8:15– 8:20, except for Sunday, and, according to Nicholas, aimed to catch women before they went shopping; however its timing was also an acknowledgement that many with responsibility for household food were also workers. Although originally planned as 'Food Front', the Ministry of Food considered that *Kitchen Front* was more housewifely. The programme contained advice about 'best buys' both on and off ration, 'tips on making food go further and always at least one recipe' (Nicolas, 1996, p. 8).

While such practices as adding baking soda to vegetables were alternatively criticized and recommended in *Kitchen Front*, on one thing – the 'assasination' of vegetables by over-boiling – contributors, principally the Radio Doctor, were unanimous about; no more than half an hour could be recommended for any vegetable and no more than 20 minutes for cabbage (Nicholas, 1996, p. 81).

Kitchen Front was not entirely focused upon cooking, when the fuel economy campaign was introduced in 1942 this was discussed; as were water-saving campaigns and there were two women gardeners, one introduced as having previously been a working-pupil of Mr Middleton. Initially food dominated *Kitchen Front* and to a significant degree *Wise Housekeeping*, and indeed much domestic broadcasting. For example, in late 1942 Mary Fergusson, in a new series *Calling All Good Neighbours*, explored 'workers' shopping problems and how to overcome them' and in 1943 Freddie Grisewood introduced a series on *Men in the Kitchen*. As Calder has suggested, by this time people's morale was at a low ebb. Clothes and household goods had begun to wear out and were almost impossible to replace, and the BBC resolved to give a higher priority to problems arising out of 'shortages in the wardrobe and the kitchen (that is to say fuel, tea towels and saucepans as well as pants and petticoats)' (BBWA memo to Ministry of Food of 7 August 1943). Nevertheless the *Radio Times* and the *Listener* sections for housewives were almost exclusively food focused throughout the war: a reflection of the centrality of food not only to the ideas of domesticity but also to national identity. The process of linking the national and domestic food supplies was carefully established by Mrs Horton in *What's in the Larder?*, which, it was suggested:

> is a question with which all of us who are housewives are only too familiar. What should I give them today? Have I got enough of this, that or the other? You know how it goes. Today the question has new and wider significance. What's in the nation's larder? How can we make the most of each of our food supplies? For to waste any one of them would be the worst kind of folly (8 November 1939).

Avoidance of waste was a theme well established in the pre-war era and an issue unavoidable to most working-class women but wartime gave this a whole new emphasis. In wartime, food consumption was intrinsically entwined with class and gender, it was not merely that the cost of food rose sharply at the beginning of the war, or that the middle-classes had more readily available access to non-rationed foods or facilities to grow food, it was also because 'The question of who gathers and prepares food is a critical problem in gender politics because the production, consumption and distribution of food always involves issues of power and cultural authority' (Brumberg, 1989). The provision of food, what sort of food, and in what quantity and style were ways of articulating and confirming class, national, regional, family and gender identities. Many of the foodstuffs rationed hit at fundamental cultural signifiers of food. Masculinity was entwined with the provision and consumption of meat. Sugar was necessary to baking, which was perceived as an important feminine skill. For the housewife, and arguably by association all women, their identity, status and power base was linked to food and cooking. Little wonder that food rationing has become an iconic image of World War II – for many, rationing was a very personal attack on who they were, their identities and their ways of being distinct from others. More problematically, the image of a family sitting around a table sharing a meal was at the heart of the domestic idyll that needed to be maintained for morale. It was this that war was being fought to protect. So the home front in a sense shifted the public space of the war firmly into the home, making the battle to provide foodstuffs in the kitchen a battle against the enemy.

Not surprisingly, food preparation remained as much of a discursive battleground as it had in the inter-war period. There was tension between the experts, housewives and their families; these were battles for power and control, and the Ministry of Food was at the heart of these battles. It actively vetted all scripts and insisted upon changes; for example, it could be demanded at the last moment that a recipe's use of apples was replaced by plums. This did not mean that the programmes were made in a spirit of calm and cooperation as all pulled together for the war effort. As Nicholas argues:

> The *Kitchen Front* liaison between the BBC and the Ministry of Food exemplified all the principal characteristics of wartime instructional broadcasting: the in-fighting between officials and programme makers, the conflicts over scheduling structure, tone and content, the problems of adapting one's message to the changing circumstances of the war, and the overriding problem of the audience: who was it, what did it need, and what did it want?' (Nicholas, 1996, p. 73).

Attempting to make the tone and content of domestic broadcasting more accessible to listeners led to the inclusion of listeners' recipes and to ordinary housewives sometimes being given the microphone; Mrs Hudson, the wife of an East End docker, broadcast on 'a weekend without a joint'. In her talk, which was then published by the *Listener*, she suggested that spreading the meat ration across the week made shopping less stressful and that an added benefit was that her husband was not so sleepy after a

Sunday meal of vegetable soup (18 March 1942). Her broadcast would at least have avoided the repeated complaints made about the cooking advice and provided recipes – that were too expensive and given by presenters who were too middle-class.

Kitchen Front provided a whole gambit of information and encouraged people to eat in the British restaurants set up by the government and off rations, and it gained '5 million listeners, 15 per cent of the available audience, and four times the audience of any other daytime talk programme' (Gardiner, 2004, p. 187). All the same the BBC might have been overstating the case a little when it asserted that: 'There is no doubt that the success of the *Kitchen Front* has made 8:15 a most memorable moment for the housewives' (BBWA memo to Ministry of Food of 7 August 1943). However, despite the efforts at popularization, it was hard to escape the strong governmental and authoritative tone that lay behind the *Kitchen Front* – when one interviewee explained: 'we only had about 2 oz butter, we got information and recipes on cookery on the radio 5 minutes in the morning, from Lord Woolton, I think' (Rose Lynch, 1 August 2002), she emphasized this. Lord Woolton, the Minister of Food, himself spoke on *Kitchen Front* at times but, whoever was speaking, it was generally perceived as 'his' voice and views. Although Cardiff has suggested that, in the 1930s, 'popular styles of presentation, originally intended to attract and inform a wide and differentiated audience in practice came to be seen as unsuitable vehicles for serious and controversial topics' (Cardiff, 1986, p. 244), in many ways domestic programming had already learned many of the lessons of popularism, although the BBC was not always able to convince the Ministry of Food of its views. The use of humour and celebrities familiar to the audience were strategies that both agreed upon; mixing education and information with rather more entertainment – Mabel Constandurous, popularly known as Mrs Buggins, and Elsie and Doris Waters – whose stage names were Gert and Daisy – were examples of this.

COMEDY AND COOKERY: MRS BUGGINS, GERT AND DAISY

Mabel Constandurous was a well established radio personality when war broke out, most famous for playing the role of Mrs Buggins and Grandma Buggins in the children's comedy serial *The Buggins Family* (1928–48) a familiarity which gave her broadcasts a comforting resonance for listeners. Her sketches for *Kitchen Front* involved a dialogue between Mrs Buggins and her grandma, positioning the listener as eavesdropping on a domestic conversation instead of being on the receiving end of a declamatory instructional talk. Their dialogue included grandma conveying the ingredients of a recipe to Mrs Buggins, who as she checked she has heard correctly cleverly ensured that the recipe was being repeated and all listeners could write it down. The humour relied upon misunderstandings, innuendo, confusion, characterization and joshing. One incident involved, for example, confusion between 'mousse' and 'mouse'. The pleasures were like those Medhurst has argued were central to Music Hall comedy and were influential in British variety entertainment on radio and later television: 'identification, recognition and celebration for working class audiences' (2007, p. 69). In so doing, they offered shared national communality through comedy in the face of adversity. Thus, when in one dialogue Mrs Buggins commented that 'it's a job to know what to give people to tempt their appetitive', grandma replied, with reference to the lodger, that "is appetite wants dampin' down not tempting'. The humour rests upon her verbalizing a common problem – having done this through comedy, arguably the solutions offered in terms of recipes became more palatable. The language used avoided correct pronunciation and relied heavily on colloquialisms and everyday slang words such as "ospital' and 'workin''. Vera Hodgon, a middle-aged social worker, stated that she enjoyed Mrs Buggins broadcasts on *Kitchen Front* (cited in Abbott, 2003, p. 61); whether she was the intended audience and whether it shifted her cooking or eating habits or acclimatized her to government policy is open to question though.

Elsie and Dorris Waters, two sisters better known as Girt and Daisy, made their radio debut in 1927 and were by the mid-1930s already regular radio performers. With classical music training and early singing careers, their path to radio celebrity came, according to the introduction to their lives in *Radio Times* (9 August 1935) when they improvised a sketch to go on the flip side of record and invented Gert and Daisy – two cockney chars. They continued successful careers on the stage in Music Halls and in radio variety programmes such as *Ack Ack* and *Beer Beer*, alongside domestic broadcasting and consequently were less willing to comply with BBC requests to contribute to domestic broadcasting and negotiated financially more lucrative contracts than most other cookery programme presenters. In a series of sketches entitled *Feed the Brute*, broadcast in the evening in 1940, they were full of suggestions for eking out or substituting meat with offal and sausages which were off rations. Again the viewer was positioned as eavesdropping on humorous banter between the pair, as the following extract on the benefits of haggis and faggots demonstrates:

> Daisy: Oh I've often had faggots.
> Gert: Yes I like them too! But some people are funny about 'em. They like sausages, but they don't like faggots. I think they're both jolly good.
> Daisy: Oh they're not the same.
> Gert: Don't forget sausages wear tights, while faggots flop about without any means of support (laughs).
> Gert: Well, anyway, sausages aren't rationed, and what's nicer than a hot sausage between two slices of bread?

Mass Observation produced a report on how effective Gert and Daisy broadcasts were, something which was and remains hard to assess. If 'popular comedy offers solace, identification, confirmation and belonging' (Medhurst, 2007, p. 205) then no wonder Gert and Daisy were popular with working-class listeners. One woman remarked: 'they're good and I like the recipes they give because they're suitable for the poorer class of people. You really can make them. Not like some of them they used to have on the wireless' (MO, Box 2 22:4:1940). The pleasures of comedy are, however, often defensive; they involve a resigned recognition of circumstances rather than a call to action. It is therefore not surprising that Mass Observation reports indicated that many listeners enjoyed listening to Gert and Daisy's banter, but had no intention of engaging with their advice. One man commented that 'we listen to them and enjoy them too. I suppose they're a help. My wife would know better' (MO, Box 2 22:4:1940). There are indications that, for many, Gert and Daisy provided entertainment not domestic governance, as evidenced in comments such as 'They're very good, fair makes you roar', 'We always listen ... We listen more for fun than anything', 'Well I think they're good but I don't go for fancy food myself', 'I just listen to the wireless but I don't give much thought to it'. Mass Observation's report rather pompously summed up their findings:

> We do however get the preliminary impression through reading carefully through the verbatim material of people's replies that to some extent the *full impact* of Gert and Daisy's talks has not been achieved. There has not been that extra something which has crystallised interested listening into universal action. If there had been a brief summary in a serious male voice at the end, this effect might have been more fully achieved (MO, Box 2 22:4:1940).

Putting the gendered prejudice of this report, which assumes that only men can be authoritative, to one side, there were some complaints that the cost of food suggested was too expensive and that their ideas would not be well received in families where tastes were already defined and the housewife's skill was assessed in her response to these tastes. What they did do, as the Mass Observation report acknowledged, was, like Mrs Buggins, through accent, dialogue and familiar cultural reference points achieve a sense of identification with the listeners – rather than with the Ministry of Food. In this the title of the series *Feed the Brute* was key. When in 1941 they gave a recipe for 'murkey', stuffed mutton intended to replace what they described as 'the almost unobtainable turkey' (Gardiner, 2004, p. 186), it was an example of the comedic operating as a 'triumph of life at its most opportunistically resourceful' (Žižek, 2000. p. 29).

It is in its rootedness in working-class culture that popular comedians can be differentiated from many other domestic wartime broadcasters who provided similar recipes but who belonged to a different cultural milieu to many listeners. For example, Marguerite Patten, one of the cookery advisers on *Kitchen Front*, who later became a television cook, went on to reach an iconic status as a representative of World War II cooking; she was also a Home Economics adviser at the up-market department store Harrods. It is the cultural familiarity with working-class life that explains the popularity of the books sold by Gert, Daisy and Mrs Buggins, and the 30,000 listeners who requested the accompanying recipes to *Feed the Brute* (Nicholas, 1996). Although one respondent told Mass Observation interviewers they thought that having to use 'comediennes for cookery programmes was a sorry state of affairs' (MO, Box 2 22:4:1940), these programmes acknowledged and brought together two elements of key significance to national culture – food and comedy (Medhurst, 2007). In so doing, these broadcasts may have assisted the population in becoming acclimatized to rationing, shortages and wartime diets, even if they did not rush to follow the recipes. Perhaps interestingly they shifted the paradigmatic framework in which food was discussed on broadcasting into the spaces of pleasure, fun and pastime – and away from 'managing' and nutrition; in this they laid the seeds for cookery programmes of the late twentieth century.

NATIONAL NARRATIVES

If the provision of adequate food was increasingly a preoccupation for housewives, the progress of the war became a national narrative which dominated many homes. Wartime radio is popularly identified with the transmission of news; the radio announcement of the declaration of war is included in many documentaries on World War II and in many oral histories. A Mass Observation survey, however, discovered at the outbreak of war that in one in ten households they visited there was no wireless, some were broken, while others said they had 'no time to listen' (MO, TC 74/2/A). Sales of radios seem to have increased in the first two weeks of the war, although spare parts were often in short supply, as were batteries (MO, TC 74/1/H). For the middle-classes, electricity enabled the radio to be plugged into the mains; for very many working-class listeners the shortage and cost of batteries and their recharging and accumulators was prohibitive, as one man remembered: 'Reception could be varied, a battery powered radio was our main source of entertainment ... reception in Cornwall was never very good especially at night times' (Harry Pligrim, PWW, 3 May 2005).

The news became a nationally shared open-ended narrative – almost a national soap opera – punctuating days, discussed in shops, influencing mood. As Anne Cresswell recalled: 'The radio was on continually and spirits rose and fell according to how things were going' (PWW, 8 September 2005). Nella Last also recounts how 'nowadays when my husband and I hear bad news on the wireless we look at each other and don't talk much about it. I read a puzzled wonder in his eyes – as if he cannot believe what the announcer says. I wonder what he reads in mine' (Broad and Flemming, 2006, p. 104). Although many recollect the news being listened to with reverence, in many cases the audience was more interactive; one memoir demonstrates this: 'Adults and children would sit quietly and listen to the news everyday on the BBC. The news reader always gave his name, and we tried to guess which of the news readers it was' (PWW, Kathleen Smith, 22 October 2003). Here a shift from the news as of national significance and worthy of hushed silence was articulated, as at the same time it was incorporated into a parlour game of 'guess the newscaster'.

A Mass Observation description of ordinary people listening to the news in their homes accompanied by an observer suggested there was an active but spasmodic engagement with news items and that there was also a process of personalizing and familiarising the news items, and that the process of creating the news became a focus of gossip. For example, when an Italian name is pronounced, the son of one household asked, 'I wonder if they have to practice for words like that?' (MO, TC 49 Box 1/D 67/6). At other times, news was seen to operate as only one of a range of sources of information; as when a Streatham household shifted their attention from listening to news items to hearing the daughter's account of a runaway balloon (MO, TC 49 Box 1/D 67/6). Furthermore, a degree of scepticism about 'accuracy' was demonstrated when, on hearing the radio announce 'No ship hit', a woman responded by saying 'that's good' and her husband snorted (MO, TC 49 Box 1/D 67/6). For others the news evoked a sense of empathy for those in danger; Nella Last explained that she was nervy, 'its a feeling of a having a skin less, of "seeing pictures" as the BBC announces the Admiralty regrets; of thinking shudderingly of boys in tents with few blankets – and what is now worse, of little children and women that are not too strong hurrying out of warm beds and cowering in shelters' (Broad and Flemming, 2006, p. 71).

Despite the national radio serial that World War II became, Hilmes has charted the tensions within the BBC around drama serials which represented the domestic experience of war. Serials such as *The English Family Robinson* (1940–6), which 'as the Blitz began and bombs fell on British families' ensured that 'the Robinsons suffered and survived alongside them' (2006, p. 14), were tolerated and maybe seen as an indication of growing populism in the BBC. Despite disapproval, *The English Family*

Robinson became part of the BBC world broadcasts including the BBC's North American Service, and at one point four million listeners tuned in daily. It moved to the Light programme after the war, 2:45–3:00 on weekdays in the afternoon, as the *Robinson Family* in 1946 but criticism continued: 'A programme of this kind which is deliberately constructed to hit at the very centre of the domestic hearth by playing variations of all kinds of domestic trivia, is bound to achieve a quite unreasonable influence' (R19/1047/2, quoted in Hilmes, 2006, p. 21). The contempt here was arguably for a fictional rather than a factual narrative which the nation could follow and discuss. One interviewee explained 'When I was at the shop they used to say 'did you hear so and so?' (Mrs Selsey, 27 July 2002). There is also an indication of a sense of contempt 'for domestic trivia' and for domesticity. During World War II the much talked-about home front suggested that domesticity and the home were very much part of the national war effort, and the language of war was extended to everything, including the patriotic potato, as the kitchen became the front line of this home front. Arguably this could be seen as an indication of the increased status and significance of domesticity. But Higonnet and Higonnet (1993) point out that in wartime the significant, high status and important work is that carried on by the armed forces. In support of this it is interesting to note that, whereas the *Radio Times* in the inter-war period frequently carried domestic scenes on the front cover, in wartime the covers portrayed military images, and very occasionally political figures. In the porous and leaky relationship between public and private that broadcasting involved itself in, many in the BBC wished to foreground the organizations associated with the nation over those of the domestic. Arguably divisions are not so clear cut; housewives were not passively positioned by discourse but were required to actively take it up; furthermore, broadcasting was becoming increasingly sensitive to consumers' tastes and demands and the national preoccupation with domesticity and domestic trivia was there to stay: domestic serials became a staple of broadcasting in the post-war era.

CONNECTED BY THE AIRWAVES – MESSAGES HOME AND SHARED LISTENING

One element of many households' focus on the news was a desperation to hear anything that would reassure them of the safety or otherwise of their loved ones who were away from home. One interviewee articulated this when she described how a son, on being sent abroad in the forces, 'sold his bike and bought his mother a radio' (Mrs Lynch, 1 August 2002). She then went on to tell an apocryphal story of another mother who learned of the sinking of her son's ship, and that he was therefore presumably dead, when she overhead the radio news at her local shop. Arguably these narratives suggest that radio was perceived to be a significant link between families fractured by war. Sometimes this was an unintended consequence of the familiarity of listening material. Nella Last recounts how 'I got a pleasant surprise when I heard the signature tune for "Scrapbook", for I had not had time to read the *Radio Times*. It brought back memories – Arthur had just passed his civil service exam and started work' (Broad and Flemming, 2006, p. 31). During the war a number of broadcasts fostered this sense that they could link members of families geographically separated by war and help to maintain domestic relationships and personal connections – especially when this separation was the result of men serving in the armed forces or children having been evacuated.

Initially a sense of contact with family members in the forces was offered by broadcasting concerts performed for the troops. A storm of criticism erupted when the BBC broadcast only 15 minutes of a 2-hour Gracie Fields' concert for 5 thousand troops in France in November 1939. As the *Evening Standard* pointed out: 'Every person in this country who has a man out there would have thought "Perhaps my son, or my husband, is in that audience shouting with the rest having a jolly good time"' (*Evening Standard*, 18 November 1939). The BBC learned its lesson, and by 1943 the British Expeditionary Force was accompanied by a recording unit which broadcast to the Forces and British radio every Saturday night. The ideal of shared listening, which had become part of the domestic idyll of the inter-war period, in wartime could continued although listeners were geographically separated. *Radio Times* provided explanations of time variations between Britain and different parts of the world where forces were engaged. Under the title 'When Will He be Listening?', instructions were provided on when men in the forces were most likely to be listening. Likewise, messages sent across the airwaves offered a symbolic and very partial replacement for conversations which had taken place by the domestic hearth to the accompaniment of the wireless.

Letters to the BBC and messages were read out on air in, for example, Vera Lynn's *Sincerely Yours* or *Sandy's Half Hour*, which was first broadcast on the Forces Service in February 1940, and seen as 'bringing together in spirit husbands and wives, fathers and children, sons, mothers and sweethearts' from the 'whole British army and thousands of homes' (*Radio Times*, 5 April 1940). *Sandy's Half Hour* was advertised in the *Radio Times* as 'a programme of requests specially to unite listeners in their homes with their friends and relatives serving with the forces', presented by Sandy MacPherson who also played the theatre organ. As Nicholas points out, these 'message programmes' soon became a characteristic feature of both the Forces Programme and the BBC's short-wave services, they were however 'periodically criticised by the BBC hierarchy for their sentimentality but their contribution to morale was considered invaluable' (Nicholas, 1996, p. 129). That their populist and low-brow feel was slightly frowned upon can also be seen in a Mass Observation report which noted: 'to the people taking part in them, or to the people for whom they are meant, they are, not unnaturally one of the most important things the BBC has ever done' (MO, TC 74/1/A). Oral testimony and press coverage also emphasized their significance; Jack Toothill recalled: 'At Christmas time ... whole families would be bent over little radio sets listening to crackling messages from all around the world' (PWW, 6 August 2004), while the *Radio Times* also reported in 1944:

> For five Christmases since war began radio reunions have linked our people at home, our fighting men, our kinsmen and our Allies overseas in a pattern that has gained permanence; through the years, it has always reflected the colour of our changing fortunes. Together we celebrated 'Christmas Under fire' in 1940. Together we toasted 'Absent Friends' in 1941, Together we reaffirmed our faith and determination in the dark days of the 'Fourth Christmas'. Last Christmas in 'We are Advancing' we could sound a strong note of achievement. This Christmas after a year of momentous victories we chart 'The Journey Home' (22 December 1944).

Absent friends – the theme of Christmas Day 1941 – both acknowledged that domesticity had been fractured and attempted to provide links with domesticated spaces in which people were celebrating Christmas – broadcasting parties from groups of 'men from the empire', working London, soldiers from India in Wales and allied troops on their bases in Scotland. The notion that, through listening to the radio, people from across the world would be able to lift up their glasses to absent friends and have a sense of connection and shared listening was strong. The connections were not just to friends and relations: Nella Last welled up with tears when she heard on the radio a Prisoner of War speak about Red Cross parcels – and felt that her war work to enable such parcels to be sent was worthwhile (Broad and Flemming, 2006, p. 257). Few would have imagined that the listeners included Prisoners of War, and yet Hubert Tuck recalls listening to a radio constructed by inmates in a Prisoner of War Camp in France (PWW, 11 February 1940). Similarly Ralph Corps remembered the excitement when, in a POW camp in Italy, one of his fellow prisoners, using headphones and a repaired radio set, announced that he could get 'Scottish Regional' on the radio:

> I can never hope to be able to put my feelings into words at that moment; I would have liked to shout the news to the farthest point of that prison camp. Every man in that room was bubbling with excitement and almost bursting to ask questions. We each listened in turn to the variety programmes broadcast that evening (PWW, 28 May 2005).

Their emotional excitement and shared enjoyment of hearing radio variety emphasizes the degree to which the radio was invested with a sense of belonging and comfort as it represented home. A programme which played to this was the series *Home Flash*, in which the outside broadcasting unit focused on a particular town, village or city to provide news of what was going on there to those in the forces. It suffered from the obvious problem that it was not necessarily of much interest to those who did not live in that particular area, and that a number of rather local mayors tended to drone on while local inhabitants tried frantically to use the programme to send messages to their loved ones (BBWA, 34/955/1) so that it was eventually axed in 1944.

EVACUATION

One of the most obvious and traumatic ways in which families were fractured in wartime was 'during the dislocation of evacuation' (*Radio Times* 17 November 1939), which first occurred 2 days in advance of the outbreak of war on 1 September 1939. Nearly 1 million unaccompanied schoolchildren and over half a million expectant mothers or mothers with pre-school children were evacuated through government schemes and it is estimated that 3 million children and mothers were evacuated privately. The process of reassuring parents and connecting them to their children began within a programme entitled *We are Evacuated*, made up of recordings from a small Lancashire mill town which was one of the reception areas. Olive Shapley's introduction to the programme explained:

> When we arrived, the streets were given over to children: the high school girls sauntering arm in arm up the main street in their tidy brown uniforms, children playing football in the steep cobbled side streets, children going shopping for their new mothers, children making friends with policemen and ARP [Air Raid Precautions] wardens. (Shapley, 1996, p. 68)

As Shapley admits, the role of such programming was twofold: 'Parents were to be reassured that the evacuation policy was for the best and receiving families needed encouragement in their wartime role and coping with unfamiliar changes' (Shapley, 1996, p. 68), going on to admit that for those working in the BBC the division between propaganda and objective reporting was not easily identified and reporters were encouraged to ensure that those coping with wartime challenges with courage and determination were adequately represented. This determination at one level contributed to the dominant, although very partial, discourses of World War II, seen in films such as *Christmas Under Fire* (1941) in which 'brave little Englanders' were portrayed as defying the Blitz and the privations of war to celebrate Christmas. In the same year a programme entitled *Children in Wartime* (1941) included the story of a 9-year-old boy describing a daylight raid and a letter to parents from an evacuated schoolgirl. The main thrust of such programmes was to encourage parents to leave their children in the countryside and to resist the urge to take them back home, as the programme *Children in the Cities* pointed out:

> But three hundred thousand children stayed in reception areas, and when the bombs were falling mothers were thankful and their courage strengthened because they knew their children were safe ... safe and happy as they began to settle down and explore the new life that was opening up before them. (14 October 1941)

Despite the broadcasts, during the period of the phoney war when no bombing occurred, many children and mothers had returned home by Christmas 1939. A second wave of evacuation was consequently needed the following year when the Blitz began and the Kent coast was evacuated after the fall of Dunkirk when invasion fears were at their highest. A final wave of evacuation took place late in the war when doodlebugs fell on London but for the many children evacuated abroad for the duration of the war there was no question of return and these children and their parents, after some negotiation with the Ministry of Information, became the focus of a number of broadcasts. At Christmastime a radio card of Christmas greetings from evacuated children in Great Britain, Canada and the USA was initially broadcast in Britain, Canada, the USA, South Africa and Australia, where children had been evacuated, but it merely involved messages being read out. At other times a selection of extracts from BBC Children's Hour was broadcast in other countries to provide reassurance and a sense of home to British evacuee children, often accompanied by 5 minutes of parents' recorded messages.

By the Christmas 1940, *From the Children* provided recorded messages from Australia and New Zealand, and the BBC began two-way broadcasts between parents and their children evacuated abroad. In January 1940 the first live linkup between parents and their nine children who had been evacuated to the USA and brought into an American radio studio, went on air and the announcer's introduction affirmed the role of radio in reuniting fractured families with the following words: 'Across the Atlantic in London all their parents are assembled and in just a few minutes warm words will be exchanged over land and sea as the magic of radio reunites mothers and fathers with sons and daughters. Are you ready London?' (1 January 1940). Each child was given 2 minutes of communication with his or her parents, although occasionally something went wrong with numbers and everything was much more hurried. Writing in the *Radio Times* about her work on these programmes, Enid Maxwell portrayed the BBC as very much providing a public service, with emotionally moved staff watching on admiringly as stiff-upper lip, emotionally restrained parents talked to their children over the airwaves (*Radio Times*, 19 December 1941). Those memos that remain in the BBC archives tell a different story and not one which necessarily portrays those involved in a good light. Their key concern was to orchestrate good listening material with perhaps rather less concern for the welfare of all the participants. Obviously some children were tongue-tied, and some parents were emotional. One follow-up memo inquired: 'I hope the Richardson's were not too upset by their daughter's tears. She sounded as if she was trying to be brave and finding it difficult. We considered it a good programme though, of course we should have liked to hit the Australian compare on the head with a hammer' (BBCWA, 24 June 1942 R 11/12).

BBC employees focus upon getting a good programme certainly matched the exploitation of any contemporary reality television programme, despite the obvious distress at times of parents, some of whom were as dumbstruck as the children. Parents were warned to try and frame their comments to avoid upsetting children; nevertheless one producer noted 'I am so sorry the R's were so dim! Poor Mrs R was in such floods of tears, and I had literally to hold her up to the mike, while her distress pre-occupied Mr R more than somewhat' (BBCWA, 12 December 1942 R 11/12). Spontaneity was not the order of the day, although there was an emphasis on the 'children and what they had been doing', but BBC producers were often disappointed in the children's performance and after one programme announced 'They were the dumbest lot of children I have ever heard ... Something must be done. For one thing the children must be coached' (BBCWA R 11/12, 31 March 1943). Despite a number of difficulties, including getting parents and children to the studios simultaneously and in different parts of the world, or American audiences being offended by British exclamations of horror that their children had acquired American accents, the programmes continued approximately once a month or once every two months until 1943.

Transatlantic Call – Family Reunion, broadcast on Sunday 26 December 1943, linked New York, Canada and the BBC in London.

The announcer introduced the programme, which had managed to capture the BBC's ideal spread of evacuees and their home regions, and explained, 'This week the programme takes the form of a family reunion. British, American and Canadian children will exchange greetings with parents in London, Leeds and Glasgow', and went on to explain that the programme included 'children from Clydeside, an American boy whose father is in London and a 15 year old from Middlesex who after 3 years in the States wants to say hello to his parents in London' (26 December 1943). Programmes were less frequent in 1944, as some children journeyed home from their foster homes abroad. Some parents had clearly found the programmes very positive; a Mrs B from Birmingham explained, 'its was a great joy to speak to and hear her children again … what seemed like an ordeal turned out to be a real pleasure' (BBWA R11/12). The trauma of these broadcasts is hard to assess and is perhaps a small issue in relation to the trauma of the evacuation itself for many parents and children. For some the reassurance of listening to familiar or shared radio broadcasts enabled the airwaves to link those separated by war, for others it just served to emphasize how fractured their families were and was a far from ideal experience as Mann has pointed out:

> Everyone always said, 'It was lovely to hear your voice'. But it was a frustrating exercise. Not only were the participants aware that every word they said was being listened to by a large audience, but in those days when broadcasting seemed an arcane and glamorous trade many of them were paralysed by 'mike fright' and refused to cooperate …
> BBC Staff invited parents to the studio with a an offer to refund travel expenses … one evacuee – Lucy Tipton recalled 'I remember my parents speaking to me on the radio on a programme called *Hello Children* following which I was terribly ill, due to mental depression. And I remember crying for hours after seeing the movie Mrs Minever … I think in my own way, as a child, I felt

guilty that I was eating and sleeping so well and my parents were not.' (Mann, 2005, pp. 220–2)

In wartime, radio served to link both domesticity and the family to spaces, places and individuals displaced from the radio's hearth, while the national significance of the home front in a sense shifted the public space of the war firmly into the domestic sphere. As the homemakers of Britain battled to provide foodstuffs in their kitchens, the wirelesses and BBC became firmly entrenched at the heart of the home and the nation; yet in the 10 years that followed the declaration of peace in 1945, television took over the central place in the nation's domestic spaces.

Chapter Five

From austerity to consumer wonderland: post-war domesticities

The Coronation of Queen Elizabeth II in 1953 was watched on television by an audience of approximately 22 million. Many of them sat in front of one of the 1,400,000 sets sold in the weeks prior to the event (Hill, 1986). One interviewee recalled the arrival of the television:

> There was great excitement when it was being delivered, just shortly before the coronation in 1953. It was in the lounge, it was only a little black and white screen but it was a big box and stood on the floor, it was quite a big thing, the speaker was at the bottom … I remember watching the coronation, it's one of my earliest memories (Mr Eldred, 8 December 2010).

Others were not so lucky, instead having to visit friends and relations to enjoy the first mass televisual spectacle in Britain. The celebrity cook, Marguerite Patten had provided housewives with advice on 'Cooking for Coronation Day' in the *Radio Times*, on *Woman's Hour* and on afternoon television. Food for the 'larger audience than usual' … gathered … 'round the television screen', it was suggested should be planned in advance so that the housewife did not miss 'a particularly moving or exciting few minutes' (*Radio Times*, 15 May 1953, p. 45). For many the Queen's Coronation and the television sets on which it was watched epitomized post-war culture. The new consumer technology, an idealized domestic harmony of the royal family and of family viewing heralded the 'new Elizabethan' age. The era has been typified in popular mythology as one of long and happy marriages, domestic contentment and harmony as the country progressed towards increasing affluence. A more careful examination of the first 15–20 years that followed World War II, and of broadcasting during this period, suggests a more contradictory and complex picture. Although there had been a boom in the marriage rate at the beginning and end of the war, the divorce rate was also climbing and campaigns for divorce reform were gathering support. Calder has pointed out 'that the paradoxical effect of war overall seems to have been that it loosened family ties and moral constraints, while simultaneously creating a yearning for a settled home life' (1969, p. 23). The gap between the yearning for domesticity and the lived experience caused problems for many: disharmony, instability, disappointment and disillusion often lay behind the domestic ideal.

Two and a half million couples had been apart for long periods during the war, and a third of a million servicemen and women and merchant seaman had been killed, as well as 67,635 civilians (Addison, 2005). Reconstructing fractured wartime domesticity with the now fragile and tentative family units was problematic in interpersonal and emotional terms; something that was exaggerated by the difficulty in finding a suitable space to turn into a place called home. Despite the speculative building of the inter-war period providing new suburban houses for many of the middle-classes, the legacy of wartime bombing was a severe shortage of housing stock. There was also a significant number of damaged houses": in London 160,000 houses were damaged but repairable; 780,000 were damaged but habitable. The Labour Manifesto of 1945 asserted that: 'Housing will be one of the greatest and earliest tests of government's real determination to put the nation first'. The 1945–51 Labour government, in allocating limited resources and skilled workers, prioritized repairs (Bullock, 2005) and 60,000 damaged houses were in use again by 1947. Nevertheless, in 1949, as *Picture Post* pointed out, a survey suggested that the Labour government's second most outstanding failure was seen as being 'too slow with housing' (Langhamer, 2005, p. 344).

The financial crisis in Britain at the end of World War II with large overseas debts, particularly to the USA, meant that a period of austerity quickly followed victory celebrations; not only did rationing remain but it got more severe with, for example, bread being rationed for the first time in 1946. The austerity was metaphorically emphasized by the hard winter of 1947, which provoked a fuel crisis. As Adisson suggests, in the late 1940s 'the Home Front ran on without a war to sustain it' (1985, p. 84) and with a legacy of pent-up consumer demand from wartime, the era of austerity was also accompanied by despondency, weariness and a flourishing black market operated by spivs. Acknowledging the spirit of the time, advertising utilized the rhetoric of weariness; Wincarnis tonic wine sold itself as a pick-me-up for 'Housewives who are wearied', while Byford men's socks with nylon in the heels were intended to help 'Darn Weary Wives'. The development of a system of welfare provided a social wage and the state's commitment to full employment provided the background for a steady rise in the standard of living for most people, while the introduction of the National Health Service in 1948 provided free access to healthcare to accompany 'free education and a residual safety net for the most disadvantaged in society' (Fink, 2005, p. 45) reduced some of the effects of personal crisis which in the pre-war era would have sent households into debt. In 1948 the *Daily Mail* was able to assert:

> On Monday Morning you will wake up in a new Britain, in a state which 'takes over' its citizens six months before they are born, providing care and free services for their birth, for their early years, their schooling, sickness and workless days, widowhood and retirement. All with free doctoring, dentistry and medicine – bath-chairs too if needed – for 4/11d out of your weekly pay packet. (*Daily Mail* 3 July 1948, cited in Fink, 2005; see also Timmins, 1995).

Despite the optimism, the new Britain of the 1940s, in which the BBC replaced its Forces Service with the Light Programme and

Radio Luxembourg, began broadcasting again, domesticity of the post-war 1940s and 1950s was full of contradictions. Television returned in 1946 but the golden age of consumerism existed alongside the persistency of poverty and class divisions. The role of the housewife was often idealized but an increasing number of women were in the workforce. Broadcasting negotiated the diversity of domesticity and struggled to reproduce representations of domesticity that were credible to its consumers; as it did so it drew attention to the performative nature of domesticity, and that these performances rested upon gendered power relations. The performances developed by the 1950s into the hysterical and over-the-top campness of Fanny Craddock.

WOMAN'S HOUR

Woman's Hour, which is now the longest running radio programme in British broadcasting, was launched on 7 October 1946. It had a male presenter, gramophone records, a fairly gentle serial, a recipe of the day and patronizing talks on 'Making the Best of Oneself', and would arguably be unrecognizable to devotees of today's programme. It owed much to its forbears: the BBC's *Woman's Hour* of the 1920s, *Household Talks* and Radio Luxembourg's *L'heure de dames and des demoiselles*, which was broadcast in 1935 (Mattelart, 1997). Given that, as Oakley (1974a) has argued, the categories of women and housewives were in many respects seen as interchangeable in the post-war era, it is perhaps not surprising that domestic topics featured heavily within the programme. Something that was emphasized when the first presenter – Norman Collins – welcomed women listeners with the words:

> Good Afternoon and welcome to our first *Woman's Hour*. It is to be a regular feature in the Light Programme – and I hope you will find time to join us as often as you can. In fact it's your programme – designed for you. There will be talks by experts on keeping house, on health, on children, furnishings and beauty care – in fact

> on everything concerned with your sort of problems in the home. Now with us today, we have first of all Mrs Mary Manton, and you are going to talk about midday meals aren't you Mrs Manton? (Quoted in Feldman, 2000, p. 66)

Perhaps unsurprisingly, *Women's Hour* had a slightly shaky start; it did, however, speedily improve to become a more varied, interesting and outward-looking programme, including not only how to knit a stair carpet, the indomitable Mrs Webb on filling the store cupboard, some shorter punchier talks on a child starting school and preparing the garden for the holidays, but also, with a gesture towards the new citizen–housewife, turgid and worthy reports of the newly nationalized National Coal Board, the Women's Voluntary Service (WVS) in war and peace, and advice on national insurance. According to Olive Shapley, who was a presenter from 1949–53, the programme developed to become 'a magazine programme for intelligent women, which would deal with keeping house, health, children, beauty care and home furnishings and finish with a short serial' (1996, p. 36). The *Women's Hour* format, whereby 'the presenter would weave together a number of disparate elements into some sort of unity: the shape of each programme would be familiar enough to regular listeners but the content ever-changing' (Hendy, 2007, p. 46), was innovative in Britain, although popular on American radio and as such often seen as populist and a little suspect.

The time slot of 2 p.m. was chosen to fit in with its perceived audience's everyday lives. The morning schedule on the Light Programme was given over to *Housewife's Choice*, a mixture of music and requests which were intended to accompany housework and distracted listening. *Women's Hour* came after the morning chores were completed and prior to the return of children from school. For young mothers it conveniently coincided with dominant paradigms of childcare, articulated by Truby King (a guest on *Woman's Hour* in the 1940s) which insisted that babies should be fed at ten, two and six o'clock. It became, in time, the time of day when housewives fed the baby, made pastry, did the mending, ironing and other household tasks that could be undertaken within earshot of the radio. Thus when, in 1990, it was proposed to move *Woman's Hour* to a morning slot, Brian Redhead is rumoured to have retorted 'there won't be a decently ironed shirt in the country' (Jenni Murray, 12 July 2010). Shapley argues that *Women's Hour* in the late 1940s and early 1950s 'tried to lighten the household chores and give listeners a new interest, albeit an appropriately feminine one. It also tried to open a window onto the world outside the home, in a way which listeners themselves may not have had the time or opportunity to do' (1996, p. 38). Within this remit, the programme in the 1950s covered topics which included: venereal disease, the change of life, women without men, coronation robes, warts and the problems of women with big feet. Such topics confirm the programme's relationship to the inter-war *Household Talks*.

The decision to title the programme according to the gender of its perceived listeners, as opposed to their role, was legitimating for women; it affirmed their place within the schedules of the national broadcasters, not because they performed a role but because they were part of society. One audience member wrote: 'thanks a lot for *Woman's Hour.* It is nice to feel that somewhere the female sex is deemed worthy of an hour in each day. It is all very nice and will be helpful to many. Here are a few tips to save precious soap ... (BBCWA, 14 October 1946). An analysis of audience on 12 and 13 August 1948 indicates that the male audience took a while to grow (BBCWA, R/51/640/5). In 1953 a 'mere man' wrote in to say that he had begun listening to *Woman's Hour* while confined to home ill and had found it interesting. 'May I suggest that the programme could be transferred to the evening, it should be called *Family Hour* because it is a family programme' (*Radio Times*, 24 July 1953, p. 47). Although his suggestion was ignored, male listeners grew, even though the programme, unusually in broadcasting history, placed them as the second sex; they now made up about a third of the audience.

Undeniably this is linked to wider car use by men in their working lives, where radios are now universally fitted. Car radios were, in the 1950s, a relatively new introduction. Nella Last, a middle-class housewife, remarked in her diary for Mass Observation with little enthusiasm on her husband's decision to have a car radio fitted in 1948 (Malcolmson and Malcolmson, 2008, p. 233).

Nella Last was not the only post-war wife who was less than totally enamoured with their husband's actions; the *Women's Hour* broadcasts and correspondence revealed the disharmony, disillusion and misery of 1950s domesticity. A BBC report on the *Woman's Hour*'s audience saw the listeners as housewives, often lonely, and suggested that 'Possibly because of this loneliness they regard themselves as having an extremely intimate relationship with the compere ... they often write amusing and sometimes touching letters about their own personal environment and affairs of a kind they are unwilling to communicate to their neighbours and families' (BBCWA, R51/642). At one point in the early 1950s there was some discussion about introducing an anonymous letters feature, which would have lifted the lid on a range of emotional problems behind the veneer of family life as a source of domestic contentment. Women wrote of problems with the menopause, period pains and spending 2 hours at each meal trying to feed a 3-year-old (BBCWA, R51/642, Eileen Molony, 5 February 1948). One letter that would have been included was a plea for sympathy and understanding by parents from a young gay man, who described himself as a male listener. These letters, while not read out, lay behind the *Women's Hour* 'policy of bringing hush-hush topics into the open, including Homosexuality in 1955, Cancer in 1956 and couples living together without being married in1967 '(Quigley, 1956, quoted Feldman, 2000).

Thane has pointed out that 'After the Second World War marriage, at least once, became almost universal' (2010, p. 7) and within marriage it was assumed that women would take on the domestic responsibilities of a housewife: one woman gave a talk on how she ran her home around her working hours, as she had her own business two and a half miles from her home and explained, 'On my way home if necessary I do some shopping and then I set off to prepare a meal' (N14/288/1). Neither *Woman's Hour* nor the media more generally necessarily assumed that being a housewife would preclude women working or being involved or interested in a range of activities outside the home. Bournvita, for example, ran a series of adverts in *Radio Times* in the 1950s featuring a range of working mothers, such as Mrs Charlotte Wilson, from Catford, London, who was described as a clippie on the buses, who 'puts just as much enthusiasm into her other job as a housewife. She is glad to do her bit to make ends meet and thoroughly enjoys her double life.' She has two children and an aunt who lived with her family helped with the housework and kept an eye on the children when she was at work (*Radio Times*, 16 October 1953, p. 52). Mrs Wilson and other women's wider horizons were facilitated by a decrease in family size and the significant number of childless couples. Although there was an immediate post-war baby boom, arguably attributable to couples choosing to delay completing their family until the end of the war, families increasingly chose to restrict their families (Thane, 2010) and the Royal Commission on Population (1949) acknowledged 'women of all classes were aware that having more than one or two children was incompatible with living what they regarded as a tolerable life' (Thane, 2010). This stimulated an acknowledgement that the aspired-for 'tolerable life' was not necessarily available to all or even many of *Woman' Hour*'s listeners. Zweiniger-Bargielowska suggested that the 1950s 'witnessed the emergence of an average lifestyle, characterised by plentiful food, fashionable clothes, household durables, do-it-yourself decorating and home improvements, cars, annual holidays at home and abroad' (2005, p. 3), but lifestyle is always an ideal, an aspiration, it differs from day-to-day lived experience. This difference in itself precipitates tension, feelings of inadequacy, dislocations and at times exasperation and anger – as *Woman's Hour* found out.

Producers seemed to be aware of the multiple, diffuse domesticities that they were trying to interact with in this period, even though they were criticized for having 'an almost laughable obsession with domestic detail' (Jenni Murray, 12 July 2010). To some extent *Woman's Hour* was consistent with both the professionalization of women's, or at least middle-class women's, domestic role as mangers of the household, which Winship (1992) argues was identified in women's magazines of the 1950s. It also endorsed the ideal of the housewife as the consumer citizen by providing consumer advice, including on how to buy a teapot. Yet an awareness of generational divisions led to special editions of the programme for older and younger listeners at times in the 1950s. In 1947 'Housewives Exchange' every Tuesday was undertaken by the regions: Northern Ireland, the North, the Midlands and Scotland on a 4-week rota. Displaying somewhat stereotypical perceptions, a well-meaning BBC employee based in London suggested:

> Could the regions supply us with some really good housewives describing the circumstances of their lives – their favourite local dishes methods of relaxation pleasure etc. I can imagine a miner's wife from Durham describing the town she lives in, what she gives her husband for dinner, whether they go to the football match together etc. (BBWA, R51/640/3)

These programmes provided a space for 'ordinary' housewives to speak about their lives while attempting to address the diffuseness of the *Woman's Hour* audience. The ordinary was not necessarily the typical, and the programme legitimated experience, but those whose lives remained marginalized from such legitimation were sometimes antagonized. When Mrs Jackson from New Maldon described the three-bedroom house she and her husband rented, she explained, 'My one big grumble is that the kitchen is a bit too compact. I think the builders lost sight of the fact that somebody might offer to help with the washing up occasionally and only made the kitchen big enough to take one person at a time' (20 July 1948). What she grumbled about would have been a palace to many potential listeners. The post-war housing shortage forced one in five households in 1951 to share a home, either with strangers or as 'concealed households' such as newly-married couples living with in-laws. In 1950 approximately one in six London households' inhabitants lived in buildings converted for multiple occupancy; often in one room sharing a sink tap and lavatory, with an allocated day for washing. The gap between this and what Langhamer (2005) has identified as the fantasy of home – offering warmth, cosiness and the ability to be one's self, which was central to post-war aspirations, led to justifiable dissatisfaction. One letter writer who listened almost daily pointed out:

> My greater criticism of *Woman's Hour* is that is seems to be directed very much at the fortunate woman who has a house to herself and enjoys an income which places her in the middle class. How about we who married during the war and are making do in rooms with perhaps no sink and very little money – we are quite numerous and that little chat on how to take care of one's curtains riled a little … and that effort about bottling peaches – we daren't look at fruit with the price it is. (BBCWA, R51/640/3)

Instead she wanted features on how to budget on say £4 … and secondly any washing expert telling us the 'best way to wash babies clothes and napkins in congested space with no sink (lots of new mothers are in this position)' (BBCWA, R51/640/3). In the early post-war years one-third of households did not have a fixed bath, more than half did not have a hot water supply, and almost 8 per cent did not even have a WC. If, as Langhamer (2005) argues, 'for women too, the circumstances of war had intensified a longing for home' or at least fantasies of home, experience often did not live up to it. A talk entitled 'What About that Empty House?', which discussed the slow pace of requisitioning and the mending of houses, pointed out that three-quarters of a million people had been re-housed and acknowledged that 'the sight of an empty house, just what you want to make life bearable, must be maddening' (11 August 1948). Housing invited controversy; other areas of domesticity, where social divisions were never far from the surface, were cooking and budgeting, as they had been in the pre-war era. In 1950 a memo wondered whether it would 'conceivable be possible to suggest to Sister Myles, who provided advice on childcare, that she at least mentioned tins of fruit puree and recommend the official orange juice a little more as it was cheaper and less time consuming than the squeezing oranges which she encouraged' (BBWA, R51). One marginalized listener from Northern Ireland wrote in following a series of *Woman's Hour* talks, which mirrored those of the 1930s by being entitled 'How I Manage':

> Dear Sir
> Having listened with interest and a deepening sense of shame to the series How I Manage, I feel I should like to be interrogated in a similar broadcast from Northern Ireland, where it has been stated the cost of living is higher than anywhere else in Great Britain. As the mother of two ravenous school children for whom I neither get cheap milk nor school meals I feel the talk could rightly have been named 'How I fail to manage'; and might be something of a solace to the working women of the country who like myself have too much month left at the end of their money and who like myself are just a little weary of the vast army of well organised and self-satisfied Rose Buchans who never waste either their money or their time.
> Yours sincerely, Dorothy Johnston (BBCWA, N14/288/3)

Recipes were criticized for being either too expensive or patronizing. Food was and still is significant for expressions of identity, which is wrapped up in fantasies of home, yet wartime and post-war conditions, such as rationing and canteen food in factories and the services, had limited such fantasies from being realized and left a pent-up sense of dissatisfaction which radio as an aural medium did a little to dispel; television in time would fill the gap. According to an audience research survey carried out in 1948:

> It was, not uncommon to hear the remark that 'the recipes and household hints either tell you things that you can't do or don't work'. This point of view was expressed even where it was manifestly untrue, and, to some extent, is likely to represent an attitude of mixed anxiety and hostility towards any giving of information or instruction which suggests that housewives are less than omniscient in their own domestic roles. (BBCWA, BR15/9/12).

Although a latter BBC audience report in 1953 noted that: 'How to buy a cabbage was slightly more favourable than usual cookery talks' (BBCWA, R51/640/16). What was perhaps indicated by the audience research is that active discerning housewives were, as ever, resistant to broadcasting's attempts at governance. Nevertheless, the serendipity of topics and viewpoints which were aired in *Woman's Hour* underlined the uncertainty and instability of scripts on femininity and housewifery being performed in this era and this domestic medium's welcome preoccupation with them.

MRS DALE'S DIARY – THE DOMESTIC SERIAL, 1948–68

The wartime had accustomed the British public to following serial narratives on the radio, both listening to the progress of the war on the news and also to the domestic serial of *Front Line Family* aired on the Forces channel as *The Robinsons.* Serial domestic drama was identified as Americanized popular culture, yet despite opposition from Val Gielgud, BBC Head of Drama, *The Robinsons* like many other Forces programmes was transferred onto the Light Programme in the post-war era. It was however masculinized; Mrs Robinson's role took was increasingly reduced. As Hilmes argues, the introduction of *Mrs Dale's Diary* in 1948 and the rural drama, *The Archers*, in 1950 'represent the BBC's belated acknowledgement of the domestic serial drama a as a legitimately British and hence acceptable form' (2006, p. 22). The original intention of the series was that, although Mrs Dale and her family should not be working-class, they should not be 'far above it' and would share similar types of problems as the majority of the country at the time, practising economy and having to save for holidays and cinema tickets. The series was broadcast between 4:15 and 4:30 a.m. daily and repeated the following day at 11 a.m., each episode opening with a brief introductory narrative spoken by Mrs Dale as if she was writing in her diary. This and the title privileged Mrs Dale's experience, despite the original editorial policy which stated: 'This serial has a simple object: to hold and mirror the everyday life of a normal middle class family. Womanhood does not have to be demonstrated invariably as the dominant sex and source of all human virtue.' Indeed not, as she seemed to be regarded by some listeners as either an awful busybody or an insufferable prig (BBCWA, R19/779/2). Whatever the intentions, the Dales represented a thoroughly middle-class domesticity. According to programme notes, they lived in an old, possibly slightly shabby, 14 to 15-room house in which Doctor Dale had his surgery, somewhere near London in Esher or possibly Richmond. A report on the social status of the family was conducted for the BBC in 1950 by a Miss Owen, who listened to the programme for 2 weeks and expressed puzzlement at the selective representation of domestic life. With the ideal of post-war companionate marriages firmly in her mind, she pointed out that: 'The Dale family spend a good deal of time at home, but there is little indication of any activity which is undertaken jointly.' She also seemed uncertain on Mrs Dale's role as a full-time housewife and as to why she would need to launch an economy drive. There was, however, a series of story lines which explored the less than stable home environments in which many listeners were living in at the time. In the 1950s, stories covered housing rackets, someone threatened with losing their house for being behind with the rent and married daughter Gwen, who returned to work after having a baby, facing financial problems as a result of hire purchase debts gained by her purchases of furniture and white goods.

Despite its very middle-class setting, the series had a significant working-class following, one housewife remarked: 'They are my friends I find myself thinking of them at all time.' The BBC audience research suggested that the appeal for regular listeners lay in 'curiosity and idealised family life' (BBCWA, 9R19/779/2). In considering this, it is important to point out that it was only Mr and Mrs Dale's family life that was idealized. Although the initial intention had been to keep the family as static (as the cartoon characters in the Simpsons now are) this caused difficulty for the scriptwriters and was abandoned in the early 1950s; after which threats and challenges to the ideal of companionate marriage, personified in the Dales middle-class family unit. The threats are represented by the lives of those on the boundaries of the community of the Dales family and friends, those constantly circling around the Dales.

Although the 1950s and 1960s has been seen as the golden age of marriage, oral history, autobiography, anecdote and, importantly, popular culture suggest a more complex picture; as does the speed with which traditional marriage was abandoned in the 1970s when legal change made divorce laws much easier. Arguably, those who had grown-up within the post-war period, which had witnessed the greatest longevity of marriages, did not necessarily experience such marriages as idealized, harmonious and supportive relationships that they wanted to imitate. A range of storylines in *Mrs Dale's Diary* suggests also that stories which had 'emotional realism' for the listeners involved them or more accurately those close to them, in less than ideal marriages (BBCWA, R19/779/). Plot lines included: a nurse from the hospital where Doctor Dale trained, who left her husband and intended to have her small son adopted, Mrs Dale's sister Sally's neighbour, who left her husband even though she had a young baby (although she finally went back to him), a young pregnant girl whose trainee doctor husband went missing when she was due to give birth and a story of an unmarried mother. Closer to home, Mrs Dale's daughter's marriage was somewhat shaky and her sister Sally had a slightly turbulent personal life (including a divorce and a dead husband who reappeared), which brought Mrs Dale's cosy domesticity into relief. Sally's long-term friendship with and marriage to Richard Fulton was also doomed to disappointment. He was an 'over-sensitive, malicious, hypochondriacal, grudge bearing writer of romantic fiction and Shaftesbury Avenue plays', with a manservant and two Pekinese (Howes, 1993, pp. 278–9) whose sensibilities were clearly gay. In 1967, just as homosexuality was decriminalized, he went to Paris to explore his homosexuality, much to Mrs Dale's shock. Another reference to social change included Mrs Dale herself having a little flirtation with the rise of feminism in the 1960s – when she responded to Dr Dale's refusal to let her have driving lessons by going on strike and not cooking meals.

Despite these storylines, the series was perceived to be too twee and middle-class. *Mrs Dale's Diary* was also both more expensive to produce and less popular than *The Archers*, which was being broadcast in the evenings and had a potentially wider and more mixed audience. BBC producers and scriptwriters constantly discussed ways of updating the serial, including at one point the suggestion that the Dales should have a car accident which would kill off Mrs Dale. Dr Dale was to be nursed back to health by a young nurse he would then marry. In the end, the attempt to update the series involved a move to a new town named Exton and the series being renamed *The Dales* but, as Hilmes has pointed out, this 'attempt to reconcile' tension between the earlier symbolic idealization of family with a realist mode led to the series' final demise in 1969, but not before there had been one or two very dreary scenes set in factories (Hilmes. 2006).

Not only were *Mrs Dales Diary* and *The Archers* populist and feminized serials, they also took the BBC once again into areas of consumerism, a number of franchised recipes and home-decorating advice columns appeared in magazines – for example, *Women's Illustrated* in 1957 included an Easter supplement focused upon Mrs Dale's advice (BBWA R, 44/975/1). *Home Chat* similarly produced a number of series by Miss Gwen Berryman (Mrs Archer) on country lore and recipes, and also a cookery book. Similarly the *Daily Mail* carried cookery features based around *The Archers*, and *Woman's Own* a serialized story. It was, however, when *The Archers* carried a dramatic storyline in which the newly married Grace Archer died in a fire the night that ITV was first broadcast – 22 September 1955 – that the commercial imperatives, which were in time to dominate television broadcasting, crept into the BBC's radio serials.

CONSUMERISM AND TELEVISION

The 'rise of television as a domestic phenomenon' in the 1950s and 1960s has been linked to demographic change, 'the post-war baby boom, the expansion of suburbs and new towns, slum clearance, new housing' (Turnoch, 2007, p. 4). Hartley also argues that 'what was needed before television could be invented as a domestic medium was "the home". TV was a lounge room medium but many working class people didn't have a lounge' (Hartley, 1999, p. 99). Housing remained a political priority in elections; the Conservative government in 1951, with the economy now adjusted onto peacetime footing, introduced the 1952 Macmillan Housing Act which stimulated house building. By 1957 two and a half million houses had been built since the war and the 1950s saw a frenzy of interest in home-making (Hoskins, 2004, p. 4). Cohen's argument that 1950s house building and redevelopment of the slums led to a new reliance on consumerism and media-defined needs, that women found themselves cooped up in suburban housing estates, isolated from families and community (1972, p. 17) has taken the status of orthodoxy. Yet there is in this a touch of the intellectual distrust of suburban estates, which Carey (1992) had identified in the inter-war period and feminists such as Betty Friedan (1963) articulated in the 1960s. Oral history and autobiography supports Tebbutt's (1995) argument that communality and gossip could be found on the new estates. Furthermore, the privatized home life that improved housing offered was the dream of many middle- and working-class people. DIY entered the English language in 1958, although a range of modernizing home improvement activities were already well established, including the desire to cover surfaces in older houses with hygienic and brightly coloured Formica, which for many was a symbol of modernity (Browne, 2000). These ideals were demonstrated in the BBC television appearances of Barry Buknell, which included *Do It Yourself* (1955) and *Bucknell's House* (1962–3). As Giles has suggested: 'Doing-It-Yourself' made a great deal of sense to working and lower middle class householders of the 1950s for a number of reasons, importantly it was a financially viable way of modernising, and applying their own judgement and creativity (2004, p. 179).

Hartley (1999) has suggested that capital investment in housing and the ideology of domesticity are precursors to popular television in the UK; for many, fridges were the priority in home technology acquisition and a highly revered item. Nella Last's diary describes how in 1947 'my husband came rushing in excitedly and said "How would you like a fridge for your birthday?" And said that a shop has four in and the proprietor who often works on big jobs my husband has, had promised him one for a long time' (Malcolmson and Malcolmson, 2008, p. 83). Steedman (1998) describes how, in working-class London, fridges came into the household in the 1950s as birthday presents for the children. During the war, as Hartley points out, adverts by, for example EKCO, Mullard and GEC, nurtured the aspiration for radios and televisions, although such items were unavailable (1999, p. 84). The purchase of a fridge and acquisition of a television were elements of the consumer boom of the mid-1950s.

Rationing ended in 1954 and, with the security of several years of full employment and easier credit, many people began to enjoy a new period of affluence: 'by the end of the fifties 4 out of 5 families were the hire-purchasers of goods worth £1,000 million' (Partington, 1989, p. 209). As Morley (1995) has pointed out, the television as an object has a meaning, role and place in domestic culture, separate from its use; to some the acquisition of the television set was, in the 1950s, a visible marker of affluence. A 36-year-old male Civil Servant respondent for Mass Observation explained, 'at the current price of sets I am inclined to think that a television set is mainly an item of conspicuous display for those who can't get a car for this purpose' (MOA, 4/f). He went on to suggest that unmistakable TV aerials were a visual display of affluence. Turnoch has argued that following the introduction of ITV in 1955, the link between television acquisition and consumer culture has become ongoing, through payment of instalments and the promotion of consumer culture to the daily viewing of adverts and images on the screen (Turnock, 2007, p. 6).

There had been pressure from advertising agencies for the introduction of advertising on television for some time; there was, however, much discussion and disquiet about the nature and influence of advertising. When ITV was introduced, regulation limited the amount of time (6 minutes per hour) dedicated to advertising, alongside when, where and how it could operate. Adverts were permitted only in 'natural breaks' within programming; as it was the advertisers who footed the bill for programmes, independent television companies needed to sell audiences to advertisers in order to function. Advertisers required niche as much as large audiences and housewives, seen as the managers of domestic spending, were perceived to be an important target audience, as they had been for commercial radio. As Pattrington points out, it had become 'commonly accepted that consumption was 'women's work' (1989, p. 206). TV advertising informed the housewife about the vast array of new consumer products which assisted housework, making washing, baking and especially cleaning apparently easier. Toothpaste, washing powders, floor cleaners, washing machines and vacuum cleaners were all promoted on television. As Hartley suggests:

> TV advertising was … obsessively artificial and alimentary – concentrating on what people put into their mouths and with the cleanest and most efficient way of getting it through their alimentary canals, and then out of the house. Everything edible was constantly harassed through its domestic career by cleansing. (1999, p. 102)

Advertising was thus predominantly targeted at housewives; that women at times responded to this should however be seen as symptomatic of their dissatisfaction with domesticity rather than an indication of their gullibility. McCracken (1988) has suggested that consumer items are often a way of attempting to reconcile the gap between their idealized lives and lived experience; consumer purchases can be thus seen as stepping stones or scaffolding towards their ideals. In the 1950s, for many, domesticity and the idealized family, so longed for during the war, did not live up to expectations. The new washing machine, toothpaste or convenience food, advertised on the television, were some of the stepping stones towards their idealized domesticity. Many of these adverts also confirmed this idealization. Arguably, the successful adoption of consumer culture confirms that in domesticity many housewives encountered a diverse and less than satisfactory lived experience.

The press were fixated by the cultural change that television would bring. The *Daily Sketch* announced, after a preview of the first adverts in advance of ITV's first night, that: 'Anything can happen now. Britain's first TV "commercials" have arrived' (23 September 1955). *Picture Post* produced an investigation on America and how 'Commercial television has Changed their Lives', arguing that it had contributed to the standization of American Life; which included the eating of TV dinners, mass produced foodstuff and children singing advertising jingles both at home and in the playground. ITV was set up as a regional service, with slow but steady development of regional companies and transmitters; it took a while for ITV to be available across the country. To begin with, like the BBC, it was very London based, with the housewife's consumer power so central to the ITV programmer's need for advertising revenue; it was also populist and feminized. The BBC, which saw its audience plummet as ITV became available to a wider proportion of the population, also had to popularize and feminize. Thumin argues, 'much contemporary discourse proposed television as a debased and therefore, by implication a feminised form, the same audiences idealised the television audience as consumer' (2004, p. 32). Women were perceived as the primary audience during the day, who also, because of their centrality to the family, had to be addressed in the evenings.

Apparently in 1958 none of the main party leaders owned a television set (Abbott, 2003, p. 90), yet by 1959 Conservative politician Harold Macmillan confidently asserted 'most of our people had never had it so good', but the consumer boom was not enjoyed by all; a persistent strand of poverty remained. Thus, although Langhamer argues that the home life and domesticity experienced by some, and 'desired by many, in the 1930s becomes a material reality for very many' in the 1950s (2005) for others it remained a dream, their television watching restricted to visits to friends and relations on a Saturday night. An important element of the consumer improvement in homes in the 1950s was the widening availability of utilities – piped water, gas and electricity – which, particularly in rural areas, were far from widespread in the late 1940s. Marwick, however, has pointed out that the 'majority of the population continued to live in late nineteenth and early twentieth century houses badly in need of updating, providing squalid and overcrowded housing' (Marwick, 1996, p. 73). Nevertheless, allegedly, Macmillan asserted that 'the class war is over and we have won it' and social scientists began to talk of 'embourgeoisement'. However, despite the rhetoric of consumer culture, class divisions and deprivation were not far from the surface, and became a more significant element of television culture in the 1960s and 1970s. The incorporation of the television into households should not be seen as a straightforward or linear narrative of consumerism. The aspiration for a home and lounge was as significant as its actuality in the purchase and, very frequently, rental of a television. Images from the 1960s of homeless families in temporary accommodation show the significance that the television acquired in constructing a sense of home by the end of the 1950s; the family grouped around the television set which defined their very limited domestic space as home. The TV became the link, the stepping stone or scaffolding towards their idealized but still unattainable home.

AFTERNOON PROGRAMMES FOR WOMEN

While the widespread acquisition of televisions rested upon a boom in both housing and consumer spending, its incorporation into domestic routines and domesticity was complex and varied. Toddlers' truce, whereby the transmission ceased for an hour at 6 p.m. each evening, is an example of how the medium attempted to fit into the perceived domestic lives of its audience. It also underlines the dominance of the discursive construction of the home and family as being composed of heterosexual couples with children; a construction that was, and is, deeply unrepresentative. If radio was in the post- war era accepted as a secondary medium within the home, a soundscape which accompanied a range of domestic activities, meaning that there was no perceived tension between radio listening and the housewives' role, the same was not true of television. As Thumin points out, programme planners at both the BBC and Independent television were aware that the potential daytime audience of women was likely to place different and competing demands and expectations on television schedulers. Although some women would feel able to take a break and sit down and watch the TV, looking for either escapist entertainment or stimulating and informative programmes, many would not. The ambivalence of housewives' relationship with work and leisure led to an awareness that many women might look for television programmes that could be combined with other activities. In the late 1940s, a housewife of 39 who like many had never actually seen a television explained, to Mass Observation, the anxiety over fitting the new medium into women's domestic life: 'I nearly always mend work when listening to the wireless, presumably I could not do these things when watching television' (MOA, 4/f). Feminine multi-tasking while television watching was however encouraged by *Women's Illustrated*, which provided a special booklet entitled 'Lady Barnet's TV Knitting – 20 Knit While You View Designs'.

Following the reintroduction of television after the war, the *Evening News* (8 October 1947) announced: 'Television is to have its very own *Woman's Hour*. But possibly remembering the shaky start of *Women's Hour* on the Light programme the Ally Pally people are approaching the subject with caution.' In her recollections of the three o'clock afternoon slot which became associated with women's programmes, Olive Shapley, who both produced and presented programmes, described the editor Doreen Stephens as having:

> spent many weeks touring the country knocking on front doors and, over innumerable cups of tea, finding out what housewives, alone in their homes in the afternoon, really wanted from the BBC. It seemed that although they were not averse to general cultural items … in reality such items were a long way from most daily lives (1996, p. 158).

The early afternoon programmes were consequently varied in content; for example, one entitled *Designed for Women* covered a range of topics from cooking to Acts of Parliament, and features which included fashion, music, a personality, a picture, a handicraft, etc. The aim was to produce an afternoon gathering of women in the news, which viewers were invited to attend with only women taking part and only women's interests discussed. *Women's Viewpoint* in 1951 included the politicians Lady Megan Lloyd George and Jennie Lee. Thumin argues that producers of women's afternoon programmes defined 'their audience partly by their ability to watch television during the afternoon, and partly by assumptions about their interests defined by gender ... the women audience was increasingly defined as domestic housewives' (2004, pp. 57–7). In this they are echoing the assumptions of radio producers in the 1930s. Furthermore, the attempt to combine assumptions of housewives primarily domestic interests with a format which relied upon auditory engagement, supplemented by distracted viewing, led to the development of a number of magazine-style programmes, which encouraged the viewer to give the television, at least occasionally, some short spells of concentrated attention without any commitment to watching for long. They aimed not to interest all of the people all of the time but some of the people some of the time.

Post-war BBC programming amounted to approximately 35 hours a week – focused upon the afternoons, evenings and weekends. ITV initially introduced a women's programme entitled *Morning Magazine*, which broadcast from 11:00–12:30 and offered 'people with gaiety and charm' to combat depression and loneliness as well as echoing perceptions about women listeners of early radio: 'Because women are above all, concerned with their homes and families, there will be practical programmes too' (*TV Times*, 22 September 1955, p. 14). Many programme titles such as *About the Home, Family Affairs, Hands About the House* and *At Home Today*, emphasized domestic topics and had features on home and garden, childcare, cooking and health. In many respects the focus and format was similar both to *Woman's Hour* and to the numerous women's magazines purchased in the period, however while magazines catered to differentiated niche markets, television did not, and the BBC prior to 1955 had to aim itself to the whole audience and at least half of the audience after 1955. Furthermore, afternoon television programming for women needs to be understood in relation to radio programming. BBC personnel, such as Olive Shapley, moved between *Woman's Hour* and television, and some had their broadcasting roots in *Household Talks* and the wartime *Kitchen Front*. In the post-war consumer-modernity of television, however, the authority of the rural housewife of inter-war radio programmes had no place and instead in these programmes the performative nature of housework was emphasized.

Like *Woman's Hour*, the programmes looked outward from the home, discussing careers, travel, the arts and reading, as well as topics as varied as relationships, home perms, planning a day's work, health and beauty, exercises and physiotherapy as a career. Like *Woman's Hour*, many of the producers and presenters were married career women and there was no assumption that listeners would not be the same, although in February 1951 a memo indicated that at least one member of the BBC staff was in favour of 'the desirability of making programmes more topical, controversial where necessary, and constructive. One topic I should like to handle is wives at work. Because of the high cost of living mothers just have to earn extra money. But the children suffer' (BBCWA, S322/72/1). Nevertheless, in a feature about family life on *Family Affairs* (19 January 1955), Mrs Smart talked about family life, living with her husband and daughter in a 38-foot caravan, as her husband works in the family business – Smart's Circus. Amidst discussion about the importance of regular routines for young children, despite her husband's irregular hours, Mrs Smart, who was a lion tamer, explained that now her daughter was two she intended to go back to work.

It was not just in the topics that the daytime television was domestically focused, the set itself, a pseudo-domestic space, presented domesticity as a performance. Specific instructions were given for the set on *Designed for Women* and the props requested included a three-piece suite, a lamp stand, blue printed curtains, light wood writing table, low bookcase and real books for the bookcase (BBCWA, S322/72/1). At one level, the audience was positioned as a friend dropping in on a domestic conversation, just as in the fireside chat of early radio discourse. The linguistic framework used, for example in this series, was of friends talking: people are introduced as if at a party, for example – 'May I introduce Marguerite?'; there is a heavy use of 'we', for example 'we'll come and meet the designer herself', which served to produce a lexicon of participation. Thus 'the hostess' introduced one programme:

> As you see it is *Designed for Women* again. This afternoon and you will find some old friends: Marguerite Patten to demonstrate home canning, Lady David Douglas-Hamilton with her demonstrators to show you how to walk gracefully and ... Mr Streeter to talk to you about horticulture as a career (BBCWA, S322/72/i).

This performance of domesticity, intimacy and friendship required the purchase of consumer items – so much more visibly on display on television. In contrast to the radio, on television the look, appearance and image were foregrounded by the presenters' performance of domesticity. BBC's programming and ITV's advertising and programming, as Turnoch has suggested, 'showed its audience new commodities through advertising, but also through a range of other programme forms' (2007, p. 148). Again, there was a particularly middle-class culture and lifestyle to the idealized consumer, as in afternoon television programming 'woman's responsibility for the moral dimension of family life translated into and was often articulated through their responsibility for the material form and arrangement of domestic interiors' (Sparke, 1995, p. 145; see also Holliday, 2005, p. 70). Initially ad-mags were allowed on commercial television, 'for example *Jim's Inn* (A-R 1957-63) had Jimmy and Maggie Hanley as a couple running a village pub in which they discussed prices and quality of various domestic products with their customers' (Thumin, 2004, p. 39).

The format was reminiscent of the BBC's *Shop at Home* in the early 1950s, and in 1955 the BBC presented a new programme called *Look and Choose*, which *Radio Times* introduced in the following way: 'In this Isobel Barnett, with the assistance of a panel of experienced homemakers, will seek information from experts of all kinds to help them find out how to get the best value for money when buying goods for the home' (16 September 1955). The anxieties that surrounded ITV leaked into concern that the audience would not be able to differentiate between advertising and the programme, and that they were a little too close to the prohibited sponsored programmes; following the Pilkington Committee recommendation in 1962, they were banned (Thumin, 2004, p. 39). Advertising on television had, however, already set up what Wernich (1991) has described as the chaining of promotional discourses; whereby a chain of interdependent promotional images are bound together through different elements of media and culture – in the adverts, in the afternoon magazine shows for housewives, in the mis-en-scene of drama and comedy. All of these promoted the more freely available consumer culture of the 1950s.

TELEVISION FAMILIES AND UNRULY WOMEN: *I LOVE LUCY*

Television's domestic audience shaped the content and focus not only of those programmes intended for housewives during the day, but also of prime-time entertainment television; the domestic household and 'family' became the setting for much television fiction. The crisis, threats, trials and tribulations of domestic life were the narrative focus of many drama series, documentaries and sit-coms in the 1950s. *The Grove Family*, often seen as the first British soap opera, told the story of 13 cross-generational characters, and first appeared on TV screens on 7 April 1954. They were significantly placed lower within the strata of middle-class life than Dr and Mrs Dale had been. They lived in a London suburb, where Mr Grove was a builder. This first television 'soap', however, had a much shorter run and ceased broadcasting in 1957; its public service role may seem very heavy handed to a contemporary audience; the narrative was halted on occasions in the first episode, when a friendly policeman provided Mr Grove with advice about security to deter burglars and gave consumer advice on the purchase of a home-safe, locks and chains. Lucille Ball graced the front cover of the first edition of *TV Times* in September 1955, and the sit-com *I Love Lucy,* in which she starred, symbolized all the new commercial channel had to offer: popular, exotic, glamorous, consumerist home entertainment to amuse and lift the spirits, often American in origin. *Picture Post* in the same week compared the American and British television families of Lucy and the Groves. Lucy Ricardo and her husband Ricky lived in a New York apartment; he was a Cuban-American, a singer and band-leader, their social life revolved around their friends and landlords, the more conventional Fred and Ethel, who operated as co-conspirators in Lucy and Ricky's antics.

The media coverage that surrounded *I Love Lucy* and *The Grove Family* set up a series of engagement and negotiations about different domestic realities which in a sense served to emphasize the performivity of domesticity. The two main characters of *I Love Lucy* – Lucille Ball and Desi Arnaz – were indeed married in real life; the birth of their on-screen son in the second series coincided with the birth of their son in real life. By the time the USA series finished in 1960, they had filed for divorce, the on-screen kiss at the end of each programme was provided by a rerun of an earlier performance. As Holmes has pointed out, a four-page article in the *Radio Times Annual* devoted much attention to the relationship between the on- and off-screen selves of the members of *The Grove Family*. Whereas Spigel has suggested that programmes like *I Love Lucy* were 'blurring the lines between electrical and real space' as 'Television families were typically presented as "real" families' (1997, p. 224), *Radio Times* was certainly keen to emphasize the producers' awareness that the domestic audience's critical gaze was based on their own domestic experience when they talked about *The Grove Family*, pointing out: 'Coming as they do before the eyes of the public ever willing to judge what it sees against what it knows, the Groves realise that one false note, one piece of out-of-character behaviour would be enough to discredit them for weeks' (25 March 1955). The idea and meaning of family are fluid, shifting, applicable in a range of situations, and in the 1950s it connotated cosy domesticity, inclusiveness and belonging which television suggested could stretch not just to family of habitat but could be applied much wider to all television viewers. A cover of *TV Times* in January 1956 showed a three-generation family in a 'TV-screen shaped frame'; the cover story was 'The Jones Family join the ITV Family' (Thumin, 2004, p. 32). But families viewing television and those represented on television were contradictory, subject to tensions, anxieties and conflicts; all was not necessarily cosy.

In *I Love Lucy*, Lucy Ricardo was caught between lived experience and the ideal of domesticity. As Mellencamp points out, 'Lucy Ricardo was barely in control, Lucy endured marriage and domesticity by transferring them into vaudeville dissatisfaction, discontent; ambition beyond and desire to escape from the domestic sphere are recurrent themes' (1997, p. 67). Her husband, Ricky, readily 'upstaged and disobeyed' (p. 69), although Lucy was invariably given the last word or look (p. 63). In one episode entitled 'Equal Rights', Ricky's assertion that Lucy should know her place, as Cuban wives do, was countered by Lucy's assertion of American equal rights. The light-hearted battle between them involved each playing a series of stunts and tricks on each other, with Lucy having the last laugh. *I Love Lucy* followed a tradition of unruly women, who were both rebellious and incarcerated with domestic regimes' (Mellencamp, 1997, p. 72) found more commonly in comedy and Music Hall in Britain. Its popularity is an indication of the pleasures to be found in transgression, in playing the boundaries of domesticity, but for comedy to work it has to operate in areas which are familiar, Eddie McGuire, writing in the *Radio Times*, tried to explain 'Why Domestic Humour is Always

Topical' and suggested: 'The humour of the home is personal war, easily understood; its roots are in family life, and family life turns house into a home. Home where small are great and the great are small, the place where we can take off our new shoes and put on old manners' (17 April 1953, p. 87). In this he articulated both the democratizing and comforting elements of home, but comedy also operates at already defined cultural tension points. The appeal of *I Love Lucy* suggests that, beneath the surface domesticity in the 1950s, all was neither harmonious nor ideal. Another element of pleasure that the series offered was consumerism for British housewives, newly released from rationing, struggling with 'a range of hand me downs ..., and worst of all ... the "social normality" of utility furniture' (Morley, 1986, p. 96). The domesticity that Lucy and her husband inhabited represented what all British housewives could aspire to. Lucy's apartment, the domestic interior from which she so frequently attempted to escape, was packed with consumer items; all her coordinated and ample drapes spoke of luxury and consumer culture, while product placement for Lucky Strike cigarettes was embedded in the text. Importantly, however, the consumer-laden domesticity of Lucy's life was not offering domestic harmony. In *I Love Lucy* the consumer lifestyle was but a stepping stone to other things; the gap between the ideal of domesticity and the lived experience Lucy dreams would be resolved if she were able to enter show business – a media career is thus presented as an alternative stepping stone to an ideal world. Celebrity housewifery thus offered the audience, along with comedy and laughter, a release and acknowledgement of the gap between their ideals and lived experience. At the very least they provided a momentary release from experience.

POST-WAR TELEVISION COOKS AND FANNY CRADDOCK

An important, although perhaps often over-looked, area of consumer culture in the 1950s was food and dining. As rationing eased, and leisure and foreign travel increased, a growing emphasis was placed upon culinary enjoyment. The gastronomic writings of Elizabeth David evoked 'moods of relaxed pleasure' and suggested that 'the search for food and description of it is a very serious matter in intellectual, cultural and artistic terms' (Floyd and Forster, 2003, p. 148). A broadening range of products became available in supermarkets (Benson, 1994, p. 69); although access to new foods and supermarkets was not uniformly available to all women, shortages of money and transport made it aspirational for some. Yet by the early 1970s two-thirds of women used a supermarket once a week, in part facilitated by growing involvement of husbands in shopping, enabling women to carry more. Films also testified to the increasing diversity and pleasure to be found in food: in *Genevieve* (1953), barrister's wife Wendy returns to their London house with a shopping bag full of exotic produce including aubergines. Warde's (1997) analysis of women's magazines suggests that the recipes in the 1960s utilized diverse and unfamiliar cuisines and readers had to be 'cajoled and encouraged' into foreign and international cuisines' (1997). As early as 1958 the Gas Council and the Good Housekeeping International Kitchen, however, published a recipe booklet which included cuisine from a wide range of countries such as India, Spain, France, Germany, the Netherlands, Hungary, China and Brazil. Thus, in the 1950s and 1960s, the kitchen changed from being a 'straightforwardly practical and functional part of the house … to a more integrated social space. It became less private and more open to family and social life' (Hoskins, 2004, p. 47).

Daytime television cooks such as Marguerite Patten and Philip Harben also introduced French recipes to the general public, but cookery programmes proved quite challenging to produce – Olive Shapley recalled:

> Recipes had to be presented slowly enough for them to be taken in, and not so slowly that the whole thing became boring. Also photographing food was not easy. I remember watching an

> attempt to get a good picture of some innocent little biscuits. 'Tilt the plate this way, Bob. No back again …' Doyley on. Doyley off. And still the biscuits continued to look like flat, grey stones from some cold, cold beach (1996, p. 158).

However, like the cooking features on *Woman's Hour* which were not well received, the television reporter of the *Manchester Evening News* commented that he had received a barrage of criticism about afternoon television programmes for women, which he claimed: 'are beginning to assume the look of a dog eared menu' according to one woman viewer. The food may be beautifully served but the very fact that one knows each day's menu by heart destroys the subtlety of taste' (*Manchester Evening News*, 20 January 1956). Food alone, particularly with the limitations of black and white television, could not produce a good television show, not without a strong television personality to carry the show.

One of the most successful post-war TV cooking personalities was Philip Harben, who having given radio talks for *Kitchen Front* during the war broadcast the first post-war television cookery series on 12 June 1946. Abandoning post-war austerity, and perhaps with an awareness that more expensive and luxurious food was not on rationing, he demonstrated 'How to make Lobster vol-au-vent'. His annual series continued until 1954 and he remained popular after 1955, when he moved to commercial television. He became well-known for instructing people how to cook what was available at the time, reputably using his own rations for his early shows. His masculinity was affirmed by his slightly gruff voice, beard and butcher's apron, emphasized by the title of his 1952 and 1953 series *Man in the Kitchen*. In one show in 1952, entering to the music of 'Come in the Cookhouse Door Boys', he addressed the audience: 'Should any ladies be viewing now, will they please switch off as I wish to speak only to the men'… changing to a more intimate tone he then adds, 'Chaps, now that we are alone'. Audience participation involved him asking a male member of the studio audience what he would like to cook, and when he reeled off a range of complicated and fancy dishes he responded that these required special ingredients and suggested they compromise on chips instead. His authority and expertise was scientific; he even explained the problems of emulsifying mayonnaise. The planning for his 1948 series included as the topic for week 3, 'Flesh foods, demonstration of the effect of various degrees of heat and a survey of cooking method', while *Radio Times* described one of his appearances on daytime television: 'Philip Harben explained how carbon dioxide gas brings about the aeration of flour' (*Radio Times*, 2 May 1950, quoted in Thumin, 2004, p. 60). Harben's TV personality, was cultivated through appearances in variety shows such as *Meet Mr Lucifer* (1953), *Man of the Moment* (1955), *Desert Island Discs* (1955) and as the back end of a cow in *Pantomania* (1956) and the *Benny Hill Show* (1957) He published books, wrote a column for *Women's Own* magazine and, like Marguerite Patten, endorsed products and appeared in a number of adverts, including for Trex margarine. His association to consumer culture was affirmed when in 1958 Harben co-founded Harbenware Limited, which produced non-stick aluminium frying pans. He later launched 'The Philip Harben Cookery Set' aimed at children; it included small-size cooking utensils, a chopping board, rolling pin, cookie cutters, mixing bowl, rotary whisk, wooden spoon, plastic weigh scales, as well as miniature toy packets and cans of food such as peas, carrots, Tate & Lyle sugar, Nestlé tinned milk and Ovaltine.

The most famous television cook of the 1950s and 1960s was Fanny Craddock, whose first appearance on television was on 17 February 1955 in a programme entitled *Kitchen Magic* at the unlikely time of 10:15 in the evening. She had already published her first cookery book, *The Practical Cook,* and in 1949 had written a column in the *Daily Express* under the title 'My Kitchen'. With her partner, Johnnie, she established her place in the British culinary discourse of the 1950s by writing a column entitled 'Bon Vivier' in the *Daily Telegraph*, for which she reviewed hotels and restaurants at home and abroad. Her persona soon developed through live *Daily Telegraph* and Gas Board sponsored cookery demonstrations held throughout the country on theatre and concert hall stages before large audiences. The Craddocks filled the Albert Hall with a high-profile show in December 1956, part of which was also televised by the BBC. In 1957 they demonstrated at the Ideal Home Exhibition and were photographed talking to the Queen and Duke of Edinburgh. Couihan has argued that:

> Because food is so often women's work and language, food symbols can emphasise the importance of women and challenge the centrality of men. Because women are sometimes forced to serve and cook for others, or because their work is devalued, food can be a channel of oppression. Yet through cooking, feeding, eating, refusing food or manipulating food's meaning, women can sometimes chart their own way around barriers. (2004 p. 167)

At one level Craddock can be presented as playing and undermining the gendered power relationships of the domestic sphere; she showed women how to carve a roast at a time when carving was a signifier of the male as provider. She usually appeared with Johnnie, who acted as her assistant and who was often banished to washing-up and has been described by the *Sunday Telegraph* as 'monocled and monosyllabic' (1 January 1995). Butler (1990) argues that gender is something actively and repeatedly performed (not natural) relying often on bodily expression, but gender trouble may be caused by drawing attention to this performance through an excessive or exaggerated performance. Craddock's performance was excessive; as BBC producers often noted, it was over the top, a female camp so exaggerated that it drew attention to its performivity. Indeed, when I showed contemporary students an extract of one of her shows, I struggled to convince them that she was not a drag queen. It is also ironic that perhaps one of the best known TV cooks of the post-war era, who popular mythology suggests shifted British cooking from drab austerity into the conspicuous consumption of the 1960s, was indeed performing her role as the perfect housewife. She had committed bigamy, abandoned both her children when infants and was pretending to be married to Johnnie Craddock with whom she lived. Her very life was an example of the problems that lay hidden behind the veneer of 1950s and 1960s domesticity.

To those who 'had suffered a long period of enforced deprivation from non-essential goods, fashion, colour and ornament' (Attfield, 1990, p. 86) there was something appealing even transfixing in the excesses of Fanny Craddock's decoration and presentation of food, which included choux pastry swans, butter curls and pagodas, sandwiches parading as chequer boards, spun sugar, chocolate leaves and orange maypoles (Craddock, 1966). It was a long way from the modernist principles of good design – there was much that was frivolous, useless and effected in her cooking, it revelled in 'the importance of 'display ... relevant to the 1950s, a period in which keeping up with the Joneses became a popular phrase' (Attfield, 1990, p. 84). The 1950s housewife was subject to a barrage of advice on good taste and how to consume, in magazines and on television, but the attitude towards this advice, the appropriation of ideas of good taste, was complex and contradictory. As Partington points out, 'The Happy housewife of the 1950s was not the happy housewife heroine ... passively and blissfully acquiring mass-produced goods and oblivious to her material conditions of existence' (1989, p. 211). Rather, she suggests, that there was a misappropriation of goods and tastes as a form of resistance, 'not a planned or thought through resistance but a playing with the advice. Women paid lip-service to legitimate notions of "good taste" (responsible consumption) while their pleasures in consumption were inevitably improper and irresponsible' (Partington, 1989, p. 212). Looked at in this light, the appeal of Fanny Craddock's campness becomes more understandable. The trademark ball gowns that she cooked in, never protected by an apron, signified her irresponsibility. As Ellis (2007) points out: her cooking and performance always looked as if it teetered on the boundary of being out of control, stories abound of whelks still wriggling as she served them and raw chicken served to guests on her show.

Television in the 1950s and 1960s took over radio's centrality to the domestic space; by the mid-1960s television was a mainstream leisure activity with 13 million television licences. It asserted cultural and symbolic power, according to Turnock (2007), with long-lasting consequences. In the post-war era both radio and television were intrinsically tied up with domesticity but the domesticity they conveyed in order to be credible for domestic audience was one which drew attention to the perfomativity of domesticity: its diversity, its tensions and the ways in which the gap between the ideal and lived experience is negotiated and reconciled by housewives. As Thumin points out, programming for women in the afternoon was withdrawn from the BBC in 1964 and the Women's Programme unit replaced by a Family Programmes unit which focused on adult and children's programmes. ITV in many respects followed suit, but the legacy of the 1950s is found in the 1970s with the introduction of *Houseparty* (which will be discussed in Chapter 7). However, *Woman's Hour*, despite some initially mixed responses and a change of scheduling time in 1998, has remained on air since the 1940s, arguably by carving out a defined feminized space on the Home Service, and then its successor Radio 4, *Woman's Hour* served to protect the masculine and higher status of the rest of the channel.

Chapter Six

Broadening domestic 'realities': soaps, documentaries and working-class domesticities in the 1960s and 1970s

By the 1960s, television could be seen as central to mass domestic culture and leisure, with one TV set per household and only two channels, until the advent of BBC2 in1964. Television was, as Ellis points out, 'something the whole family shared or argued over' (2000, p. 46). The single television set provided domestic routines and repetition; the regular broadcasts of programmes, like *Coronation Street*, were both structured and were structured by the domestic lives of their audience; domestic lives which were, in the 1960s and 1970s, subject to significant changes. The 1960s have been seen by some historians as a period of cultural revolution (Marwick, 1999), of upheavals in class, race and family relationships, with a new concern for civil and personal rights. In 1963 Harold Wilson, as the Labour party leader and soon to be prime minister, gave what is known as his 'white heat of technology' speech to the Party Conference; domestic technology – washing machines, fridges, television and cars – were becoming more widespread and by the mid-1960s the Labour party predominantly assumed 'that its working class past had been subsumed into a new alignment with a modernising technological society' (Laing, 1986, p. 219). Neither this nor the 'cultural revolution' were necessarily greeted enthusiastically by all the population; not least, perhaps, because the growing economic crisis that Britain faced in the 1960s meant that many were excluded from personally experiencing a lot of the advantages of technological or social changes. Arguably it was not until the 1970s that changing attitudes to marriage, divorce and sexuality touched the everyday lives of many. In the meantime, in what Ellis (2000) has called the 'century of witness', social change was worked through in the media, particularly television where it was amply demonstrated that a home, and the post-war dream of contented domesticity, remained for many only a dream.

Silverstone has suggested that 'those re-housed from urban slums in Britain after the 1939–45 war were offered a bourgeois solution to the problems of the city: a home of one's own with a little garden, both spaces to cultivate' (1997, p. 9) and that this produced a new hybridized suburban class culture based upon consumption. Following the introduction of commercial television in the 1950s, consumption was a key discourse of television but it was by no means the only one, or necessarily the dominant one. That television became a particularly suburban medium was suggested by Spigel, when examining USA television, she argued that in its 'ability to merge private and public spaces ... television was the ideal companion' in suburban homes (1997, p. 213), where it 'gave people a sense of belonging to the community' (1997, p. 212). Television was, it has been suggested, expected to be a unifying force; a 'fantasy of an antiseptic electrical space' (1997, p. 215). Spigel argues that 'at the centre of the suburban space was the young upwardly mobile middle class family. Older people, gay and lesbian people, homeless people, unmarried people and people of colour were simply written out of these spaces – relegated to the cities' (1997, p. 214). Spigel's arguments do not translate straightforwardly to the UK; the homes into which broadcasting went were perhaps more diverse and contradictory than the suburban paradigm in which TV is so often discussed (Hartley, 1999). In the equally diverse representational practices of television texts suburbia is not necessarily dominant or sympathetically presented. Medhurst has argued that 'the television genre which has centred its attention on suburbia is the sit-com' comedies were frequently focussed on those 'concerned with maintaining genteel values against threats from outside' but they interrogated suburbian values, the rule was 'know your place'

(1994, p. 261). He goes on to suggest that the 'British television suburbia belongs primarily to comedy; and if it strays into soap it is liable to be laughed at' (1994, p. 262).

British television retained a space for the ordinary and the mundane, as did British politics and popular culture. Making a speech in 1968, the British Prime Minister, Harold Wilson, disclosed that his personal television favourite was *Coronation Street* (*Television Today*, 24 April 1968). In what was arguably a calculated bid to identify with the 'ordinary', to be seen as a 'man of the people' he claimed to watch this twice-weekly soap-opera in which 'reality was guaranteed by the northern setting' (Laing, 1986, p.185). A preference for this soap also linked together the relatively new popular technological medium of television and an association with the working-class community of the Labour Party's past. Little wonder perhaps, for as television became mainstream, its emerging popularity did not correspond with a mass working-class move to privately owned suburbs but to a very different sort of 'suburbia' emerging around towns. In post-war Britain large working-class estates of local authority-owned social housing surrounded many of the main conurbations, accompanied in the 1960s by tower blocks, while many of the working-class remained in overcrowded and sub-standard urban housing.

Although early broadcasting has at times been criticized for its middle-class bias, it had always provided some space for representations of working-class domesticity; the 1960s and 1970s, however, saw a significant broadening of class and regional representations of domesticity in soap-operas such as *Coronation Street* in drama, documentaries and even in some comedy such as *Steptoe and Son* (1962–74). Furthermore, as Hartley suggests, in the 1960s 'the so-called masses – were beginning to find their way into parts of the body politic and folds of the social fabric that had previously been thoroughly disinfected against them … Democratisation was reaching into culture, education, lifestyle and intellectual life' (1999, p. 172). This democratization gave expression to the cultural rights of the working-class to have their 'experiences, beliefs and aspirations represented in the major fora of public culture': television (Murdock, 1999, p. 30). However, a note of caution is perhaps required, how such representations are constructed and consumed is contradictory and complex. The challenge presented in the 1960s and 1970s by an increasing visibility of working-class domesticities was mitigated in a number of ways. For the middle-classes, working-class representations on television in drama and documentary, as Paget (1998) has pointed out, often then and now offered merely 'cultural tourism'. Shifting paradigms of representational practice in this era owed much to the changing institutional frameworks within which television was produced. ITV was made up of regional companies which sought advertising revenue but remained restrained by public service requirements to inform and educate; thus, as Murdoch points out, it 'developed a 'populist ethos. Less inclined to defer to cultural and political authorities, more disrespectful, more engaged with popular experience'. Consequently, it developed spaces in which voices spoke with regional or working-class accents 'of the contemporary experience of dislocation and change' (Murdoch, 1999, p. 32). Granada television produced both *Coronation Street* (1960) and the documentary series *World in Action* (1963–98), which included programmes such as *A Wedding on Saturday* (1964), thus bringing northern working-class domesticity onto television. Such changes were not restricted to ITV; the BBC explored social issues in documentaries such as *Living in Sin* (1966) while *Play for Today*, which included the award winning *Cathy Come Home* (1966) sought to encourage political debate, resulting in complaints from protestors who were certain that the Corporation 'was hell bent on systematically undermining the morals and values of mainstream society through its drama output' (MacMurraugh-Kavanagh, 2002, p. 150).

Many of the drama and documentary programmes produced in the era explored shifting patterns of ordinary people's domestic life facilitated by growing legal and social changes that included the introduction of the birth control pill. The period – known as the long 60s – between 1958 and 1974 saw suicide and homosexuality decriminalized, the death penalty abolished, a relaxation on the laws on gambling, abortion and homosexuality, alongside divorce reform which introduced divorce by mutual consent or after 5 years without the consent of an ex-partner. It was, as Bocock (1998) has pointed out, a historical moment at which moral governance moved from being the responsibility of the legal system to one of self-discipline. Self-discipline, which was simultaneously encouraged and undermined in the watching and discussing of television programmes, which, particularly following the introduction of BBC 2 in 1964, began to represent more varied domestic experiences, and portrayed a multiplicity of incarnations of marriage, family and personal life. In both the production and consumption of these texts the gaps between idealizations of domesticity and the lived experience of many, stimulated debate, opposition to change and controversy. Television rapidly became a battleground for 'nothing less than the future shape of British Society' (MacMurraugh-Kavanagh, 2002, p. 150). Legal changes and controversy should not be mistaken for a universal shift in attitudes or a greater moral leniency. The responses evoked by drama's such as *Cathy Come Home* (1966), documentaries including *Seven Up* (1964), *Living in Sin* (1966) and *The Family* (1974) indicate that for many these representations of working-class domesticity evoked anxiety. An anxiety which was felt more acutely because once such representations had been witnessed through the liveness and intimacy of television viewing, it was no longer possible for the suburban middle-classes to deny knowledge to 'say that we do not know' (Ellis, 2000, p. 1) anything about the living conditions, problems and cultures of the working-classes.

It is important to remember, of course, that the visual representations provided by television were certainly not reflections of or even windows into working-class 'realities' but rather constituted and constructed the working-class in popular imagination, drawing particularly on three tropes: nostalgia for disappearing working-class communities, the working-class as victims of material circumstances – especially housing problems – and finally the ever present trope of the working-class as sexually amoral or aberrant. These were not initiated by television, but rather television borrowed, reworked, played with and consolidated already circulating discursive frameworks for the representation of the working-class in order to produce entertainment. These tropes, sometimes used together, sometimes competing with each other, provided a focus and perhaps a way of managing anxieties about working-class domesticity for many years. The significance of such tropes should not be ignored, their residue helped to frame potential political solutions, not only in the period but well after.

NOSTALGIA: *CORONATION STREET*'S COMMUNITY

When introduced in 1960, the popular drama *Coronation Street* focused predominantly on the domestic lives of the residents of a fictional street in 'Weatherfield' (Salford). Scenes were frequently set in living rooms which opened out into a kitchen or scullery at the back of the house. The solid tables, which families were often seen eating or chatting around, stylistically owed more to wartime utility furniture than 1960s consumer culture. The two-up, two-down terraced houses with their mismatching and mundane furniture, were often cramped. Yet almost from its inception *Coronation Street* was discussed as presenting a nostalgic view of working-class life, in so doing it drew upon discursive strategies that were not restricted to soap-operas or even television, and were far from straightforward. The *Observer*, which regarded the series as, 'One of the very few original contributors to television' (2 December 1962), talked about *Coronation Street*'s nostalgic appeal and by the end of the decade Wolsley, writing for the *Financial Times*, affirmed that the attraction of the programme was based upon nostalgia, suggesting that 'surely when you examine it, the trueness to life is sheer nostalgia, especially in absence of discussion on money and work' (19 March 1969). However, a momentary pause to compare the assumptions of this quote with the early episodes of *Coronation Street* suggests this dominant trope for understanding the representation of the working-class was and remains problematic. Even within the first episode, Elsie Tanner accuses her son of stealing money from her purse while he laments the problems of finding work with a prison record. Indeed a number of early narratives focus upon work and money, often linked to domestic life; Florrie is caught and fined for selling firelighters in her shop after hours; and when Elsie's son Dennis gets a job at a club, he runs into his father who left the family years before.

Coronation Street does not offer an idealized domestic world which serves as a refuge from discussions of work or money, rather, as Thumin suggests, 'the home and the workplace are conflated and the home itself is clearly acknowledged to be a workplace in its own right … the separation between the public self of the workplace and private self of the domestic environment is refused' (2002, p. 218). Arguably, the community of the street, the friendship networks of different households, replace those of the 'family' and individual domestic spaces. The bar of the local pub, The Rovers Return, stands in for the domestic sitting room. Whilst the personal and relationship concerns of domesticity are transferred into the workplace when, in the 1970s, the factory is firmly established in the centre of the narrative following the arrival of Mike Baldwin as the factory owner. From then on, the factory, like the shop, operates as both a public place of work and space for domestic–social interaction within which the irritations of personal relationships of pseudo 'families' are played out. Gossip is used 'for dramatic effect' and indeed Tebbutt suggests a narrow interpretation of women's lives was reinforced by 'strong female characters who were signifiers of an ideal community' (1995, p. 176).

Like all popular texts, *Coronation Street* was and remains polysemic; its widespread popularity rests upon the ability of diverse audiences to watch the same text but see many different programmes. The reactions of the above *Financial Times* writer (Wolsely), for example, contrast with those expressed by *The Times* television correspondent who understood *Coronation Street* as a comedy and featured the programme in an article entitled 'How true to life is television comedy?' He acknowledged that the programme was not 'entirely comedy' but it suggested that it:

> chronicles the day to day existence of a group of cantankerous neighbours in another town ... here is the true stuff of life – in the north specifically but in effect anywhere where a street of terraced houses form a close knit community and everybody knows everybody else's business (21 June 1961).

This take on the programme emphasized both the idea of community and of northerners as more down to earth than effete, insincere southerners (Laing, 1986, p. 185), as regional working-class domestic concerns were brought into the centre of cultural life of the whole nation. Although, perhaps, previously unknown, this representational paradigm was not restricted to television; a range of films – including *Saturday Night and Sunday Morning* (1960), *A Taste of Honey* (1961) and *A Kind of Loving* (1962) – were also set among the northern working-class.

Academics have also affirmed this nostalgic interpretation of the programme, suggesting that the nostalgia for working-class communities reproduced within *Coronation Street* echoed one of the founding texts of Cultural Studies: Hoggart's *Uses of Literacy* (1957) (see Dyer, 1981; Laing, 1986). Nostalgia for, supposedly, tight-knit urban working-class communities was a significant strain in the new intellectual framework of sociology, cultural studies and social history that developed in the 1960s and 1970s. To regard a text as nostalgic is, however, only a beginning, for nostalgia, as Wheeler (1994) has pointed out, does not necessarily carry negative connotations, rather it is a critique of the status quo, a rejection of the prevailing cultures and values, and to some degree an attempt to suggest a different preferable way of organizing society, albeit one that draws upon and reworks representations of the past. There is a potential radicalism in this: in the refusal of the nostalgic to accept the contemporary social organization as a given.

Arguably, then, *Coronation Street* offered a critique of 1960s working-class alienation which was juxtapositioned against a sense of community that apparently existed in the past, but this was not the only meaning the text offered. The concept of community is singularly elusive, open to numerous interpretations – many linked to shared norms and self-sufficiency. It can be, as Raymond Williams (1983, p. 66) pointed out, a warmly persuasive word to describe a set of relationships. Communities are, however, often understood in functionalist terms, as made up of interrelated and dependent parts or people. Despite the positive connotations of the term community, in soap opera narratives communities are full of conflict and tension to encourage audience engagement. The 'gritty realism' of *Coronation Street* thus arguably reworked easy idealized perceptions of working-class domestic communities, the characters have been described by the series' creator, Tony Warren, as like family and friends, people the audience would be able to describe in terms of 'know your faults and love you still'. Furthermore, personal relationships in the fluid and extended domestic world of the street were portrayed as full of anxiety, strife and conflict. The community was often seen as restricting people who were quick to resort to verbal and at times physical aggression, as the drama of their lives unfolded. Much of the audience's pleasure came from the characters' circumnavigation and rejection of social norms, and from the flawed characters' articulation of views and opinions that viewers would have been more restrained from expressing in their own communities.

The very concept of community is almost always associated with something that is lost, under threat or disappearing. In the 1960s and 1970s working-class communities were perceived as under threat, passing away or already destroyed. There was a range of potential culprits responsible for the destruction or at least threatened destruction of working-class communities. These included consumerism, individualism, Americanization and rehousing, and more problematically immigration, the welfare state, and the domestication of men and television itself. Significantly the nostalgic working-class communities of the past were invariably perceived as white. The unspoken structuring absence of the nostalgic trope was of a past prior to post-war immigration. Not until 1983, when Shirley Armitage became a machinist in Baldwin's factory, did *Coronation Street* even begin to embrace the multi-culturalism of many post-war urban areas.

The 'sprawling suburban' council housing estates, such as Leigh Park (outside Portsmouth) or Bethnal Green (east London), which were intended to alleviate the housing crisis, were often in popular discourse seen instead as having destroyed working-class communities and as a signifier of the failure of the welfare state and government spending which aired to create the longed for dream of domestic contentment for the mass of the population. Local authority estates were presented in the media as far from ideal, perceived as alienating, liable to lead to a range of social problems because they lacked community spirit, and the inhabitants had been uprooted from their extended families and friends. The television documentary *A Marriage Today: A Social Institution* (1964), for example, opened with a women's voice explaining 'I was born in Liverpool', as the visual imagery shifted from Victorian terraced houses to a woman and child on a contemporary low-rise housing estate, the voice-over continued: 'I don't think the estates are old enough to have fostered any community sense.' Discussion of 'new town blues' experienced by young mothers, separated from their families in standardized, small semi-detached or terraced properties led to a government report in 1961 and the following summary in *Time Magazine*:

> Take a working-class family living in a grimy, overcrowded urban slum. Move it to a spanking-clean, new garden city, cheerfully

> designed and well planned, where there are plenty of lawns, light and airy schools, spacious, rainproof shopping centres, no heavy traffic to menace the children. Would the family be happy in its new surroundings? The answer, as published last week in a report by Britain's Ministry of Housing: Not very. (18 August 1961)

There was a not inconsequential dose of cultural snobbery towards the working-class in these critiques, which suggested that privileges which once belonged to the middle classes, a home of one's own and a garden were wasted on the working-class, for whom 'The isolation and anonymity of the modern family in new housing estates is compounded, by the cultural uniformity imposed by television' (Thumin, 2004, p. 108). Evidence suggests a range of more complex responses to the new estates; Roberts, for example, has suggested that even during the third quarter of the century 'women's aspiration towards better accommodation for themselves and their families was stronger than their attachment to a friendly and supportive neighbourhood' (1995, p. 230). Nevertheless, *Coronation Street* with its cobbled streets can, at one level, be seen as a rejection of new housing estates. In the series the 'community is retained through the physical stability of the street itself' (Laing, 1986, pp. 184–5). The perceived uniformity of the new estates was in sharp contrast to the 'character acting' of *Coronation Street* and, reassuringly perhaps for a middle-class audience, the working-class appears to know their place. Consumerism had bypassed the domestic interiors of 1960s *Coronation Street* and pretentiousness or embarrassment about working-class culture is frowned upon, as demonstrated in early episodes by the discomfort of the young Ken Barlow about his background; the modestly and working-classness of the domestic space in which he lived. Ken's unwillingness to display his home to his more middle-class girlfriend contrasted and drew attention to the confidence of the *Coronation Street* series itself, which brought a construction of working-class domesticity into the homes of television viewers of all classes. It was however a particular version of working-class culture: of beer and stout drinking, flat-capped pigeon-owning earnest white people, unpretentious 'down to earth' or more importantly not influenced by Americanism, consumerism and mass produced popular culture.

Anxiety about consumerism can also be identified in the documentary *A Wedding on Saturday* (Granada, 1964), which captured the experiences of the families of two young people getting married in a northern mining town. It is suggested that the social cohesion of the miners who 'tend to find they all stick together' is threatened by 'selfish and rotten to the core' youth who have been corrupted by money. Indeed money is represented as more plentiful and the consequent disappearance of pawnbrokers, once a traditional part of working-class communities, is remarked upon. In contrast to *Coronation Street*, in this documentary the camera visually dwells upon the strong friendship and communality among this 1960s working-class community which utilizes the artefacts of their contemporary popular culture : the bingo hall, the one-armed bandit, pop music and a modern pub were all portrayed as part of a new version of working-class communality. Television was also presented as playing a part in constructing working-class communality in the version of domestic space which evoked most criticism in the 1960s and beyond – the high-rise tower blocks built on the edge of urban centres such as London, Manchester, Birmingham and Glasgow. To encourage their construction and the quick provision of multiple homes, subsidies had been provided by central government to local authorities that built high-rise flats, although the policy was undermined in 1968 when the corner of a 22-story block in the East End of London collapsed killing seven people and making 80 families homeless. High-rise flats did not figure predominantly in the televisual landscape of working-class domesticities but rather television was perceived as able to offer a domestic community to those alienated in high-rise flats. *Television Today*, drawing upon the trope of nostalgia for working-class communities, suggested that *Coronation Street* provided for the elderly:

> a link with a past that can never return, a reminder of a time when there were friends and neighbours, children running past the front door, endless cups of tea and chat, instead of loneliness in a high rise council flat. In Manchester there are pensioners who are living in flats built on the site of the old Coronation streets, who spend days without seeing another face. For these people 8:30 is a very important time on Monday and Wednesday evenings. (28 April 1968)

To this critic, the working-class community represented on television has a role to play in replacing a previously idealized community, it provides companionship to the lonely in their domestic spaces – just as radio had been perceived to provide companionship and friends for the lonely in the 1930s. The pleasures of being part of the 'imagined community' (Anderson, 2006; Moores, 1998) of the *Coronation Street* audience were not however confined to the lonely elderly; in 1975 the Poet Laureate Sir John Betjeman likened *Coronation Street* to Dickens' *Pickwick Papers*, proclaiming, of its two episodes a week, 'I live for them. Thank God, half past seven tonight and I shall be in paradise.'

HOUSING CRISIS: *CATHY COME HOME*

When 23.6 per cent of the population tuned into to BBC1 to watch *Cathy Come Home* in 1966, they witnessed a 'dramatisation of everyday life' which was far from paradise. *Cathy Come Home* depicted Cathy and her husband Reg's struggle to gain access to basic housing in which to create a stable domestic life for themselves and their three children, and drew attention to the continuing housing crisis that many of the working-class faced in the 1960s. For Cathy and many like her. the high-rise flat, the 'sprawling council estates and new towns' were an unattainable dream not to be despised or critiqued. Given the symbolic significance of the post-war home, there was something ideological about homelessness, it symbolized exclusion, a hopelessness and desperation which gave the play a particular cultural poignancy. The *Sunday Observer* described *Cathy Come Home*, one of the BBC's series *The Wednesday Play*, as 'A programme to remember', while *The Times* suggested, 'Few can have watched ... without being deeply moved' and the *Daily Mirror* described it as 'Dynamite ... a magnificent piece of observant sparse writing, direction and production'. Such comments no doubt contributed to 42 per cent of the population watching the repeat eight weeks after the original broadcast. Since then the play has taken on iconic and mythical status in the history of television, credited with starting a national debate about housing (Ellis, 2000, p. 46). Similarly, Biressi and Nunn suggest that ordinary lives in docudramas like *Cathy Come Home* 'merge journalistic characteristics with fictional forms' being issue based they 'depict ordinary lives ... not simply to afford them recognition but to make a point' (2005, p. 59); however, the housing crisis was already well established and had been part of the political landscape since World War II; although certainly the housing charity, Shelter, utilized the public attention roused by the play and ran adverts under the by-line 'Did you see Cathy last night?' after the repeat.

The play's narrative charts the story of Cathy 'just up from the country and in the big city she meets Reg and falls for him. She dreams of settling down, building a home and having some babies' (*Radio Times*, 10 November 1966). As their children are born, the steady increase in the family is matched by the steady decline in their housing. As the play ends, their marriage is over; Reg has disappeared, Cathy's children are taken into care and she has no option but to hitch a lift back to her home town. Both the title and the narrative privilege Cathy's experience, endorsing Thumin's critique of the inequitable representation of women on the television in the 1950s and 1960s where 'opportunities are for men, problems are in women' (2004, p. 118). As the BBC in their press release pointed out: 'All she wants is a husband, a home and babies in that order. That's all, not much for a young girl to want from life. After all she and her husband are respectable.'

Respectability had been in the nineteenth and early twentieth centuries the qualification to be one of the 'deserving poor' able to access charity. Reg and Cathy are unable to access council accommodation, the only secure option for the working-class, despite Cathy's respectability (they do not have children until they are married, and they are devoted to one another and their children) hence her dreams are destroyed. Importantly, however, these are not just *her* dreams, but they are arguably endorsed by the BBC as the 'reasonable dreams' of all of the 'ordinary' working-class; the particularity of her fictional narrative came thus to stand for a social phenomenon. Importantly Cathy and her husband maintain their ordinariness; producer Tony Garnett emphasized that 'what Cathy's about is ordinary people wanting to live ordinary lives'. And much of the discourse around the programme focused on the ordinariness of the couple, emphasizing that, as the *Telegraph* explained, the text powerfully conveyed 'the suffering of decent, bewildered' (17 November 2006) members of society.

It was the acceptance of Cathy's representativeness and the 'truth' claims of the play which created its impact; something that relied upon the discourses which surrounded the text both in other BBC broadcasts and the press. *Radio Times* assured viewers in advance of the broadcast that: 'Everything in tonight's play the author Jeremy Sandford has seen with his own eyes' (10 November 1966, p. 35). The BBC followed the broadcast with a discussion on BBC2 and had broadcast a number of programmes on housing in the period before the play. This included a *Man Alive* series entitled *A Roof Over Your Head*, which looked at some of the problems of those trying to buy their own home; as *Radio Times* explained 'Twenty-five million people live in homes owned by landlords and, as was seen in the first three programmes on this theme, it causes problems' (10 November 1966). Furthermore, the previous week *Woman's Hour* had explored whether natural parents should have the right to demand the return of a child that had been in a foster home for 3 years, since the child's family had found themselves unable to cope after they were evicted from their home (8 November 1966). Similarly the *Evening News*, in an article entitled 'Cathy Can Come Home', highlighted the work of housing trusts to re-home one woman who had been living in a 9 feet by 9 feet square damp basement with her two children (who had been in care for a while) and paid £2 and 10 shillings rent (£2.50p). This came out of her earning of £8 a week earned by winding lengths of wire to make transformers (16 January 1967).

Consequently one housewife responded to the BBC audience research unit by saying: 'In my opinion this was one of the best things ever done on TV. The playwright's skills bludgeoned home the points he wanted to make in such a way that I was left squirming in my seat wanting to say "this is rubbish" but having to face the fact it was true' (BBCWA T5/965/1).

The 'truth' was affirmed by the use of 'documentary style' footage shot in hostels for the homeless, on caravan sites and in gypsy camps. In so doing the text redefined and challenged the images of home and domesticity on television. Cathy's description of the cramped conditions of one flat, where the lavatory led off the kitchen such that 'You can sit on it and do the cooking' shocked the audience. The proximity of food, dirt and faeces and potential contamination symbolically defined her living space as a slum and tapped into concerns about mothers' inability to provide hygienic homes for their children – which had surfaced in World War II (Webster, 1998, p. 95). The tenements referred to in *Cathy Come Home* were in Islington and the borough's public relations officer was quick to point out that these tenements had been built in another age when there was no restrictions on housing density and that the borough had purchased them and was pulling them down but it was a huge job (BBCWA, T16/696). As Hartley points out, 'the urge to pull down the slums represented a strong strand of modernist reformist thought in British Public life that lasted for more than a generation' (1999, p. 114). The iconic early documentary film *Housing Problems* (1935), as he suggests, 'glimpses television's intimacy and involvement by going into the homes of ordinary people' (1999, p. 97) and is indeed a significant forerunner to the exploration of the housing crisis in a number of 1960s and 1970s texts, including *Cathy Come Home* (1966).

The trope of working-class as victims of their material circumstance, and in particular cramped and inadequate housing, also circulated in some of the popular discourses on wartime evacuation and the election campaigns of the post-war era. From the 1945 election through until the 1980s, as Macfarlane argues, 'Party election manifestoes, candidate election addresses and the opinion polls all indicate a high sustained level of public concern with housing as a major political issue' (1981, p. 60). This issue was addressed by a significant increase in the provision of housing by local authorities and in new towns. Between 1947 and 1966, not only did the proportion of owner-occupier households increase from 27 to 46.7 per cent but state housing increased from 12 to 25.7 per cent (Macfarlane, 1981, p. 62). This represented 'a significant material gain for certain sections of the working class by reducing the cost of shelter without a commensurate reduction in wage levels' (Stewart and Burridge, 1989, p. 66). However, the increasing desire to participate in domestic consumer culture, widely circulated by television, arguably also led to an increasing number of couples who sought to set up separate households at a younger age – as Cathy and Reg had done early in the play. This, alongside older people staying put in familiar surroundings, added pressure on the limited housing stock and as the population grew from 38 million in 1921 to 46 million in the 1960s, the number of private households almost doubled from 8.7 to 14.9 million. The housing crisis can arguably be seen as a direct consequence of increased expectations that went hand-in-hand with the welfare state, consumerism and the post-war settlement, which Sinfield (1997) suggests was premised on a continued improvement in living standards. Furthermore, a significant amount of the housing stock was old. The Ministry of Housing and Local Authorities classed approximately 1,800,000 houses as unfit for human habitation in 1967 (Macfarlane, 1981, p. 63), just one year after *Cathy Come Home* was broadcast.

That improvements were occurring, alongside poverty and deprivation, was conveyed in the documentary *Morning in the Streets* (BBC, 1959), which also included images of working-class domestic overcrowding and substandard housing. A family of seven was shown waking up, all having slept in one room; the father and son in one bed, mum and two kids in another bed, another child had their own bed, as did an elderly grandfather. Attention was also drawn to homes with leaking roofs where water dripped from the roof into a pail, to rats, cockroaches and ceilings falling down in 'homes'. Nevertheless, a housewife's voice explained with a strong condemnation of nostalgia : 'You've no idea how we used to live, five of us in one bed, five of us, mother used to try and cover us and she'd have coats to cover us. The good old days, there were no good old days, they were cursed.' Davis (2001) has pointed out that conventional politics was, however, slow to give space to the extensive social grievances of the housing crisis during the 'age of affluence'. Indeed when *Cathy Come Home* was shown for the third time in 1968, it was preceded by a Labour party political broadcast, which failed to address housing at all. Arguably popular culture continued to place housing on the political agenda and *Cathy Come Home* tapped both into and fuelled popular political discourses circulating about housing. For example, the *Guardian,* when it reviewed the play, referred to how, following Reg's accident, the family's life was 'diverted towards living in a Rachman world, sinking deeper into slumland' (17 November 1966). The activities of Peter Rachman had come to light during the Profumo scandal in 1963, and become a focus of media attention. Rachman had, in the wake of the Conservative government's abolition of rent controls in 1957, bought properties in Notting Hill, forced tenants out and rented them to Caribbean immigrants who consequently found themselves living in some of the most squalid and overcrowded slum conditions in Europe. The Rachman scandal did little to alleviate the widespread racism in the housing market or discursive narratives of white people denied housing because of immigration, which fed into the almost casual racism in some of the dialogues in the hostel in *Cathy Come Home* and some documentaries of the period. As Webster argues, the 'vision of "ordinarily" English People threatened in their homes by "immigrants" is a central motif of Enoch Powell's infamous Rivers of Blood speech in 1968' (Webster, 1998, p.183). Indeed the trope of working-class as victims of their material circumstances and housing crisis was thus able to be utilized by a range of political groups.

When *Cathy Come Home* was broadcast in 1966, *The Wednesday Play* had already established a reputation as edgy and challenging, which led to a number of letters from irate listeners who were concerned about the representativeness of the plays, of the BBC and of the plays' writers, directors and producers. In one letter a viewer pointed out that: 'we feel that we, and people like us, represent the majority of people who pay for the privilege of having a television in their homes', going on to point out:

> On returning home last Wednesday evening Mar 2nd my husband and I found our teenage children watching an apparently harmless play dealing with a school war memorial. We joined them but very soon, with no warning, we found ourselves watching rape, gloatingly presented. We were very embarrassed and horrified to have such a scene in our sitting room.
>
> There must be many thousands of parents, like us who are deeply disturbed and distressed at what is being brought into our homes.
>
> If you had to watch this with your wife and family I feel sure you would have been embarrassed. (BBCWA, T16/733)

The Controller of Programmes – Television, in a confidential memo about *The Wednesday Play*, emphasized that the series aimed to 'reflect the changing pattern of life today, the plays concentrate mainly on the here and now' and that new writers were told to 'illuminate the truth, not to "pontificate" or propagandize' (3 October 1966, BBCWA, T16/733). Yet the viewer's letter and the reference to the 'scenes in our sitting room' encapsulates the domestic intimacy into which television is broadcast and the anxiety that images of working-class domesticates evoked. Another Wednesday Play, *Up the Junction*'s (1965), portrayal of working-class girls sexuality and an abortion taking place in a working-class living room also caused controversy; 400 viewers complained and Mary Whitehouse started the National Viewers' and Listeners' Association as a response to it. The depiction of a very domestic abortion made uncomfortable viewing, but so did a similar scene in the film *Alfie* (1965). It was such scenes' entry into the living rooms of the once protected middle-classes through the medium of television which was problematic.

The *Birmingham Post* complained that *Cathy Come Home* did not focus on 'what was being done to improve things' (17 November 1966) and when the play was repeated in January 1967 the *Daily Mirror* reported that 2,000,000 councillors and council workers from across the country were encouraged to watch and spot blunders – many of which they had already spotted as 'the play gives the false impression that the local authorities could not care less about the homeless'. BBC 2 followed the repeat with another discussion which included several young couples from Birmingham who confirmed their poor treatment from council officials (*The Times*, 12 January 1967). Furthermore, the critique of the play by Laurence Evans, Head of Local Government Information Officers, in their Journal suggests that the less than sympathetic attitude Cathy received from council officials had some credibility, when he argued:

> The play failed because of its highly emotional attempt to encourage sympathy for a feckless and irresponsible young couple who entered marriage, took on an expensive flat and started having babies without one whit of a thought for the future. There are many other people far more deserving of sympathy than Cathy and Reg. (2 November 1966)

Although response to the play was generally far more supportive than this, there were other critiques. One letter writer to the *Guardian* suggested that, 'As heart rendering as *Cathy Come Home* was, it was patronising in the assumption that the working class is irresponsible, unthinking and incapable of taking care of itself' (17 January 1967). Irresponsibility was a not uncommon critique, as in one letter which argued that: 'irresponsible attitude to marriage and procreation seems to ensure that the problems and the suffering it involves will be with us for the foreseeable future' (17 January 1967). In this there is the suggestion that it was working-class behaviour rather than material circumstances which created social problems, something that underlined the trope of the working-class as sexually amoral or aberrant.

DOCUMENTARY DISCOURSES: *SEVEN UP*

The significance of material circumstances was also emphasized in the series *Seven Up*, originally a Granada's *World in Action* special when first broadcast in 1964, which put forward the premise that a child's home background, his or her class and the material circumstances of the domestic world in which he or she grew up would shape his or her future. Working-class lives were one focus of the resurgence of television documentaries in the 1960s as a result, according to Willis, of 'the relative portability of handheld 16 mm cameras' (2000, p. 100), which enabled current affairs programming like *World in Action* to move away from studio question and answer sessions and out into the lives of ordinary people. *Seven Up* was based upon interviews with, initially, 20 children from contrasting social backgrounds who were brought together for a day out in London, visiting the zoo and having a party for the benefit of the cameras. The 7-year-old children discussed their hopes and expectations for the future as 'members of a generation who would be running the world in the year 2000' and, as Bruzzi points out, ITA was overt in the programme's intention to emphasize the social divisions in society and education through the selection of participants and through editing (2007, p. 22). Importantly the series was broadcast in 1964 when the election of the Labour party, in what was initially a minority government, indicated a shift away from the consumerist consensus of 13 years of Conservative rule. Although Macmillan reportedly claimed in the early 1960s 'the class war is over and we have won it', for many a vote for the Labour party was both an acknowledgement and a rejection of the class divisions in British society. Initially *Seven Up* emphasized the significance of education in creating social divides; children such as the Eastender Tony were predominantly filmed in school or at least outside their home. The iconic image of Tony falling over as he ran from his home to school was symbolic of the pitfalls that working-class children were seen as likely to encounter in life and education.

Domesticity thus operated as a structuring absence rather than the visual focus in the initial documentary. In returning to re-interview the children, or at least some of the original group of 20, approximately every 7 years until 2005, the series became a unique television programme – a lengthy docusoap with huge gaps between episodes and, like so much of British cinema and television documentary, became 'fixated upon the quotidian and the personal' (Bruzzi, 2007, p. 22). By *Twenty-One Up* in 1977 and *Twenty-Eight Up* in 1984, the cameras were taken into the participants' homes; the mis-en-scene for the interviews provided a narrative of their relative material success or lack of it. From Peter's student flat at 21 to Suzy's middle-class house in the Home Counties at 28, their domestic setting is used to define the characters and tell the narrative, propelled by the individual stories of changing work and personal relationships of the participants. As the series progressed, the under-representation of women in the initial series was counteracted by a greater emphasis on some of the partners of some participants and by an increasing focus upon the three girls – Jackie, Lynne and Sue – who had attended a primary school in a working-class district of London together.

Jackie and Lynne are both married by *Twenty-One Up* and the cameras and viewers are introduced to Jackie's semi-detached house on a new estate in Essex. The series became something of a docusoap, and viewers were offered the pleasures, as Kilborne suggests, of 'the chance of witnessing ordinary folk operating in familiar environments and thus, supposedly becoming privy to the everyday challenges they confront' (2000, p. 111). In latter episodes the significance of class, so central to the initial programme, is sidelined by the growing focus upon Neil, who initially as a 7-year-old was full of life but had by 21 dropped out of university and was living in a squat in London and an emphasis on Tony the Eastender lad who is first a jockey, then a cabbie who buys a holiday home in Spain. Tony's story and the centrality of Neil's struggle with homelessness and mental illness, despite his involvement in local politics, shifted the text from the social to the particular. *Seven Up* became less political, as the cultural landscape of Britain shifted; and at the end of the millennium *Seven Up* arguably become more individualist.

Interestingly by the second programme *7 Plus Seven* (1970), one of two researchers for the original programme had started a career on *Coronation Street* and was involved in both drama and documentary. Indeed much critical focus on the series has explored the degree to which the interviews were a performance and two of the participants, Nick and Bruce, have suggested that 'It is possible that what the *Seven Up* children offer up to the camera, far from being a considered and accurate distillation of who they are and what they are feeling, is a series of occasionally random statements that pop into their heads because of the pressure to say something for the camera' (quoted in Bruzzi, 2007, p. 60). Arguably this serves to undermine the stark reality of class divisions that are highlighted by edited snippets of earlier programmes used in later programmes. Upper-class children muttering that the working-class children smell, or proclaiming from their private schools that the working-class have just as many opportunities they had, rendered more palatable for late twentieth and early twenty-first century audiences; by emphasizing the performivity of all concerned producing a pleasurable negotiation of otherwise challenging material.

As Kilborn points out, the basic appeal of a docusoap is that it offers the prospect of a voyeuristic encounter with 'real life' (often larger than life) individuals (2000, p. 112): a voyeurism involved in all documentary viewing. The pleasures that documentaries offer, which include a licence to watch the private, hidden and what would otherwise be forbidden intimacies, predictably perhaps led it into the domain of sexuality (Freud, edited by Gay, 1995). The *Man Alive* documentary, *Living in Sin*, broadcast in September 1966, started with a voice-over explaining:

> In a society geared to an image of family life, more and more couples today are deciding to do without the blessing of church and state. Increasingly people who CANNOT marry and people who WILL NOT marry are choosing to live together … for the increasing number of couples who decide to do it, life is different living in sin. (T 14/2/469/1)

The documentary mixed titillation with social inquiry; couples whose life stories were featured included a man unable to get a divorce who had a baby with his new partner. His loss of moral respectability, implied by the programme's title, was underlined by his work as a park keeper, although he had previously been a teacher. In the 1960s and 1970s respectability was an economic necessity; divorce or an 'irregular' private life could cost people their job. The programme determinedly struggled to get the cohabiting couples to draw attention to disadvantages in their domestic arrangements and condemn their actions. The degree to which these couples challenged dominant paradigms of domesticity is limited; rather they actually reinforced a fairly traditional view of heterosexual relationships. External factors were held responsible for their inability to marry; previous partners who would not consent to a divorce or parents who withheld consent to the marriage of their children who were still under the age of 21. It was not until in the 1970s, when *The Family* was broadcast, that viewers' perceptions of domestic sexual morality were really challenged.

THE FAMILY: CONTROVERSY AND THE TROPE OF ABERRANT SEXUALITY

Franc Roddam and Paul Watson's 12-part observational documentary *The Family* (1974) focused upon the everyday life of the Wilkins family from Reading. As their day-to-day interactions were followed by a camera crew and then, in edited form, by the general public, the working-class home was placed again into the cultural centrality by the television (Biressi and Nunn, 2005, p. 66). As Asa Briggs pointed out 'many viewers told a BBC Lister Research audience panel that they were bored by the series' (Briggs, 1995, p. 963), nevertheless the programme gained regular audiences of six and a half million and won a number of awards including the Broadcasting Press Guild's 'Best TV documentary of year'. However, like much reality TV, *The Family* evoked controversy, not least for its disregard of the bourgeois boundaries of public and private (Lisbet Van Zoonen, 2001, quoted in Holmes, 2008). Terry Wilkins, a driver-conductor on the local buses, and his wife Margaret Wilkins, who were both 39, had been married for 22 years when they applied to be the subjects of the documentary, as she explained in a television discussion of the programme: 'I thought it would be better for ordinary people to do something, instead of things done by actors and actresses, made up and set up. They've got *Coronation Street* but people don't live like that.' In retrospect it could be argued that the family were very much set up by the editing of Watson's team. The credits of each episode focused upon a photograph of the Wilkins family on their mantelpiece and the iconic image of each member of the family 'suggest a sentimental attachment to the family ... and underscores the emphasis on the personal and domestic life in Watson's film' (Biressi and Nunn. 2005. p. 65). The opening scenes of the first episode were shot as the Wilkins ate around the kitchen table chatting with Watson who, with his camera crew, had by then spent 2 months filming in the household. His visible inclusion in the family, sharing a meal, symbolically suggests that the general public are also being invited into the private world of the Wilkins' domestic space.

The programme focused on the Wilkins' domestic lives, although not exclusively. Margaret worked in a greengrocers shop below their rented and somewhat crowded three-bedroom flat, which housed nine people, a dog, cats and numerous budgerigars. As Jimmy Saville remarked in a televised discussion of the programme: 'you could see them all crammed in that house, there seemed to be about 47, it was like a cartoon'. The housing conditions were far from ideal; on one occasion their young grandson reached from his cot in the cramped room he shared with teenage parents and emptied the entire contents of the nearby food cupboard onto the floor. The struggle to move into council accommodation by the eldest son, Gary, his teenage wife Karen and their baby, was one of the structuring narratives of the series; for the Wilkins family council provision offered the only hope of domestic security. Many of the viewers saw the allocation of a council flat to the young couple as favouritism, influenced by the presence of the television cameras. Within and beyond the text there was discussion about the allocation of one of the most prized resources of the post-war welfare state – housing. Margaret Wilkins, however, articulated a familiar anxiety that women who split up with their husbands and became single parents were prioritized for council accommodation. Teenage mum Karen is presented as a conscientious and diligent housekeeper, constantly cleaning and tidying, careful with money, although an inexperienced and worried young mother. The council flat Karen and Gary eventually moved to and the Wilkins' home did not suggest that domestic diligence was rewarded by the goodies of post-war consumer culture. Karen is shown struggling to purchase second-hand furniture and even when Terry re-wall-papered the Wilkins' kitchen it too was in sharp contrast with the images of domesticity portrayed in advertising and lifestyle programming during the period. Furthermore, in the Wilkins' flat, the only bath was under a worktop in the kitchen and when daughter Marion wanted to take a bath, as she dressed for her wedding, she is shown first asking everyone to clear out of the kitchen. As Margaret Wilkins explained when interviewed by Jimmy Saville: 'You see all these kitchen sink dramas with beautiful kitchens nothing out of place no dirty pans and what-have-you, all sparkling. Well people's kitchens aren't like that, well maybe a small percentage' (BBCWA, T66/55/1).

It was not, however, the housing conditions or overcrowding which caused controversy, they were generally uncommented upon. It was the rather outspoken Margaret Wilkins who was criticized both for her past sexual misdemeanours and for condoning the behaviour of her children: her eldest son Gary had married at 16 when his girlfriend Karen was pregnant, her eldest daughter Marion lived with her boyfriend in her parents' flat and her youngest daughter Heather, a teenager of 15, had a black boyfriend. Whether Marion and her boyfriend Tom would marry, was set up as one of the series structuring enigma narratives. The representational trope of working-class sexuality as amoral or aberrant structured the debate about both the programme and the Wilkins family themselves. When Margaret Wilkins explained, in the very first episode of *The Family*, that her youngest son, 9-year-old Christopher, was not her husband's child but rather the result of an extra-marital affair, controversy and condemnation erupted. Arguably, it was not by the 1970s that such situations were uncommon but what was controversial was the public disclosure. Historians, however, cannot gauge in how many families the fathers were not biologically related to the children, without DNA testing few could be sure at the time. In the wake of the greater overt representation of sexuality and adultery that the 1960s heralded, young Christopher's paternity represented a public reminder that behind the idealizations of the domestic family were many messier and untidier lives; as Briggs points out 'if some viewers were shocked by what they saw others were sympathetic' (1995, p. 963). Despite the apparent sexual revolution of the 1960s, Gorer's 1971 survey of sex and marriage had indicated that a double standard continued in attitudes to men and women's sexuality, and that one-quarter of married men and nearly two-thirds of married women had been virgins when they married (Stanley, 1995). The reliability and representativeness of such interviews is hard to gauge; they are perhaps an indication of a version of sexual behaviour that interviewees felt it was acceptable to present in a public arena, while *The Family* presented rather different versions of sexuality to a very broad cross-section of the public.

In her autobiography, Margaret Wilkins laid the blame for the marital crisis that resulted in Christopher's birth on the material circumstances of working-class life: 'My unsettled lifestyle, an early marriage, the strain of being hard up and not having a decent home, being tied down too young with children, had all had their effect on my marriage and contributed towards the problems that Terry and I had faced' (1975, p. 156), but the controversy focused upon aberrant sexual conduct and which, according to one local newspaper, portrayed a 'degraded impression of what a family should be' (BBCWA, T66/55/1).This responded to growing anxieties over 'the family' and domesticity in the wake of more widespread access to divorce, abortion and birth control, more married women in the workforce, single parenthood being on the increase, while 'the proportion of "traditional households" comprising of a couple with dependent children had been falling since the 1960s' (Hughes and Fergusson, 2004, p. 55). Furthermore, *The Family* was based upon Craig Gilbert's *The American Family* (1972), within which the central couple had a much publicized marital split and ultimately divorced. The shifting cultural landscape of sexuality in the 1970s, coupled with a widespread awareness of the fate of the 'American family', framed viewers' engagement with the Wilkins, drawing attention to the fragility and tenuousness of the Wilkins' domesticity. Indeed Terry and Margaret did divorce 4 years after the series was completed, as Briggs suggested: 'the impact of television on the Wilkins family proved as complex and controversial as the impact of television on society as a whole' (1995, p. 962).

Although *The Family* contained scenes of domestic harmony and a companionable marriage, when the Wilkins were shown eating together, watching television or going on their first foreign holiday, such moments were fleeting, brief respites from the squabbles and arguments that made up this version of working-class domesticity. Such tension could be seen as an inevitable consequence of so many people living in such close proximity, so that artist Gillain Wearing saw watching *The Family* as a child as: 'surprising watching normality ... There had been nothing like it on British television. There was *Coronation Street* but that was too acted, too nostalgic to be real' (Jeffries, 2006). Her interpretation of the Wilkins' version of working-class domesticity as normality was not necessarily shared by other viewers. If the significance of *Cathy Come Home* lay in the cultural acceptance of the text's representativeness (enabling the problems of a particular family to be seen as social problems encountered by many), the reverse occurred in the discourses that surrounded *The Family*, all their social problems were particularized. Rather than being interpreted as symbolic of changing definitions of family and domesticity, the Wilkins' cultural values, codes of conduct, ethics, ideologies and life choices challenged bourgeois notions of domesticity; the Wilkins were defined as a problem family and castigated for their unrepresentativeness.

Over 190 letters of criticism were received by the BBC, from viewers expressing disgust at the choice of the Wilkins and disapproval of their way of life; only three letters expressed appreciation. One reader of the *Radio Times*, focusing upon the sexual ethics of the Wilkins, postulated: 'The average working class family does not regard illegitimate children as something to be found in every working class home and reluctance to get married to the woman you are living with as the typical reaction of the British Male' (*Radio Times*, 13 September 1974). However, as one member of the public waiting to see the wedding of Marion and Tom in episode 11 explained to the television cameras, 'A lot of people have said they're the wrong sort of people but I don't think there is the average family in England.' Critiques of representativeness were from a range of social groups, although those who had access to the media to express their disapproval were predominantly middle-class: as a letter published in the *Listener* pointed out that a panel assembled on Jimmy Saville's programme to discuss *The Family* was 'entirely male and middle class … a basically patronising attitude to wage earners, women and older citizens could not have been more aptly expressed' (11 July 1974). The representativeness of *The Family* continued to be questioned, and consequently opened up a debate about the representation of class on television and about the nature of working-class domesticity.

Murray and Ouellette have suggested 'one of the most compelling aspects of reality TV is the extent to which its use of real people or nonfactors contribute to the diversification of television culture' (2004, p. 8). Such diversification inevitably caused controversy if *Cathy Come Home* suggested that not only had the consumer revolution escaped significant swathes of the population but the basic necessities of life were beyond their reach without significant state intervention, the controversy about *The Family* suggested that bourgeois discourses of domesticity and respectability were being disturbed and dislodged. In the 1960s and 1970s ideas of domesticity within broadcasting were changing, this responded to, reiterated and constituted changes in the very domestic spaces within which radio and television were consumed. In the years that followed, broadcasting continued to be both preoccupied by an increasingly diverse range of domesticities, to idealize domesticity and recognize that it was often the site of controversy and conflict.

Chapter Seven

The personal becomes political: domesticity in turmoil and as a political project

The 1970s saw the removal of the BBC's monopoly of radio in Britain, leading to the emergence of commercial stations such Capital and Virgin. Social change, in the wake of feminism and the cultural revolution of the long 1960s, contributed to the shifts and changes in the domestic spaces in which broadcast media were consumed. The 1980s and 1990s brought together both an unparalleled expansion of broadcasting hours and a growing political obsession with the family and domestic spaces. Channel 4 was introduced in 1982, Channel 5 in 1997, and satellite and digital technology became increasingly popular in the 1990s; shifting television into an era of abundance but also uncertainty. Soap-opera, reality television and talk shows gave what would once have been private (domestic even feminized) emotions and experiences an airing in the public domain. The inter-relationship between broadcast media and society's increasingly therapeutic and confessional culture, also found in tabloid newspapers and social media, led to the 'domestic' sphere being constructed as: fragile, in crisis and turmoil. Politicians increasingly became concerned to spread governance into domestic spaces; however, as politics became increasingly concerned with the private sphere, so too domestic aesthetics, issues and concerns seeped into politics. Domesticity overlapped, merged and entangled itself in programming once identifiably focused on the public sphere such as *Panorama* (BBC, 1953–) and *Newsnight* (BBC, 1980–). Consequently political discourses about war and remembrance, for example, became simultaneously re-routed to a growing concern with domesticity.

HOUSEWIVES AND *HOUSEPARTY* (SOUTHERN TELEVISION 1968–81)

In the 1970s, second wave feminism's presence had become visible on the political landscape following the first Women's Liberation Conference held at Ruskin College, Oxford, on 13 March 1970. The Women's Movement overtly dislodged and unpicked the dream of domesticity; thus, in the same year that *The Family* (1974) was broadcast, Anne Oakley published two books, *Housewife* and *Sociology of Housework,* which explored and condemned women's unpaid work in the home. For Oakley, housework – unpaid domestic labour – was the particular domain of women who had withdrawn from the labour market and become economically dependent on their husbands. Consequently domestic labour was interwoven with the low status of women and 'the problem with no name', which Betty Friedan had previously identified in the USA – identifiable in alienated, despondent and depressed housewives. The 'Wages for Housework Campaign' in the 1970s was one attempt to draw attention to the lack of recognition for domestic labour. Jill Nicolas reported for the feminist magazine *Spare Rib* how one speaker at a campaign rally argued: 'We appreciate the cards and flowers, but they're just not enough – we want a wage for our work' (*Spare Rib,* No. 58, May 1977). The rally, held on Mother's Day in 1977, went on to consider the Icelandic housewives' strike, while also demanding higher family allowances – the precursor to child benefit.

Oakley's research, which conceptualized housework as work, while questioning its low status, suggested that 'housework is the most disliked aspect of being a housewife' (1974b, p. 183) and questioned the belief in 'natural feminine domesticity' (1974b, p. 185). Broadcasting's emphasis, since its inception, on the performivity of domesticity and on domestic education had arguably already dislodged the 'naturalness' of feminine domesticity and was arguably as significant in rupturing the ideal of domesticity in the 1970s as the emergence of the women's movement. Particularly as, by Oakley's own admission, most housewives she interviewed 'had the idea feminists are not interested in housewives – that they look down on them' (1974b, p. 194); a position which had some credibility. For example, Caroline Freeman, writing in another feminist publication *Red Rag*, had said of housework: 'We see it as unacceptable, as wasteful and limiting in itself ... the situation of dependence in which it is usually done destroys all taints of possible satisfaction' (No. 5, 1973). Sally Jordon – who Oakley describes as living in a three-bedroom council house in a bleak and isolated area and as 'extremely oppressed as a woman' – indicated the problematic relationship between feminism and housework when she explained:

> I think of myself as a housewife, but I don't think of myself as a cabbage. A lot of people think they're housewives and they're cabbages. I don't like to think I'm only a housewife ... These days people look down on housewives. There's more women fighting for equality and doing men's jobs, and a lot of women don't like staying in the home. There's more work full time than part-time. I wouldn't like to work full time and run a home as well. (1974b, p. 154)

Yet Oakley's interviewees found that, despite monotony and loneliness, autonomy and satisfaction could be found in housework – in part through women specifying and adhering to their own standards, routines and rules (1974b, p. 183).

In the 1960s and 1970s lonely housewives were not well served by television, especially during the day. *Television Today* berated programmers in 1970, asking 'why are women overlooked by the planners?', while pointing out that sport dominated Saturday afternoons and most channels on other afternoons also (16 July 1970). A growing critique of the male dominance within television institutions was also expressed by Jill Tweedie writing in the *Guardian*, who asked 'Why is Auntie run by Uncles?' (4 October 1971) and 5 years later a Helen Taylor suggested in the *Guardian*: 'For all the companies women's programming is a low priority and thus a low budget area' (15 July 1976), echoing Virginia Ironside's plea 'Why won't TV spend a little on ME?' (*Daily Mail*, 3 March 1969). Although to some analysts and critics the problem lay in women's limited role in the television production process, arguably programmers faced more complex problems.

Radio accompanied women's domestic tasks; *Woman's Hour* continued, as did *Housewives' Choice* until the introduction of Radios 1 and 2 in 1967. *Woman's Hour*, as *The Times* pointed out, went 'from strength to strength, a finely balanced hour of broadcasting able to switch from current affairs to currant buns with seamless grace' (30 December 1987); however, attempts by both the BBC and ITV to provide daytime television programmes for women struggled to navigate the complex and contradictory terrain of women's interests in an age of feminism. Although the BBC heralded the return of 'television for wives' in the 1960s and in 1970 Thames Television announced a show for women viewers, which promised 'to be unlike other women's programmes' as it would 'not include the usual recipes, chats on knitting and nappy pins' (*Sunday Mirror*, 24 May 1970); the *Guardian* queried: 'Do women want corndollies or contraceptive advice?' (15 July 1976). Certainly programmes were criticized when they concentrated on women's continuing domestic role. To be popular, a programme aimed at housewives had both to articulate women's continuing domestic responsibilities and their questioning of this domestic role. Southern Television's *Houseparty*, which was broadcast three times week from the late 1960s, did exactly this and over the next 10 years its popularity grew until it was broadcast on every ITV network. Set in a studio reconstructed to look like a modernist open-plan house, with a kitchen-cum-lounge, Formica surfaces and Hessian wall-weave which connoted middle-class style in the 1970s, the programme was structured to appear as if the audience was eavesdropping on a group of friends who casually met to share a cup of coffee or tea. The illusion of peeping into a domestic space was re-enforced by the door-bell occasionally ringing and participants answering it, with protestations of surprise or at least lack of knowledge about who might be there. The programme ended with a credit inviting viewers to 'drop in again', which suggested friendship and intimacy to the high proportion of women viewing on their own, which Southern Television's research had identified as making up the majority of the audience. For these viewers, the participants of *Houseparty* were constructed as friends.

Some of the 25 participants, who appeared six at a time and were paid only £20 a show, were already established household names, including Cherry Marshall who had run a model agency and Mary Morris a television cook. Although some critiqued the programme for operating at a trivial level (*Western Mail*, 22 November 1972), others were aware that the text was more contradictory and complex as the *Daily Mail* explained:

> The atmosphere is middle-aged, middle-class and very pleased with itself. But appearances can be deceptive. The *Houseparty* regulars included: a shop steward's wife, a plumber's wife, even a Franciscan nun and in amongst the recipes and the flower arrangements they have shared with the audience such personal problems as breakdowns and illegitimate children. One woman virtually had her divorce on the programme. (16 April 1977)

The do-it yourself divorce of Lucy Morgan, who had been married three times, provoked much discussion around the kitchen table, indeed as a glamorous yummy-mummy, some 30 years before the term was invented, she did much to undermine the taboo about divorce. Many of the discussions were framed by the feminist discourses of the 1970s and 1980s; David Wilson, Chairman of Southern Television, remarked that 'I wouldn't let my wife appear. Those women say the most dreadful things about their husbands' (*Daily Mail*, 16 April 1977). Indeed the programme made 'no concessions to male viewers'.

> Anne Ladbury, whose conversation often slipped into guidance on dressmaking or children's clothes, recalled: 'We had to forget

> about the cameras and were told not to say anything that you wouldn't say to your best friends. We used to get letters from women saying we had saved their lives as we had discussed the type of problems they were facing and we had made them feel they were not alone. A lot of the time it would be no-holds-barred' (*Craven Herald Pioneer*, 10 January 2010).

Newspaper reports suggest that Southern Television staff were sometimes overrun with requests for recipes, advice or pictures of the *Houseparty* group, while interviews with the producer and director Peter Egan suggest that viewers' identification with the women superseded their middle-classness, he recounted how a 'would-be suicide' had rung up, talked to the switchboard for half an hour and 'found the programme of some help' (*South Wales Argus*, 24 September 1980). Alongside *The Family* (1974), *Houseparty* heralded the emergence of the confessional and therapeutic culture which came to dominate daytime schedules with multi-channel broadcasting at the end of the twentieth century.

FAMILIES IN CRISIS

Lucy Morgan's television divorce on *Houseparty*, like the domestic arrangements of the Wilkins in *The Family* (1974), responded to wider cultural shifts in domestic relationships. The percentage of traditional households made up of two parents and dependent children was falling at the end of the twentieth century from 38 per cent in the 1960s to 23 per cent of all households in 2001. A corresponding increase took place in the number of children living in single-parent households, which went up to 20 per cent by 2001. These shifts were accompanied by a decrease in the popularity of marriage (Hughes and Fergusson, 2004, p. 56) and an increase in divorce which became easier following the legal changes introduced in 1970. These shifts were, however, ones of slight emphasis rather than ruptures, the vast majority of children continued to be brought up in two-parent families, not necessarily by both their biological parents but this was not a historically new phenomenon. Step-parenting and 'reconstituted families' as a result of the death or the disappearance of one parent were, for example, common in the Victorian era and very much in evidence in fiction of the period.

In the 1970s and 1980s, broadcasting culture similarly embraced a multiplicity of domestic relationships which included families of either birth or marriage but began to include single parents, step families and singletons sharing flats. This was particularly visible in sit-coms with, for example, the long-running series *The Liver Birds* (BBC, 1969–79) about two young girls who shared a flat in Liverpool, *And Mother Makes Three* (Thames, 1971–3) featuring a single mum, and *Man About the House* (Thames, 1973–6) where the domestic arrangements involved a flat share between two young girls and a young man. Arguably each of these texts constructs a surrogate family, albeit one of choice, reinforcing Chaney's argument that 'although aspects of moral, social and political order have been relaxed, they have changed character rather than disappeared' (2002, p. vii).

Moves towards a greater plurality of domesticities on television were given a further boost with the introduction of Channel 4 in 1982; the broadcaster's remit to be innovative, to cater for groups hitherto unrepresented on television, its status as a publisher rather than a maker of programmes, all contributed to the development of a more cutting-edge broadcaster which took more risks in programme content. The channel commissioned a new soap-opera set on the suburban outskirts of Liverpool: *Brookside*, which was first aired on the new channel's opening night 2 November 1982. *Brookside*, and the BBC's response to it, *Eastenders*, which was introduced in 1985, both built upon *Coronation Street*'s already established tradition of placing domestic relations and drama and what was perceived, perhaps incorrectly, to be a woman's genre in prime-time television. Fictional dramas set primarily in domestic spaces were the broadcaster's response to the critiques of the 1970s that the female viewer was ignored. Like *Houseparty*, their success came in both recognizing women's domestic focus, or at least role, while acknowledging that domesticity was fraught with problems, contractions and trauma. The longevity of soaps and the need for drama and character change, narratively inclined them to present families as precarious, full of hidden secrets, that are disclosed to the audience and the fictional families' neighbours for critique, discussion and judgement. In so doing the soaps endorsed a cultural perception of families in crisis and domesticity as tumultuous. Viewers of *Brookside* in the first 10 years witnessed the slow destruction of two of the main families, the Grants and the Corkhills, as they experienced debt, disclosure, deceit and violence. There is a momentary more upbeat storyline when divorced Billy Corkhill and Sheila Grant marry although they soon leave the series, but, as it is later disclosed, not to live happily ever after.

The very modernity of the houses in Brookside Close, and the more mixed-class backgrounds of the inhabitants, suggested a newer version of domesticity than *Coronation Street* had, but the tidy, planned façade was emblematic of late-twentieth-century domesticity, a veneer on an altogether messier world lying beneath, that middle-class niceties, epitomized by the Collins family, struggled to come to terms with. When their son came out as gay and their daughter had an affair with a married man, their reactions articulated the panic of a 'morality' which was slowly beginning to realize it might no longer be in the majority. *Brookside*'s most infamous storyline, 'the body under the patio', ran from 1993–4; during which time the murdered Trevor Jordache lay under the patio of his wife's house metaphorically encapsulating the soap-opera version of domesticity as well as wider cultural discourses which articulated increasing anxiety about domesticity and families. In *Brookside* Trevor Jordache was not merely a hidden signifier of his wife's desperate act of violence when she killed him but of other darker secrets; he had sexually abused his daughters and physically abused his wife. Beth Jordache's lesbianism and her on-screen kiss with a neighbouring family's nanny all fed a fear and fascination with what went on behind closed doors in the domestic interior of the home and a growing political will to exert governance on the family.

A political emphasis on the family's and individual's domestic arrangements can be identified alongside the growing economic crisis of the 1970s; with inflation, rising unemployment, repeated balance payments deficits and industrial unrest, the family became an area that politicians scrambled to associate themselves with. Addressing the 1977 Conservative Party Conference, Margaret Thatcher declared 'We are the Party of the Family' (cited in Durham, 1991, p. 13). The underlying assumption of this rhetoric was that what constituted the family was, despite evidence to the contrary, somehow fixed, uncontested rather than historically and culturally shifting. Under Thatcherism the family was seen as needing protection from the threat of homosexuality and sexual permissiveness as identified with the 1960s and it was argued there was a need to return to 'Victorian values', yet the abortion, illegitimacy and divorce rates rose. The responsibility for this was not associated with economic hardship; rather Norman Tebbit, a minister in the Thatcher government, argued that 'The broadcast media scorned self-restraint and portrayed family life as a straightjacket' (cited in Durham, 1991, p. 123). Despite this, broadcasting continued to broaden its representations of domesticity, sexuality, the family and what went on behind closed doors – particularly when the Aids crisis in the 1980s brought open discussion of gay sex into mainstream broadcasting well before the watershed.

The 1980s rhetorically saw an attempt to shift the terrain of welfare from the public section to the private domestic sphere and to families. Whereas in the 1960s it had been assumed that the state had a responsibility for providing houses, for enabling domesticity to function for many of the population; this was replaced by a new domestic responsibility to support the functioning of the state. Arguably, politicians hoped the family would pick up the slack as the growth in welfare budgets was halted in the 1980s. When interviewed by *Women's Own*, Margaret Thatcher asserted

'There's no such thing as Society there are individuals men and women and there are families' (cited in Fairclough, 2000, p. 25). The response of Labour voters surveyed in March 1986 suggests the discursive centrality of the family was not aligned to any one political party: 'It's nice to have a social conscience but it's your family that counts' (cited in Abbott, 2003). Thus, when the period from 1979 to 1990 saw those dependent on means-tested benefits rise from 4.4 to 7 million, the political opposition to Thatcherite policies placed the destruction of domesticity and the family rhetorically at the centre of their critique. In Alan Bleasdale's *Boys from the Blackstuff* (BBC, 1982) the most poignant episode is Yosser's story emphasizing the emotional consequences of unemployment, the crisis is very much played out in terms of domestic disarray – his furniture is repossessed, his wife leaves him, wallpaper is coming off walls conveying the emptiness, and the hollowness and misery of his life. The disarray in his house increases until his children are removed by social services with the assistance of the police.

Family life has also been a central theme of the New Labour Project, identified in Blair's 1994 leadership campaign as the cornerstone to effective government, when he argued that: 'The values of a decent society are in many ways the values of the family unit' (cited in Fairclough, 2000, p. 43). Arguably, the priority given to 'family life' was one of the strategies employed to build alliances between Labour's traditional core voters and the middle-classes. Domestic life and family life, which were frequently rhetorically converged, however actually experienced, were seen as fragile, in crisis and became the tenuous projects of governance. New Labour's approach to 'family life' can be seen as an example of what Fairclough terms 'cultural governance', 'governing by shaping and changing the cultures of the public services, claimants, the socially excluded and the general population' (2000, p.12) utilizing language and developing discourses to effect change. Central here is the concept of 'parenting' as a set of discursive skills, techniques and dispositions conceived as fundamental to the construction and maintenance of family life. While New Labour has attempted to target such skills directly to 'vulnerable' or problematic families, through schemes such as Sure Start, in doing so it built upon an already well-established rhetoric, which problematized single parenthood and poverty (Andrews and Carter, 2008).

With the benefit of 25 years of hindsight, Oakley's book *Housewife* was unexpectedly prophetic in seeming to point to what is perhaps one of the unexpected and unintended consequences of the women's movement: the rise of women prepared to raise children on their own rather than within poor relationships. In sharp contrast to some of the media imagery in, for example, *Cathy Come Home* (BBC, 1966) and *A Wedding on Saturday* (1964). Oakley argues that women are socialized 'to want children not marriage' (1974a, p. 191) and goes on to explain how this was demonstrated in a study of adolescent girls where 'over a third of the 600 girls who wrote essays on the theme of their imagined future lives fantasised the death of their husbands before middle age' (1974a, p. 192). Oakley interprets this to mean that 'Once the men had provided them with children, and the children were past the age of dependence the men were dispensable' (1974a, p. 192). Kath Woodward (1998) has argued that the single mother was not necessarily seen as problematic in the new individualistic agenda of Thatcherism, and indeed middleclass career women with a child and/or a partner became an icon of the post-feminism, emblematic of the choices that women had gained. However, women who relied upon benefits and, it was assumed, looked to the state to act as providers when men were not able or willing to, were frequently stigmatized. The demonization of single mums, who apparently used children to give them a passport to domestic independence in the form of a council house or flat, often converged with moral panics about teenage pregnancy. As Libby Brooks argued: 'Since the 1990s, when the Conservative government specialised in attacks on young mothers as a main plank of their "Back to

Basics" crusade, there has been the impression that the country is facing an epidemic of teenage pregnancies' (*Guardian*, 12 May 2006). Any statistical data which might challenge this became irrelevant, as wave upon wave of moral panics in the 1980s, 1990s and the noughties positioned single motherhood as a problematic lifestyle choice rather than an unintended consequence of unprotected sex or relationship breakdown: the way it might have been understood at the beginning of the twentieth century.

DOMESTIC AND SEXUAL REVELATIONS – JEREMY KYLE AND THE CHATSHOW

The political focus on family and domesticity was discursively constructed by, re-enforced and reiterated in a new staple of daytime television in the 1990s – the talk show. These shows, which discussed and debated domestic issues – relationships, the petty power struggles of domestic life, the everydayness of ordinary people lives when faced with setbacks and adversity – as Wood points out 'tended to reflect – if with some considerable time lapse – developments in the United States' (2007, p. 8). The *Daily Mail* in horror criticized them: 'We are being assailed into a new era of chat shows ... we live in the era of sound bite that glibly constructed easily digested morsel that neither challenges or informs' (9 August 1994, p. 19). Such a critique is itself far too glib and misses the complexity of pleasures and problems that these shows embrace or the particularities of developments in the broadcasting landscape which facilitated their growth at this particular historical juncture.

The 1990 and 2003 Broadcasting Acts enshrined a move towards a more free-market liberal agenda, rather than a public service ideal for broadcasting, while the abundance of television channels and broadcasting hours necessitated a regulatory framework which responded to complaints rather than attempting to prohibit certain content or maintain contested notions of 'good taste'. This, as Arthurs argues, 'Along with other cultural influences' led to a 'loosening of restraint and a greater desire to appeal directly to "popular" tastes, dispensing with normative values to address a culturally more diverse audience' (2004, p. 9). Chat shows give space to working class participants in the public sphere, although negating the material circumstances which govern and shape their domestic lives for, as Wood has argued, 'Telling a life becomes more important than dealing with the material constraints that surround and condition it' (2007, p. 12). Thus, although at one level the chat show allows working-class cultural representation, it is, as Shuttac (1997) points out, a limited, framed and in many respects a highly constrained representation. With an eye to audience figures and sensationalism, chat shows repeatedly conveyed the domestic sphere as in turmoil, fragile, fluid, temporary, sexually unregulated and distanced from the middle-class ideals of the family life that were portrayed by Linda Bellingham, as the mother of a very middle-class family, in over 40 Oxo adverts in the 1990s.

Turner has pointed out that: 'It is important to acknowledge that there is a significant dimension of popular media content that sets out to offend middle-class standards as a deliberate commercial and discursive strategy, not as an inadvertent failure of taste' (2010, p. 30). Certainly, in a competitive media environment and fragmented audiences in an age of narrowcasting, the likes of Vanessa Feltz, Kilroy-Silk, Trisha Goddard and Jeremy Kyle have, since the late 1980s, encouraged the guests who appeared on their show to 'confess all' as the *Western Morning News* (15 August 1994) suggested. The confessional culture of the later twentieth and early twenty-first centuries was not restricted to broadcasting, but it was in evidence in magazines, newspapers, autobiographies, social exchanges and the internet. Revelations about domestic life have, as has been argued, a long-standing place in the history of broadcasting, the exchange of fictional and apparently factual intimacy is part of broadcasting's appeal. What is significant in the chat show is how much further they entered into the domestic domain. Their growing preoccupation with sexuality, paternity and intimate relationships took them not merely into the kitchens and living rooms but into the bedrooms of guests, just at the point that multiple television ownership took the television into the bedroom in many households.

Arthurs argues that by the early noughties there was a growing diversity of representations of sexuality on television, a culmination of Plummer's argument that the post-war era has seen a growing democratization of intimate relationships (1995, quoted in Arthurs, 2004). Feminism and gay liberation in the 1970s had challenged the social construction of sexual behaviour while the de-criminalization and legal liberalization of sexuality both facilitated and necessitated their public discussion; for if the law was not going to set boundaries, then individuals and communities must, but where, on what basis and according to what ethical frameworks remained unanswered. Debates about sexuality converged with political and cultural concerns and anxieties about the family – given that sexual behaviour and lifestyle choices were perceived to contribute to welfare expenditure particularly in relation to single parents. As Wilson points out: 'Characteristically talk show studio audiences are simply one step away from the domestic, prompting those who watch at home to note similarities between themselves and those who appear on screen' (2004, p. 141). Similarities rested upon sexual and familial moral positioning, as broadcast media became by the early twenty-first century a key site for ethical contestation over the responsibilities, expectations, and boundaries of domestic sexual relationships worked out by an engagement with the individual stories of participants who appeared on chat shows. The dominant format of chat shows is confrontational: competing narratives and moral frameworks are presented for the studio and home audience to examine, unpick, interrogate and ultimately judge. Much of the ensuing debate can be seen in terms of 'competing overlapping expectations, interests and powers' (Chaney, 2002, p. 13). Consequently, Tolson suggests that the personal-problem format of talk shows involves two levels of discursive practice: moral judgement and the establishment of values, and then the opportunity to work through these problems (2006). The working through moves from the confessional culture to a therapeutic one, which emphasizes personal responsibility and self-help with individual, rather than social, causes and solutions for domestic problems.

In contemporary chat shows the telling of the story is a precursor to individual change, part of the talking cure espoused by Trisha Goddard (whose BAFTA winning *Trisha* was produced by Anglia Television from 1998–2004) and who repeatedly stressed her own training as a counselor. However, if Goddard empathized with her guests and disclosed her own emotional and personal problems, when she left ITV for a new show on Channel 5 in 2004 she was replaced by Jeremy Kyle, who had begun his broadcasting career on commercial radio with late-night confessional shows on both Virgin and Capital stations. He utilizes what Ouellette and Hay (2008) suggest is a judgemental approach which stigmatizes dependency and evokes a neo-liberal agenda of taking care of yourself, albeit with the support of 'Graham and the after-care team'. He chastizes the show's participants for having unprotected sex, or, if the participants are women, for engaging in sexual behaviour which leads to uncertainly about a child's paternity, for reticence to establish paternity or facilitate access for fathers to their children, while young lads are critiqued for not working, for failure to wear a condom, not contributing to the upkeep of their children or not visiting them and occasionally for domestic violence. The imposition of an ethical code which emphasizes a strong work-ethic, self-discipline and the avoidance of unprotected sex is frequently politically justified by the economic stake Kyle and his audience have in the ethics of others by virtue of paying taxes which support the domestic lives of a many of the welfare recipients that are guests on his show. In the post-Thatcher era the politics of sexual ethics frequently has an economic basis. It is important to note, however, that whatever Kyle's clearly articulated views, his viewers are not passive recipients of his ideology, rather they engage in heated discussion and debate about the ethical positions of Kyle and his guests while watching, and subsequently on a range of social network sites.

In the miasma of cultural relativism that ethical debates of personal lives evoke, the 'truth' of Kyle's viewpoints is affirmed by the use of DNA testing and lie detector results, revealed usually after a commercial break has elongated the enigma narrative and encouraged audience speculation and engagement. Utilizing a therapeutic discourse of change and self-help necessitates participants' adoption of a recognizable discursive pattern of ritualistic and arguably meaningless phrases which establish participants' willingness to adopt Kyle's ethical code and gains them access to resources at Kyle's disposal, such as DNA testing, psychotherapy or time in a rehab centre; expensive resources that may otherwise be inaccessible to those on low incomes. Participants narrativize their lives – there are significant absences in these narratives; in opposition to much of the politics of right-wing politicians, single parenthood is never presented as a lifestyle choice but as a consequence of relationship breakdown, accident and carelessness. Furthermore, there is frequent reference to having had a 'few problems' and a willingness to change, coupledom (although not necessarily heterosexuality) is desirable, as are children, and participants explain that their partner or child 'means all the world' to them and all fathers are keen to 'step-up' if their fatherhood is affirmed by a DNA test. The use of the term; 'step-up' is an interesting one, its origins lie in soldiers waiting to go out of the trenches and over the top to potential death in World War I and suggests a battle-ready mentality is required for fatherhood; an indication perhaps of the tenuousness and uncertainty that surrounded men's role in post-war domesticity.

REALITY SHOWS AND DOMESTIC GOVERNANCE

It is perhaps not surprising that fatherhood required stepping-up to, as, under New Labour, family life increasingly became subject to the same culture of performance as the public service industries and caring professions, involving 'apparently objective systems of accountability and measurement' (Dent and

Whitehead, 2002, p. 20). While New Labour increased funding and resources in areas such as nursery provision and after-school care, this was expected to be matched by improved performance and productivity from parents whose failures were externally verified through statistics on truancy and anti-social behaviour orders. Historically, private, domestic space has been subject to intervention by an army of experts, in the form of health visitors and social workers, surveying and regulating working-class mothers throughout the course of the twentieth century. More recently, and facilitated in no small part by Thatcherism's dismantling of welfare provision and discursive emphasis on the 'welfare-consumer' self-reliance and the concept of enterprise, such strategies of population management have given way to 'governance at a distance', whereby: 'Norms of conduct for the civilised are now disseminated by independent experts ... They operate a regime of the self where ... one is encouraged to understand one's life, actually or potentially, not in terms of fate or social status but in terms of one's success or failure acquiring skills and making the choices to actualise oneself' (Rose, 1999, p. 87).

The discourse of parenting within a regime of cultural governance appeals directly to this model of subjecthood, prioritizing self-management through the acquisition, practice and self-monitoring of specific knowledges, techniques and skills. Parenting is conceptualized as an ongoing process of learning, reflection and, importantly, self-appraisal, arguably because in contemporary culture – where parenthood is positioned as a choice and as one of many multiple sometimes fleeting identities or lifestyle positions – the identification of oneself as parent is like other identity positions: always tentative, unstable, a process never completed and always in process (Hall, 1996). As Carter and I have argued, a central element of governance was 'parenting as a set of discursive skills, techniques and dispositions conceived as fundamental to the construction and maintenance of family life' (Andrews and Carter, 2003, p. 41). These include the regulation of time and space, the use of rules and rewards, and an emphasis on family meals. Charles and Kerr's study of mothers of young children suggested that:

> The provision of a proper meal seems ... to symbolise the family. This symbolic significance is partly reflected in the way a proper meal was defined by the women we spoke to. They defined it in terms of the familiar meat (or fish) and two veg. But this was not all. A proper meal was defined by the social relations within which, it was consumed. Thus for a meal to be proper ... all family members had to be present to consume it. (1988, p. 226)

Ouellette and Hay have suggested that 'a cadre of reality programs have emerged to teach individuals how to diagnose problems of everyday life so as to better manage their children, households, health and leisure time' (2008, p. 86). However, that is too sweeping. A differentiation needs to be made between those lifestyle and reality programmes within which a strident breed of experts is seen repeatedly entering the ordinary individuals' private domestic space to pass judgement and sort them out and offer the promise of ideal domesticity and programmes such as *Wifeswop* (Channel 4, 2003–9) which alternatively suggested that domesticity was in turmoil, an endlessly imperfect and confrontational space.

Wifeswop involved two 'wives' swopping houses for two weeks, living according to the other's provided rule book in the first week and introducing their own rules in week two. The show's producers selected couples who were as diametrically opposed as possible, so that the preshow publicity was able to offer viewers the prospect of conflict, at rule change time if not before. Thus in introducing the Mendsawi-Imanis and Wilkinsons it was explained, 'A mum who believes in structure and routine swaps with a mum who puts fun first and education last' (http://www.channel4.com/programmes/wife-swap/episode-guide). The matching of extremes enabled the viewers to position themselves as ordinary in opposition to the participants. Occasionally one partner was positioned as 'other' by class, nationality, religion, sexuality or lifestyle; for example, a German woman married to an engineer or the mother of eight children who with her husband lived on social security. Overall, however, *Wifeswop* offered a democratization of rules and regimes rather than ones externally imposed by experts; all wives seemed keen to articulate their views of childrearing as if experts. But their attempts to impose their own rules were rarely more than even partially successful. Viewers were liable to be left with the suggestion that there are no easy answers to domestic turmoil, and an affirmation of their own attempts at muddling through.

FLUIDIFYING THE DOMESTIC AND THE POLITICAL: THE SARAH KENNEDY RADIO SHOW

If the discursive influences of the state were increasingly entering the domestic spaces of the home, so were the discursive and personal preoccupations of the domestic space increasingly merging with those of the public sphere of politics, as broadcasting in a strongly competitive environment increasingly acknowledged the domestic environments in which it was predominantly consumed. Sarah Kennedy's early morning radio show, broadcast on Radio 2 from 1993 until her departure in 2010, epitomized a new ebb and flow between the public and private, which was acknowledged when it was awarded the prestigious Sony Gold Radio Award in 1995. Her broadcasting style rested upon a strangely whimsical and middle-aged femininity in a station which had a strong predominance of male presenters, many of whom, like Terry Wogan, Steve Wright and Chris Evans, were refugees from the equally male Radio 1. The 5 million listeners, who tuned in to the early morning show (initially from 5:00 till 7:00, moving to 6:00 to 7:30 and then back to 5:00–7:00 in 2009) were provided with a diet of music, gossip, news and a summary of the daily newspapers; however requests, usually a mainstay of establishing the personal interrelationship of listeners and DJs, were absent. Personal relationships were instead fostered through correspondence: letters and emails around themes and holiday postcards which shared the personal life of both the DJ and her audience, and built up a synthetic community or surrogate family defined as' Dawn Patrollers'. Like many families, the show utilized and developed a series of phrases and expressions or versions of words which became familiar to listeners, for example 'busticles', 'chesticles' for breasts, 'colleag-wees' (colleagues) and reputably coined the phrase 'White Van Man', earning Kennedy recognition from the Ford Transit Owners' Club, which she became the honorary president of.

The timing of the show, well before the dominant pattern of the working day begun, was emphasized by reference to cleaners or coffee and buns to sustain everyone, as Broadcasting House was presented as waking-up in synchrony with homes across the nation. The timing suggested and licenced intimacy and informality; audiences were in their bedrooms and bathrooms engaged in the intimate rituals of washing, dressing and cleaning teeth. Listeners were encouraged to 'swing a marbled limb' to get a leg in a pant while sympathy was expressed on Monday for those leaving their home and familiar loo seat to work away for the week. The assumed intimate spaces in which the show was heard enabled it to develop a uniqueness which rested upon bringing the mundane unsaid and unseen facets of intimate domestic life into a public forum. Themes of correspondence also focused upon intimate activities and included: a lengthy discussion on the problem of 'being caught short' or 'needing a place to pee', followed by another heated discussion in Autumn 1999 on how frequently bras should be washed – and whether those who changed their bra only once a week were 'dirty girties'.

Discussion of the private, domestic and personal spheres flowed in, out and around debates about politics. In its most successful format between the mid-1990s and mid-noughties, the show put the tribulations of domestic households on a par with the political world of news and politicians. It moved between discussion of how to deal with piles of letters and debris that accumulate in the home, cooking disasters and the problems of making a reliable Yorkshire pudding, to extracts from the newspapers. Neither area was privileged over the other: all were referred to through frivolous and gossipy discourse and exchanges with the female newsreaders which could leave the listeners with the impression that bulletins about the broadcasters' health or choice of clothes might be as important as those on political leaders. Indeed, the show was peppered with comments about the mundane of Sarah Kennedy's own life: what she's cooking for friends, or events of the previous day and comments such as 'I got back from the cricket – it was so blinking cold I had to light a fire'. The linguistic style was of chatter and gossip, which has already been identified as broadcast talk; however this show took it to a new level, conveying a feminized and domestic mundaness which did not even bow to the rationalized discussion of the powerful, but instead revelled in transgression and gossip. In the later 1990s Kennedy remarked: 'Talking of girls there's a picture of Kate Howe, the sports minister. She won't like that photo I don't think. There's a picture of her with a horse and unfortunately they look just the same.' Her selections of news items from the newspapers emphasized trivialization of news stories. Indeed a story about a keep-fit enthusiast who attempted to cycle across the world, without leaving his bedroom, by watching videos, led her to comment in a concerned way that she hoped he has a banana down his shorts to avoid suffering from lacerations. At times politically incorrect personal opinion and gossipy style created a democratizing discourse which allowed audience engagement. A discussion in 2000 explored what the Pope should be given for an eightieth birthday party should he drop by. Alongside suggestions that he should be given a loaf and two fishes and left to sort it out for himself, she added the comment that she quite liked this Pope but that he was wrong on birth control, bringing together private standards of morality, values and emotions in a democratizing and equalizing discourse (Hermes, 1995).

Such 'off the cuff' comments endorsed a distinct element of the show in its heyday: the illusion of the precariousness of its presentation; the performance included comments that she is sorry she sounds a bit distracted something just fell on her head; and references to her having to hunt for the travel news or newspaper extracts caught behind the paper clips. Occasionally, unexpectedly the wrong music appeared to come on or she made comments about needing to clean CDs on her skirt, and shared her anxiety about getting up and getting to the show on time. On top of these arguably scripted 'slips', which were complemented by occasions when Sarah's slurring of her words could well be mistaken as a consequence of alcoholic overindulgence, the famous un-PC slips led at times to controversy and condemnation. They all, however, suggested the precariousness of her style of broadcasting and negated of the usually 'absent script writer' of radio, adding to a sense of intimacy.

The programme conveyed an assumption that the private and the political are equally important and entwined: her political judgements, based upon private premises and prejudices, invited viewers to also make judgments. As one *Evening Standard* writer suggested: 'Sometimes she just witters on about her auntie's cat ... but – come on – this is why her fans love her. She is surely an antidote to the clinical side of modern life ... long may she ramble!' (12 August 2007). The uncertainty of her presentation and her intimate style led to tensions with the BBC, which became increasingly nervous about her idiosyncrasies, and her programme ended in 2010. The *Daily Mail* suggested that 'Sources at the BBC say that in the end her time had come because she was simply too posh, too old, too dotty, too Right-wing and too much of a loose cannon. To say she did not fit in with the prevailing culture at the institution would be an understatement' (23 September 2010). Other programming was already increasingly merging public and domestic spheres and styles.

NEWS AND *NEWSNIGHT*: ETHICAL MAN AND *WAR ON TWO FRONTS*

In the era of availability, television and radio news does not give explanations, the multiplicity of news sources renders this impossible, instead it attempts, as Ellis (2000) suggests, 'to work through' problems or issues. Thus broadcasting 'exhausts an area of concern, smothering it in explanations from almost every angle'. (Ellis, 2000, pp. 79–80). The working through of issues which can occur in fictional or non-fictional texts, through images, talk and discussion, is not an even or impartial process. It is subject to institutional, economic and generic constraints, which are as likely to produce uncertainty, confusion and alienation as informed and engaged citizens. News in the late twentieth and twenty-first century is delivered through a multitude of media outlets: the press, the internet and mobile phones all compete for viewers with broadcasting channels and 24-hour news channels. The personalities of newscasters, and the style and treatment of news stories differentiate broadcasters. The personalities and experts who discuss economic policy, foreign affairs and sporting events both provide a unique element of a particular broadcaster's news coverage and extend the air time that this coverage takes up. Hence the gossip which 'occurs in exchanges between journalists, where previous news, already known to the participants, is up for further discussion' (Tolson, 2006, p. 64) has become a feature of news coverage, 'Journalists familiar with one another address each other on first name terms, humour, banter and colloquialisms may be part of a conversational, intimate and gossipy exchange' (Tolson, 2006, pp. 68–9). The speculation of the broadcasters, who utilize an informal, domestic and even feminized discourse, fits more comfortably into the domestic setting in which news is consumed – more comfortably than the formal modes of address of the immediate post-war era.

The domestication of political news and British politics was given an extra impetus by the reintroduction of breakfast television in 1983 which provided a new pseudo-domestic environment for the interrogation of politicians as guests on the sofa; their views were interspersed with celebrities from show business, musicians, sports personalities and 'ordinary people' with extraordinary lives. Furthermore, in the contemporary celebritized culture, the domestic lives of the famous and the powerful have become news items in themselves: a phenomenon which was perhaps most obvious during the 'Diana era' of British cultural politics, which included the Martin Bashir 1995 *Panorama* interview with the Princess of Wales, who discussed her marriage, post-natal depression and self-harming. That *Panorama,* which could have been categorized as a hard news current affairs programme, aired this interview is indicative of a new fluidity about what was private, tittle-tattle or entertainment and what serious news was. Broadcasting had played a significant role in these shifts: fluidifying as it does the boundaries of public and private, for communications technologies have themselves, as Morley argues, 'simultaneous capacity to articulate together that which is separate, to bring the outside world into the home' (2000, p. 87).

The soft-sofa interview, which celebrity-politician Tony Blair enthusiastically embraced following his election to the leadership of the Labour party in 1994, included interviews on radio and television with Des O'Connor, Steve Wright and Fern Britain, further blurred the boundaries of the domestic private world and that of politics. Blair's legacy as a celebrity politician was also enthusiastically embraced by David Cameron who invited TV cameras into his home, was filmed doing mundane domestic tasks such as making coffee, or looking after his disabled son Ivan. His wife's interview about his domestic untidiness and inability to turn off his Blackberry during the 2010 election campaign were arguably a contrived presentation of himself as an 'ordinary guy'. What is interesting is that this required him to be situated domestically, as if the domestic space gave him a connection with the viewers at home. Media texts are however polysemic, viewers sceptical and knowing, the degree to which viewers responded positively to images of a wealthy politician's domestic spaces is debatable.

The domestication of political news has also been facilitated by significant developments in the technology used to produce news; the miniaturization, transportability and mass production of new media technology has accelerated news formats' reformulation so that not only do they emphasize informality but also an increasing use of audience/'ordinary people', and a focus on the personal and domestic in news stories. Government spending and budgets are explored at the personal level, camera crews enter viewers' homes to discuss what government action will mean for them and their domestic lives. It is now rare for either the news or documentary to be without the almost obligatory vox pops or amateur footage captured on a mobile phone. If, as Ellis (2000) argues, the twentieth century was a century of witness, the twenty-first century has significantly widened the possibility of who does the witnessing.

A further blurring of domestic and news agendas occurred when television cameras entered the domestic life of the investigative reporter Justin Rowlatt and his family as they were challenged to live as ethically as possible for a year and to significantly reduce their carbon footprint. As he explained on his blog, which along with spasmodic reports on *Newsnight* updated viewers throughout the year:

> Ethical living ... means thinking through every single aspect of my life and considering the impact all my actions and decisions have on the environment and on other people ...
>
> What we want to explore is what a pretty ordinary family can do to reduce their impact on the environment without – in my case – moving out of my terraced house in central London. (http://news.bbc.co.uk/1/hi/programmes/newsnight/4736228.stm, 22 February 2006)

The resulting film owed much to the traditions of docusoap and reality television and led to him being accused of exploiting his wife and family with the intrusiveness of the film cameras.

The film was edited and featured in *Newsnight*, and its personal domestic focus gave a much higher profile to debates about climate change and what was an ultimately pessimistic discussion on the possibility of individual's actions influencing global warming.

Alternatively, the effects of political decisions on domestic lives were explored in a documentary entitled *Helmand: A War on Two Fronts* (BBC 2, 19 July 2010), which featured Second Battalion A Company of the Yorkshire Regiment, as the soldiers and their families began a six-month tour of duty in Helmand Province, Afghanistan. Shown at 9 p.m., it was followed by a discussion on *Newsnight* with some of the participants – conducted by Kirsty Wark, herself a mother of a son of army recruitment age. The title's reference to two fronts gave equal status to army personnel fighting against the Taliban and the wives and mothers fighting to survive on the Home Front. On *Newsnight* Wark commented: 'One of the striking elements of the film is that it is harder for the people back home.'

The disruption to domestic life that the soldiers' tour of duty in Helmand created is explained by one wife describing the last time her husband came back from Afghanistan: 'in his head he leaves me before he goes and doesn't come back when he returns'. This disruption is emphasized by film of wives saying goodbye to their husbands on their doorsteps at 2 in the morning. Listening to soldiers' vox-pops of their everyday lives, video diaries and letters to families, positions the television audience on a par with the families at home, as do images of the soldiers receiving parcels. The interrelationship of home and war fronts is indicated when one soldier explains: 'I'm really starting to feel homesick, I miss my son, sometimes the only thing that keeps you going is thinking about home.' Life at the front is domesticated by images of soldiers on Christmas Day donning Father Christmas hats and sitting around a large 'family' table to eat Christmas lunch: a carved bird and crackers on the table operate as the symbolic icons of home.

None of the company lose their lives, but one mother describes in detail how her only son phoned her to say he'd been shot by a sniper. The domestic is represented by women and children – fathers and brothers do not have a voice – rather the strength of the community is represented as the women, many of whom are in married quarters and are contrasted with an alternative family of men in the army under A company's paternalistic officer. The company are mentoring Afghan soldiers; when one of them had his arms and legs blown off by an IED (improvised explosive device) stressing the threat that hung over all the men and whether they would ultimately return to their everyday domestic lives.

The documentary moves between the Helmand and home but it is the wives' and mothers' perspectives which dominate the homecoming at the end of the soldiers' six-month tour of duty. The camera remains with waiting wives, mothers, families and children, as a small baby with a 'My Dad's a hero' t-shirt on, families holding balloons, banners and cameras, all assemble on an army base. The pain and anxiety of waiting at home is laid bare by the reassurance provided from a soldier informing them he will let them know when the soldiers are 10 minutes away, and the tears and anxiety are not obscured as families catch their first glimpse of their husbands' and sons' arrival. The structuring absence in such coverage is, of course, the iconic and familiar media images of the Union Jack-draped bodies of soldiers killed in Afghanistan, repatriated at RAF Lyneham and driven through the Wiltshire market town of Wootton Bassett, which paid silent respect in a very televisual tribute to the dead. Compared to the death toll in previous military conflicts, or the annual death toll on British roads, the numbers killed in Afghanistan may seem small but emphasis on the domestic effects of war in *War on Two Fronts* and images of weeping mothers and wives at funerals of service personnel give the deaths a new political significance.

REMEMBRANCE TELEVISION; *THE FALLEN* (BBC, 2008)

By the mid-1990s, newspaper critics were expressing concern about the state of broadcasting, with anxieties growing that, as a result of market-force ideas, video and satellite technology, a particular sense of British national identity, experienced through shared television viewing, was coming to an end. Ian Irvine lamented in the *Evening Standard* that 'television which never did threaten the death of conversation now really does threaten the death of a shared national TV culture' (29 August 1991, p. 7). Yet with the Afghan and Iraq Wars in the early twenty-first century, television became a focus for national shared viewing around the growth in the broadcast programming that accompanied Remembrance Day, such that Billen, writing in the *New Statesman*, remarked: 'at this rate, Poppy Day is going to end up bigger than Christmas' (20 September 2006). In this, broadcasting reflected a national obsession with remembrance which was a consequence of convergent and sometimes contradictory cultural forces: opposition to the wars in Iraq and Afghanistan, a yearning for a sense of both national identity and a preoccupation with the horrors of war in a period of cultural relativism. Remembrance, along with some sporting events (such as the Football World Cup), offered a national television culture but one which although connected with the very public sphere of war was strongly linked to the domestic spaces in which those who died were mourned.

Remembrance television, with its domestic focus, contributed to a growing preoccupation with the wives and families of those serving in the forces, evidenced in the introduction of the Elizabeth Cross in 2009. It continued to provide access to the traditional ceremonies at the Cenotaph and the British Legion's Festival of Remembrance from the Royal Albert Hall – as they had since the inter-war era. This became, however, only part of what with the ninetieth anniversary of the armistice in 2008, the BBC began referring to as its 'remembrance season'. Television with its 'public and all inclusive nature' ... and 'tendency to collapse formally distinct situations into one' (Meyrowitz, 1985, p. 92), was able to create remembrance texts which merged the public and the private, the political and the critical, the formal and the informal icons of remembrance and also offered a more domestic and emotionally unrestrained form of remembrance than traditional ceremonies.

The documentary *The Fallen* (BBC 2, 2008), screened on the eve of Remembrance Sunday, drew unashamedly upon the intimate revelatory style of chat shows and reality television, in remembering contemporary combatants who have died in the Iraq or Afghan wars. It contained approximately 3 hours of their families, almost exclusively positioned in their homes, narrating their stories of the lives, deaths and mourning for those who had died. The camera accompanied the narration with exploration of the family home, dwelling on pictures on the wall, mantelpiece and sideboard, empty bedrooms, and mementos which emphasize that a young life has been cut short. There is strong emphasis in the *The Fallen* on how families create domestic shrines to their sons and husbands who were lost in war; the camera dwells on memento cabinets in their sitting rooms, images of the deceased on the wall, on mugs, on clocks and in picture frames, at one point on a memorial in the corner of a garden, and rituals such as a regimental flags placed on the dining table during meals or a dead lover's shirts kept under the pillow.

One father was accompanied by the camera and the viewer into his son's bedroom where a football shirt and boots, a Christmas present to his son, were displayed. The objects were unused and metaphorically refer to the potential lives of killed young soldiers. The visual style of the text is set by home video extracts and vox-pops. *The Fallen* celebrates individual feelings and intimate revelations, utilizing therapeutic and confessional discourses of storytelling, enabling 'everyday experience to be transformed from a private to a public forum' (White, 1992, p. 385). This is not to suggest that the text offers the unmediated narratives and experiences of the bereaved families: far from it. It is an edited, structured and produced text. For example, one of the first interviews focuses on a young boy whose father was the first British soldier to die in Afghanistan; he is playing with transformers in his bedroom. It suggests both the human cost of war and critiques cultural attitudes to war learned at an early age in the home; a point emphasized later by a soldier, whose brother had been killed, explaining: 'we were about four years old and we'd go walking over Salisbury Plain and we'd see tanks and troops on the ground ... we'd go and play at army in the woods and as young boys I think it was installed in us then.'

The Fallen's construction of a chronological roll call of names of those who died accompanied by their age and date of death, in a white print with a golden hue on a black background, grinds relentlessly on, interspersed with individual narratives, which simultaneously personalized and universalized the experience of bereavement for families shattered by war. It also contributed to the creation 'a new mixed public sphere where common knowledge and everyday experience play a much larger role' (White, 1992, p. 383). Arguably the producers crossed the boundary into exploitation of private emotions when they chose to broadcast young teenagers whose father had committed suicide while serving in Afghanistan. Their anger, while understandable, produce emotive interviews that should arguably have remained in the private domestic sphere in which they were expressed rather than be aired on television (and latter streamed via YouTube on the internet) for wider public consumption. Nevertheless *The Fallen*'s emphasis on the brutalizing effects of war, the turmoil and destruction it wreaks on domestic lives, articulated a strong criticism of armed conflict and contributed to political debates about the Iraq and Afghan wars.

From broadcasting's earliest period in the inter-war years, the domestic space in which it was primarily consumed shaped its discursive strategies and mode of address; at the end of the twentieth century and into the noughties, this inter-connection and these inter-relationships went further. Areas of intimate, personal life were discussed in broadcast media and became the subject of political discourse and governance. The concerns and experiences of domestic personal lives, however, also entered spheres in political debates and programming.

Chapter Eight

Still contesting and idealizing domesticity

Domesticity has always operated both in the imagination and as a lived experience, through both discursive and everyday practices. It has been structured and shaped by housewives themselves, experts, laws and governments, and by economic constraints, class and race. It has been suggested that broadcasting, as a domestic medium, has both shaped and been shaped by the discursive practices and the lived experiences of domesticity. At the end of the twentieth century, as the last chapter argued, broadcasting increasingly represented domesticity as in turmoil. Simultaneously domesticity both became the focus of political governance and debate. The boundaries between public and private, always porous, fluid and shifting became even more blurred, and yet the discursive construction of home as the heart of the nation, or as Morley suggests 'the "symbolic family" of the nation' (2000, p. 3), a haven of tranquillity, and a retreat from the anxiety, uncertainly and stress of the political and public spheres continued to hold an allure. Home continued to be idealized as a healing substitute for the everyday anxieties and experiences of both workplace and the personal relationships of contemporary post-modern culture.

The domestic turmoil portrayed in chat shows, soap-operas, reality television and drama in the latter part of the twentieth century did not result in an abandonment of the ideal of domesticity. Broadcasting, having increasingly given space to a range of the 'realities' (albeit constructed realities), was faced with negotiating the contradictions between these realities and the idealization of domesticity within which broadcast media have striven to take up a central place, replacing the hearth as icongraphically the heart of the home. As McCracken has pointed out,'the gap between the "real" and the "ideal" in social life is one of the most pressing problems that culture must deal with' (1988, p. 105). Rather than give up on the ideal of domesticity arguably broadcasting mirrors the broader culture in resorting to 'displaced meaning' as a strategy looking to find 'a place for its ideals' to be located (McCracken, 1988, p. 105). The idealized meaning of domesticity, rather than be abandoned, may be displaced either into an idealized domesticity in the future, obtainable through consumerism, human effort and attitudes or displaced onto a nostalgic supposedly golden age of the idealized domesticity of the past. This can be seen in the increasing popularity of costume dramas such as *Lark Rise to Candleford* (BBC, 2008–11) and historical reality programmes such as *The Coal House* (BBC, 2007) or the nostalgic element of cookery programmes such as *Nigella Express*. However, these idealized versions of domesticity which emerged were emphatically performative – neither natural, private, calm or necessarily feminized. Close examination of the contradictory and complex nature of texts such as the cookery programmes of Jamie Oliver or Nigella Lawson, or costume drama such *as Lark Rise to Candleford* and the discourses that surround them, suggests that in contemporary culture, just as in the 1930s, domesticity remains problematic. Idealizations were illusive, contested, fragile and insecure; domesticity, as the recent success of the Channel 4 programme *Come Dine With Me* (Channel 4, 2005–) demonstrates, remains a contested concept: the subject of ethical debates.

NOSTALGIC DOMESTICITIES: IDEALIZING THE PAST IN *LARK RISE TO CANDLEFORD* (2008–11) AND REALITY TV

The end of the twentieth century saw the emergence of a new genre of historical programming – historical reality TV – which required participants to re-enact the past by living for a fixed period of time in the physical setting and material circumstances of another era. Given that the limitations on reconstructing the public worlds of the workplace or battlefield within contemporary health and safety regulations, perhaps it is no surprise that the focus of filming within these programmes has had a tendency to dwell upon domestic life and spaces. Within such texts clothes, food and domestic constraints are used to signify a sense of differentiation from contemporary culture, as are very clearly defined gender roles and class divisions. *The 1900s House* (Channel 4, 1999), *The 1940s House* (Channel 4, 2001) and *Edwardian Country House* (Channel 4, 2002) and *The Coal House* (BBC, 2007) constructed versions of the past which clearly predicated upon the general public's fascination with domesticity and in which intensive domestic labour was central to survival.

Domesticity, however, is signified as a displaced ideal through a number of strategies, the 'ordinary' people who take part are chosen for a television role, they momentarily become celebrities. As they discuss their views and thoughts with the rest of the viewing public, their experience is idealized for a media-saturated confessional culture. Their participation in the programme is presented as a 'holiday' from everyday life; indeed the programmes often draw attention to the very different roles that they have had in non-TV lives, for example Lady Olive Cooper, in *The Edwardian Country House*, viewers were told was a GP. In the opening credits of *The Coal House* contestants are seen initially wearing contemporary clothes, moving towards Stack Square, where *The Coal House* was filmed. Through editing they morph into 1927s costumes so the show can begin. Another element of the domestic ideal in such texts is the emphasis on communality; although tensions add to the audience's prurient pleasure in viewing, the nostalgic ideal is invariably linked to a sense of 'all in this together'. The families in *The Coal House*, or the surrogate family of servants below stairs in *The Edwardian Country House*, are portrayed as having an affinity: a communality which constructs a domestic community. The significance of 'attitudes' to constructing communities is emphasized when, those perceived to be aloof or have the wrong attitude, such as the tutor in *The Edwardian Country House*, while producing eminently watchable television also draws censure from the voiceover. To maintain audience interest and vary episodes, special events are introduced, nationally or personally recognized moments in time which emphasize communality, for example the celebration of a birthday in *The Coal House* or Bonfire Night in *The Edwardian Country House*.

At one level the increasing popularity of costume dramas such as *Lark Rise to Candleford* and historical reality programmes such as *The Coal House* rests upon their ability to displace the location of ideals of domesticity on to some point in the past, but they do not do so unproblematically. Performing ideal domesticity is seen to rest upon a significant level of effort and the right attitude of mind. In *The Edwardian Country House*, which highlights the class structure of 'the belle epoch', the effort is almost totally undertaken by those playing the roles of domestic servants. Indeed, so extreme was the effort required that two scullery maids quickly left the series – one in the middle of the night. In *The Coal House* or *The 1940s House* domesticity required intense labour by all participants; keeping the stove going, managing the washing, shopping for food on limited incomes and then cooking it, without recourse to contemporary technology, were all core elements of the housewives days in *The Coal House*, while in both programmes children were expected to undertake domestic tasks. The ideal of domesticity was attained in some way by the communality of domestic labour and more importantly by an attitude which valued domestic labour as significant. In this they mirror some of the arguments of inter-war and second-wave women's groups. However, arguably partaking in domestic labour in reality television is leisure distanced from 'real' life; it is an escape to domestic labour rather than a life sentence of drudgery.

The emphasis on effort and attitudes mirrors the lifestyle programme *How Clean is Your House?* (ITV, 2003–9), within which in each 30-minute episode Kim Woodburn and Aggie McKenzie enter a filthy house on the request of the homeowner's family, friends or neighbours and elicit a make-over of the property via determined cleaning and clearing out of clutter. At one level it was an alternative make-over programme against the prevailing consumerist spirit of the era, as idealized domesticity required little expenditure; instead it drew attention to importance of effort and attitude in creating the ideal. Furthermore, the 'recipes' for cleaning owe much to a bygone era – lemon juice or bicarbonate of soda are more likely to be used than contemporary wonder products such as Mr Muscle. However, a nostalgic emphasis on domestic labour is open to a range of readings, in *The Coal House* it is all-consuming, leaving women little scope to do anything else, while *How Clean is Your House?* required an army of cleaners to sort out a house. Questionably such texts suggest that a barrier to ideal domesticity is time, which has of course been an important discourse in the selling of much domestic technology, such as washing machines or food mixers, in the twentieth century. Arguably the structuring absence in this discursive construction, suggesting a conservative tradition of thought, is that time for domestic labour is restricted by the increasing number of women in the workforce. The Office of National Statistics points out: 'Over the past four decades, the proportion of women in employment has grown markedly. At the start of 1971, the employment rate for women was 56 per cent compared with 70 per cent in the three months to December 2008' (National Office of Statistics, 2009). Alternatively, the particularity of the idealization of domesticity offered in *Lark Rise to Candleford* is centred around the lives of the inhabitants of the post office in the small Oxfordshire market town of Candleford, where the boundaries between public and private spheres, paid work and domestic leisure are seamlessly merged and blurred together.

Television is a commercial enterprise and, at a time when Britain has struggled for exports, British heritage production dramas such as *Lark Rise to Candleford* have been sold successfully on the international market. Inevitably the commercial imperative shapes the selectivity of historical and heritage texts:

foreign sales may require an 'attractive cultural representation of the past which is shaped by the need to produce tradable goods and which connote an England that exists outside TV only in the historic imaginary. As Samuel points out: 'The weather … has improved out of all recognition … Poor are sanitised – well scrubbed and with no trace of physical deformity … Even shabby genteel are upgraded' thus 'the past can never be transcribed, it always has to be re-invented' as it become 'a plaything of the present' (1996, p. 124). Jameson has criticized the 'mesmerising new aesthetic mode' – 'the waning of our history', which he suggests 'denies us the lived possibility of experiencing history in some active way', suggesting that heritage becomes the present in costume, with seduction imagery (1991, p. 19). Jameson is not alone in his attack heritage and the nostalgia industries. Higson (2003) was vociferous in his criticism of the 1980s heritage films – such as those produced by Merchant and Ivory – suggesting they were an argument for Thatcherism. The complexity of the gender representations and the gendered consumption of heritage texts, as Monk and Sargeant (2002) suggest, is often underplayed. Indeed Samuel has pointed out that 'heritage baiting is an exclusively male sport' (1996, p. 272), which has had little influence on broadcasters who have produced a plethora of adaptations of Dickens, Hardy and Gaskell novels in recent years.

Drawing upon Wheeler's assertion 'that nostalgia isn't nasty' (1994), rather it suggests a rejection of the status quo, it can also be suggested that there are moments and fragments of recognition that heritage texts address. Their themes are culturally familiar – even if only in the regime of the imaginary – and they operate as critics of the contemporary status quo. Certainly *Lark Rise to Candleford* which *The Times* has described as 'shamelessly heartwarming Horlicks TV made with extra sugar, double cream and chocolate on' (12 November 2008) is based upon Flora Thompson's book that charts heroine Laura's shift from her childhood, in the rural village of Lark Rise, to the commercial retail sphere of the local market town of Candleford, where she becomes an assistant in the post office. Laura epitomizes upwardly aspiring, but insecure working-class girls of the era who, as Winship argues, focus upon being 'nice and neat and nice and tidy' (2000). Her incorporation into the Candleford retail culture and transition from her rural family of origin to independence in the retail sphere, operate as a metaphor of society and cultural change at the end of the nineteenth century.

In late nineteenth-century retail spaces, both played with and blurred the boundaries between not only the rural and the urban but also the nineteenth and the twentieth centuries, and most importantly the domestic and commercial worlds (see Rappaport, 2001). Arguably it is this blurring which facilitates a representation of retailing as a space of possible female power, not as consumers but as retailers, providing a source of income without compromising the gentile femininity expected of middle-class women, *Lark Rise to Candleford* suggests that retailing offered women the potential to be: employers, property owners, gossips and opinion makers. The commercial and retail culture of Candleford is personified by Ruby and Pearl Pratt's dress shop, also particularly by Dorcas Lane who owns and runs the post office and the accompanying forge and whose pleasures lie in a little gentle flirtation, meddling, gossiping and life's little luxuries including well-fitting, flattering clothes. Indeed, meddling, gossip, talk, charitable acts, hospitality and displeasure are the weapons of Dorcas's power. Retailing spaces are frequently represented on television as backdrops for style gurus on lifestyle programming such as Trinny and Susanah on *What Not to Wear* (BBC, 2001–5) who enacted what McRobbie (2004) correctly describes as 'symbolic violence' on misguided and hapless members of the general public, whose tastes did not match their own upper-middle class ones. In drama and comedy, where the focus is more often on the retailer, the retailing space – as in *Lark Rise to Candleford* – is domesticated; there is a focus upon the personal relationships, symbolically families, epitomized in the retailing spaces of sit-coms such as *Open all Hours* (BBC, 1973–85) and *Are*

You Being Served? (BBC, 1972–85) or the shops in soap-operas such as *Coronation Street* (ITV, 1960–), *Eastenders* (BBC, 1985) or *Emmerdale* (ITV, 1972–).

The people who worked in Candleford post office – Dorcas and Laura – Zillah the cook/servant (superseded by Minnie in series 2), Thomas Brown the head postman, Matthew who ran the forge, function as a surrogate family, further emphasized when Zilla explains, 'I've never had a family except this post office' (series 1, episode 6). Indeed the text offers a new millennium version of an elective family made up of unattached individuals indicative of the increasing proportion of single people living alone in the twenty-first century. The boundaries of the post office's 'family' unit are, however, porous – visitors and children come and go in many episodes, eating and/or sleeping at the post office. One postwoman and her son depart in series 1 but not before her escaped convict husband has also been offered the hospitality of food and a wash before handing himself in to the magistrate and police. Furthermore, on a number of occasions children stay at the post office (Emma Timminns' baby, James Downland's son), emphasizing the maternalistic as opposed to paternalistic in the domestic modus of operandi that governs this retailing space under Dorcas Lane's control. The post office version of family life is portrayed as both a nostalgic ideal; yet Dorcus and the post office are also narratively positioned as offering a future ideal of domesticity within the text. Interestingly, once Downland's son – 'Little Man' as he became known – came to live at the post office, Dorcus became to all intents and purposes a single mother, suggesting another reworking of the ideal of domesticity.

The text interweaves the daily activities of the post office – the delivery rounds, sorting of post, selling stamps, sending and receiving telegrams – with personal daily domestic activities – bedtime discussions, eating, interfering with other people's lives and gossiping – endorsing Silverstone's (1994) argument that it is 'dailiness' which is the key phenomenological characteristic of television. The fluidity between the dailiness of work and domestic life – the 'family relationship' – is signified by the sharing of plentiful meals around the kitchen table in all episodes. Indeed this table is just as central as the post office counter and the postman eats while wearing his uniform, suggesting the integration of work and domestic spaces.

The significance, indeed poignancy, of *Lark Rise to Candleford*'s portrayal of the central role of a community post office at historical juncture when many local post offices were threatened with closure, is just one facet of the complexity of representations in this text in which Dorcas Lane explains in a discourse any contemporary community could articulate in opposition to post-office closures: 'the post office is more than stamps and postal orders – it is the soul of the community' (series 1, episode 5). The costume drama's ability to raise contemporary political discourses is not unique. Threats to the post office or to the domestic households of Lark Rise and Candleford residents – whether from post office inspectors, absentee or unreasonable landlords, violent husbands or debt the inevitable change which are all accompanied by anxiety – are, as Sturken (2008) argues, familiar themes in heritage texts through which audiences simultaneously both consume fear and are sold comfort.

The post office offers not only retailing domesticity but a contemporary family of consumers, befitting the commercial culture in which it will be consumed, and Laura is quick to admit she 'couldn't help falling in love with the luxuries of Candleford' (series 1, episode 1). While Dorcas Lane describes baths, food, jugged hare, morning cake, feather pillows and fine shoes at various times as 'my one weakness'. Although Colin Campbell (2005) argues that modern capitalism is influenced by a protestant work ethic of delayed gratification and righteous virtue, as opposed to a consumer ethic of novelty individualism and desire framed by the spirit of romanticism; in the Candledford post office these apparently opposing strands are reconciled, so too are the worlds of work and domesticity reconciled. The popularity of these idealized reconciliations suggests much about the tensions of the very different experiences of mundane domesticity which many viewers encountered in their everyday lives.

HOME-PURCHASING SHOWS: PROPERTY A STEPPING STONE TO IDEALIZED DOMESTICITY

Drawing upon McCracken's work it can be suggested that another way of negotiating the gap between the ideal and the mundane experience of domesticity is, in consumer culture, through the purchase of goods. Consumer goods, McCracken (1988) argues, have the potential to act as bridges to 'an ideal' displaced into an elusive future. In the post-Thatcher era, domestic houses themselves became *the* consumer purchase, offering a bridge to an idealized future domesticity in a property-owning democracy. A range of television programmes, including *Location, Location, Location* (Channel 4, 2001–11), *Homes Under the Hammer* (BBC 1, 2003–), *Escape to the Country* (BBC, 2007–), *A Place in the Sun: Home or Away* (Channel 4, 2006) and accompanying web browsing (particularly since the founding of the RightMove website in 2000) have enabled, even encouraged individuals to covet property, offering if not the realization of idealized domesticity, at least a stepping stone or bridge towards this ideal. Correspondingly the proliferation of television hours facilitated by the popularization of digital and satellite technology since the 1990s has brought about an expansion of cheap, lifestyle programming. Shot on location with a small production team and an endless supply of C-list celebrities lining up to be presenters, the genre of 'house programmes' is indeed cheap programming. Furthermore, as it is classed as 'factual' programming' no repeat fees are paid to the presenters and the audience's appetite for property porn can be catered for even more cheaply on channels, such as More4, with schedules made up entirely from repeats.

The increasing centrality of home ownership to idealized domesticity owes much to the political agenda of the Conservative government that was elected under Prime Minister Margaret

Thatcher in 1979. A series of measures shifted the balance within housing provision away from the state towards private-owned and rented accommodation. A central tenet, of what was both a discursive and practical shift in the understanding of home, was the introduction of local authority tenants' 'right to buy' their houses, introduced in the 1980s. 'This measure enabled council tenants who saw the advantage of owner-occupation to achieve that goal at a very substantial discount. It was a vote-winner and proved very popular with the skilled working class' (Stewart and Burridge, 1989, p. 70). Pressure on local authorities to release land for housing was also increased, as previous legislation such as the Community Land Act of 1975 was repealed. The economic recession of the 1980s and local authority public spending cuts led to limited house building in any sector. Furthermore, council house rents rose substantially as the council houses' ownership was transferred to Housing Associations. For a significant proportion of tenants, rent rises were alleviated by housing benefit, for others buying their council house became more attractive, particularly on smaller, rural and suburban housing estates. These policy changes, and the rhetoric which accompanied them, served to make the ideal domestic space an owner-occupied home (albeit with a mortgage). Thus, as Brunsden points out, 'the last 20 years of the twentieth century saw the consolidation and proliferation of everyday discourses of value and investment associated with the purchase of housing' (2003, p. 8). For many the 'distant location for his or her personal ideals' (McCracken, 1988, p. 113) were seen as one stage closer when they stepped onto the property ladder and, according to the Office of National Statistics, between 1971 and 2002 home ownership increased from 49 to 69 per cent. Most of this increase occurred in the 1980s, and it levelled off after that. Importantly, property purchase was a ladder. Property was increasingly seen as something to be bought and sold for profit. Indeed, despite occasional slumps in the housing market, average house prices rose from an average of £23,497 in 1980 to £54,245 in 1990, while by 2010 the average house price was £163,244

(Nationwide Building Society, 2011). A corresponding 'explosion in home improvement programmes', as Holliday notes, became a 'remarkable phenomenon on British Television …' which 'can be effectively split into two categories – interior decorating and house buying and selling – and both categories claim to add value to your home, either through its immediate sale or purchase, or through its future sales potential' (2005, p. 65).

As the construction of the ideal domestic space began to be seen in more economic terms, so it became the terrain increasingly of male as well female expertise. In *Location, Location, Location* (2001–11), having first established the material circumstances which render domesticity as less than ideal – not enough space for recent or imminent additions to the family, too much time spent travelling to work, living in rented accommodation – 'professional property experts Kirstie Allsopp and Phil Spencer scour the country on behalf of house-hunters' (Channel 4 website). The search for potential properties that, even if not actually matching couple's requirements at least come some way to doing so or to renegotiating these requirements, takes place off camera. Kirstie, Phil, the camera crew and the audience all then view the properties together and the audience is invited to speculate upon the prospective owners' reactions and decision over their property purchase. Although occasionally featuring individual purchasers or gay and lesbian couples, a significant element of the programme's dynamic and audience engagement rests upon exploring the tensions between couples, predominantly a 'husband and wife', and their reactions to houses. There is often an assumption that men are holding the 'purse strings' and occasionally that the house search is framed by the need to facilitate male hobbies, for example provide space for a sports car to be restored, or motorbikes to be parked in the garden. However men are not in the main positioned only as providers but also as active players in domesticity, expressing views upon the style of house or the sort of kitchens they wish to cook in.

A recurrent theme in *Location, Location, Location*, however, is the unattainability of the ideal: the gap between financial reality and the idealized is addressed directly at some of point in the show, as Kirstie gives the potential purchasers the 'talk' which emphasizes compromise. Couples are asked to prioritize from what would otherwise be a range of unattainable dreams. They are shown homes which meet their criteria but are on busy roads, further from their desired neighbourhood or require significant remodelling, and they are encouraged to see either the prospective house purchase as a step on the way to their ideal or something which could be reworked into their ideal. In one episode the wife moved from bursting into tears on first sight of house to enthusiastically looking forward to moving in. Her reconciliation with the offending house was brought about by her gaining an understanding that it was but a step on the way to her still-held ideal. As the British property market hit uncertainty following the world financial crisis of 2007, the discourse of the show moved towards construction of home and lifestyle and placed less emphasis on getting on the property ladder. The programme sometimes ends with a visit from Phil and Kirstie to the couple ensconced within their new home, endorsing the attainment of their domestic ideal, occasionally emphasized by the arrival of a new baby, while the success of the relocation is frequently verified by the couples who affirm they have more 'quality time' with each other or their children.

The financial resources of many of the participants of *Location, Location, Location* placed their decision making and *A Place in the Sun: Home or Away* dilemmas well beyond the experience of their viewers. For example one young couple toyed with how best to spend three-quarters of a million pounds on a house in Kent. The participants are encouraged to buy into the desirability of Thatcher's legacy of a property-owning ideal by the show's discursive endorsement of a predominantly right of centre political agenda, which is further developed by Kirstie's open political affiliation to the Conservative party. For many of the viewers, the allure of the ideal of owning their own domestic space was perhaps exaggerated by its unattainability.

For example, according to the Nationwide Building Society, for a first-time buyer the typical price of a UK house 'was 2.9 times average earnings in the first quarter of 1985, rising to 3.9 in quarter 2 1989, 4.8 in quarter 3 2004, 5.4 in quarter 2 2007 and 4.5 in quarter 4 of 2010' (2011). Alternatively the programme can be seen to suggest that idealized domesticity is unattainable even to those with significant amounts of money.

This idealized domesticity is frequently displaced geographically from many of the audience's urban and suburban milieu onto the rural; in *Escape to the Country*, so frequently a repository of domestic idealization (see Andrews, 1997) or onto locations in other countries in *A Place in the Sun: Home or Away*. The structuring paradigm is that a move to another country, or the countryside, can facilitate a shift to a different way of life, and a different version of domesticity closer to the viewer's ideal. The proposed move offers a reconciliation of number of forces which were perceived as responsible for a less than idealized everyday life. These might be about work-life balance, a different pace of life, integration into a community, thus the move is seen to facilitate couples retiring, running their own business from home, being more self-sufficient or having more leisure time. A key facilitating component is maybe the cheapness of property in other countries which enables a greater realization of ideals, alternatively in other programming this is to be brought about by the strenuous efforts of home owners themselves.

REMAKING THE HOME: MAKE-OVER AND RENOVATION AND BUILDING STEPPING STONES TO THE IDEAL

In the late 1990s and early noughties, television provided guidance on how, through home improvements, renovations or building, ideal domestic spaces could be attained, in programmes such as *Room for Improvement* (Channel 4, 2006) and *Grand Designs* (Channel 4, 2001). At one level these programmes were driven by the commercial needs of the growing consumer culture of DIY, evidenced in chains such Homebase and Focus, and, as Taylor points out, they were part of the endless search by the media industries for increased market possibilities (Taylor, 2008, p. 105). Lifestyle programming offered endless scope for advertising and sponsorship deals, even if until 2011 product placement was strictly speaking forbidden. The idealization of the domestic space on display was obtainable by financial expenditure, suggesting that economic gain went hand-in-hand with the lifestyle choices such programming explored. Such popular factual programming was, as Hill has pointed out, 'a key weapon in the BBC's successful ratings and scheduling war with its rival ITV' (2004, p. 18), particularly the popular *Changing Rooms* (BBC, 1996–2004) which was structured around couples swopping houses with friends and neighbours for twenty-four hours during which time with the help of designers, they would redecorate one of their friend's rooms.

Broadcast initially on BBC2, the show's transfer after three series to a more popular BBC1 primetime evening slot signalled the centrality of domestic lifestyle to primetime (see Medhurst, 1999; Mosley, 2000). The focus on couples emphasized that as domesticity was no longer necessarily the prerogative of women, indeed as Putnam (1992, p. 195) suggests increasing investment in DIY was seen as a conjugal project. As lifestyle, gardening, home improvement and cookery entered prime-time evening schedules, these activities were constituted as the concerns of men and women, gay and straight, although culturally at least they remained predominantly the prerogative of the middle-classes. Good taste is as Bourdieu (1984) argues, both defined by and defines middle-classness. The middle-classes are, however, diverse and many of these programmes portrayed the tensions and frictions between factions of the middle-class.

Putnam points out however that 'conflict between cultural values … is a recurrent feature of home making' (1992, p. 202), consequently the 'big reveal' at end of *Changing Rooms* produced a range of emotional responses, the more extreme of which gained mythical status. As Bonner suggests 'A person's lifestyle is a concrete expression of self-identity, not a trivial addition, and the components of that lifestyle are substantially what ordinary television is concerned with, tastes, practices and possessions are all seen to reveal the self' (2003, p. 214). The suggested selves offered by redecorated rooms, given the increasingly outrageous and performative style that the *Changing Rooms'* designers revelled in, affronted many. One couple expressed their dislike of Laurence Llewellyn-Bowen's redesign of their living room with the pronouncement that it had been turned into 'a tart's boudoir'. In another show Anna Ryder Richardson's choice of framed erotic French undergarments around a room was greeted with the response 'why would I want this shit in my room? / I've got children'. At one level, in decorating a room the friends were expressing a judgement not merely of their friends' tastes but on their identity and selves; although usually over-influenced by the designer allocated from the *Changing Rooms'* team. The strength of emotional responses and the popularity of the programme provide an indication of the centrality of taste to identity construction at the turn of the new millennium.

Some social analysts had predicted that the conspicuous consumption of the 1980s would 'give way to a more thoughtful and cautious form of leisure in the 90s, whereby indulgence gave way to active and purposeful leisure which was time rather than money intensive' (Leisure in the Home Consultants, 1993). The 1990s, however, saw a huge rise in the UK DIY market which was by 2003 worth over £23 billion and funded to a significant degree by £13.6 billion of borrowing by householders (Holliday, 2005, p. 69). Property programmes and the shift to lifestyle in the prime-time slot that occurred at the end of the twentieth century can also be seen as a response to changing ideas about the gendered division of labour in the home, the feminist movement, increasing participation in the labour market by women, and more uncertain and fractured work-patterns for men which had all chipped away at the discursive construction of housework as a female responsibility. Practice was another thing – many men, as oral histories and autobiographies indicate, were involved with domestic tasks in the inter-war period and many looked after children or grandchildren, cooked or cleaned in the 1980s and 1990s but women continued to burden the greater responsibility for domestic labour.

There had been a long tradition of home decoration and DIY within British media and culture, for example within women's magazines and DIY magazines, in *Housewives Talks* and Mr Middleton's broadcasts in the inter-war years or *Women's Hour* and early television shows of the post-war era; what is distinctive about many television shows in the 1990s and noughties is the financial stake that was involved. Whereas *Changing Rooms*' make-overs were cheap, tacky and arguably easily removable, other programmes involved more structural and costly make-overs. Estate agents were frequently brought in to provide input on the financial return that home-improvements had brought about. In *Homes Under the Hammer* (where homes are bought at auction and then revamped or renovated), the boundary between those buying and doing-up homes to live in or as a business is straddled by participants. Many saw home renovation as a financial project and possibly the first step on their way to running their own business. *Property Ladder* (Channel 4, 2001) focused exclusively on individuals renovating property for profit, however as the property market became more precarious it was retitled *Property Snakes and Ladders* in 2009.

The uncertainty of the property market has not, it would appear, deterred participants to *Grand Designs* (Channel 4, 1999–) from their attempts to bring about the realization of an idealized domestic space. The scale and extra-ordinariness of their projects is signified by the title, as the Channel 4 website explains, they are 'Castles in the air'. 'Presenter Kevin McCloud follows some of Britain's most ambitious self-building projects, as intrepid individuals attempt to design and construct the home of their dreams.' High modernism and eco-friendly properties feature strongly but the range of buildings has included, for example, the renovation of a Newport folly with views of nine counties, a London house centred around a water garden, the renovation of a Yorkshire fourteenth-century castle, a Sussex woodman's cottage made entirely out of natural products and a kit house imported from the USA. Narratively each episode is centred on one build and always incorporates a degree of false jeopardy. Participants struggle to complete their building or renovation, threatened by spiralling costs, weather, late arrivals of core materials, building or planning regulations, technical problems, indecision or their own lack of knowledge and skill or unwillingness to take advice. Projects almost always however seem to be completed eventually, albeit often over time and budget.

Unlike many programmes on television, *Grand Designs* endorses the highly individualist, quirky and frequently extravagant tastes of the participants who are constructing both their homes and their identities through, it suggests, work, innovation and expenditure. Despite the appearance of occasionally environmentally friendly sustainable buildings, the series endorses a strongly capitalist ethos, where the only judgemental paradigm operational within the text is that of taste. Although Kevin McCloud questions taste and aesthetic choices, there is not one hint of questioning when one couple unwrap and install the £1,000 tap they have ordered explaining that it is definitely worth the money. Arguably the audience themselves may well question the extravagance and conspicuous consumption of the participants; particularly perhaps in the noughties – an era of unemployment and mortgage crisis – when for many property ownership had opened up yet another gap between 'an ideal' and lived experience. Nettleton, Burrows, England and Seaver's 'Study of Home Ownership and Poverty in Britain', carried out for the Joseph Rowntree Foundation (1999), concluded that half of those living in poverty in the UK were indeed home-owners – minority ethnic groups and single parents or divorced people making up a disproportional amount of these.

A more uncertain property market led to programmes such as *Room for Improvement* (Channel 4, 2004–), which guided home-owners through costly planning and restructuring of their homes as an alternative to buying and selling property. The unattainability of the domestic ideal for many is emphasized in *Room for Improvement* and a range of other DIY programmes. Participants frequently admit that their home improvements have gone over time and over budget, but a further acknowledgement that the 'task of self-improvement' is beyond many of the population is evidenced in *DIY SOS* (BBC, 1994–2005) where, following an audience vote, a professional team of decorators enters the private domestic space to clear up a bungled DIY project. Alternatively *Sixty Minute Makeover* (ITV, 2004) operates within a slightly different paradigm: the team of decorators who give homes a make-over are there to assist the worthy poor who have been nominated by friends and relations. They have not been able to undertake the appropriate work that home and identity construction require themselves because, for example, they have been ill or have a disabled child, are always looking after others or are involved in charitable work. Importantly they 'attempted self-sufficiency and an ethic of volunteerism', the show thus is 'rewarding those who struggle without expecting or asking for help' (Ouellette and Hay, 2008, p. 48). However the sheer number of decorators and workman who descend upon the home to provide the make-over affirm the enormity of DIY transformations, as does the articulation of the financial costs involved.

RETHINKING DOMESTIC LABOUR: NIGELLA'S COOKERY PROGRAMME FOR THE NEW MILLENNIUM

Lifestyle increasingly became, as Medhurst has pointed out, the genre of the 1990s, whereby 'dreamscapes have become domesticated' and people 'looked for fantasy and escape in back gardens and dinner tables' (1999, p. 26). Idealized domesticities were reworked in the imagination as they were in the spheres of politics, culture, house purchase and renovation; Forster suggests the domestic sphere, the home, was out 're-idealised as a haven of harmonious order and tranquillity' (2008, p. 104). Furthermore, domesticity was reconfigured to become the renewed focus of a range of pleasurable leisure activities: cooking, entertaining, gardening, renovation, and DIYing. Although this appears to concur with social analysts of the time who suggested that 'Partly as a result of the wide range of home electronic equipment now available, the function of the home has been and still is changing. Both house and garden are shifting from being utilities to being leisure locations' (Leisure in the Home Consultants, 1993).

The domestic genre which has perhaps more than others emphasized the notion of domestic work as leisure and the re-imagining of the domestic at the end of the twentieth century was the cookery programme. This is at one level unsurprising, since food production and consumption has a symbolic significance in the creation of the home and domesticity. In television advertising, drama and documentary, the meal table is often constructed as the heart of the home, food consumption epitomizes ethnic, regional, age, class and lifestyle choices and identity positions (Bourdieu, 1984; Beardsworth and Keil, 1997). The reworking of domestic labour into a leisure pursuit also meant it was not necessarily associated with women in television cookery programmes at the end of the twentieth and early twenty-first centuries' cookery. In 1999 *Nigella Bites* (Channel 4) and *Naked Chef* (BBC 2) had, with more relaxed broadcast personae, visual style borrowed from pop videos and a significant dollop of sexuality, suggested that cooking was a desirable pastime. They offered a 'relaxed' post-modern style of cookery, a fusion of European influences with a heavy emphasis on fresh, or at least pure, ingredients which came to define particularly the urban and younger middle-classes.

Domesticity and cookery have, as has been argued above, always been a focus on broadcast media; what is new in the late twentieth century was the way in which they moved from the margins of the schedules within daytime and women's programming into the mainstream and prime time. A pivotal moment in this move was the shift from setting programmes in the studio to locating them in the home of the presenter. Delia Smith, who rose to prominence broadcasting for the BBC in the 1970s, set the majority of her programmes within her home, and in doing so shifted the programmes from an educative discourse (Strange, 1998, p. 302) to one of personality and lifestyle, whereby, as Strange suggests, 'the specificities of mis-en-scene domestic, private, enclosed, secure – serve as an extension of Smith's personality, reinforcing her solid rooted and reliable presence' (1998, p. 305). Smith's series offered not just instruction but identity, and her first name was included in the *Collins Dictionary* as 'Doing a Delia' became understood to mean down-to-earth performance of domestic cookery.

Delia's down-to-earthness begins to address what Forster (2008) describes as the dichotomy for feminism for decades between housewife on the one side as a desirable status and alternatively as domestic labour which was frequently tedious, unrewarding and relentless. The shift to lifestyle and personality in TV cookery programmes enabled, as Feasey suggests, domestic labour to be 'reclaimed as a masculine leisure activity' (2008, p. 124) and housework was 'reinvented in domestic lifestyle programmes as something more than the drudgery exposed by feminists. In twenty-first century parlance, being a housewife has become a lifestyle choice' (Forster, 2008, p. 112) one of range of lifestyles and identities offered to viewers through broadcast media.

The popularity and multiplicity of cookery programmes is evidenced not just by the mainstream channels, but in the new millennium by the rise of related magazines, road-shows exhibitions and dedicated digital channels. The Good Food Channel won, for example, 'Best Specialist Channel' at the Broadcast Digital Channel Awards 2007 and a plethora of magazines including the BBC's *Olive* all ensure that, as Solier argues, 'The targeting, promotion and production of foodie viewer ... must be considered in the economic and cultural context of the "foodie boom" of which it is both a cause and effect' (2008, p. 75). The leisure component of food programmes is further emphasized by the generic hybrid food and travel programmes and the sexualization of television cookery shows. A number of series in the 1990s by Keith Floyd entitled *Far Flung Floyd* (1993) and Rick Stein's *French Odyssey* (May 2005) followed restaurateurs and chefs travelling to foreign countries in order to sample and teach the viewer about the local food. The camera work in such texts moves from positioning the viewer with the Floyd or Stein as exercising the tourist gaze, talking to locals, watching them acquire, prepare and cook food and the more direct address to the camera as viewers are instructed in how to cook the recipes. Consuming the tastes of foreign foods via television, the accompanying cookery books and occasional actual home cooking, facilitate the redefining of the domestic labour of food production as leisure. In so doing cookery is able to be seen as an enjoyable masculine pastime (see Feasey, 2008).

A further indication that food preparation is now a pleasurable pastime, rather than a chore, is the increasing sexualization of the food genre epitomized by both the success of Jamie Oliver's *Naked Chef* (BBC, 1999–2001) and a number of series featuring Nigella Lawson, beginning with *Nigella Bites* (Channel 4, 2000–2), which present a sexualized version of cookery, through the *double entendre* of the titles, the sensual visual style and the constant tasting, nibbling and cameras dwelling on Nigella placing food between her parted lips evoking fellatio, which led the *Guardian* 'TV Guide' to announce: 'Food is the new sex' (3 November 2001) and a *Daily Mail* headline to inquire 'Nigella Goddess or Gastro Porn Star?' (17 December 2001) (see Andrews, 2003). Food and sex have long been intimately linked, as Pullar's (2001) history of appetite and food has suggested, but the broadcast media embracing of this has positioned in the forefront of culture that the domestic space is an area of leisure and sexual recreation – especially if men and women can be involved in such domestic tasks. Indeed, to Hollows, the constructed personae of Nigella as 'Domestic Goddess' provides an 'alternative way of imagining the women's relationship to food based on the pleasures of cooking and eating rather than pleasing others', a pleasure which is consistent, as Hollows goes on to argue, with the calculated hedonism of the new middle classes (2008, p. 179).

Cookery and food programmes have traditionally presented men as legitimate in their expertise through this public sphere in their role as chef, restaurateurs or scientists, while women's expertise rested upon the private spaces, domesticity, tradition handed down from relations and their experience. In many respects this is so of both *Naked Chef* (1999) and *Nigella Bites* (2000); however, arguably, the setting of both programmes within domestic kitchens of each presenter, cooking for family and friends, domesticates both male and female leisure cooking. Interestingly Oliver's broadcasting career has continued to emphasize his public and political significance of food production. *Jamie's Kitchen* (Channel 4, 2002) attempted to train 15 disadvantaged youth to work in his new restaurant *Fifteen*, while *Jamie's School Dinners* (Channel 4, 2005) launched a campaign to improve the quality of school dinners provided in state schools in Britain.

Another key element identifiable in the expansion and morphing of the cookery genre of the late twentieth and early twentieth centuries' cookery programming was indeed the merging of the public and private in reality-TV series. *Ramsey's Kitchen Nightmares* (Channel 4, 2004–) utilized the generic elements of make-over television on restaurants while other programmes were narratively constructed around the possibility of contestants turning cookery as a leisure pursuit into a foodie career. *Masterchef* (BBC, 2009–) has since 2009 provided a range of amateur cooks with the chance to win the 'coveted *Masterchef* trophy', which is perceived as a fast route into a career in the food industry; something that was emphasized when in Spring 2011 contestants cooked for a range of previous *Masterchef* finalists who were working as food journalists, caterers or restaurant owners. The lack of success of the winners of Raymond Blanc's series *The Restaurant* (BBC, 2007–10) who after a series of weekly trials emerged as potential restaurant operators in partnership with Blanc, suggests that in reality the expansion of domestic leisure into the world of work was less than ideal.

Alternatively Nigella Lawson was seen at the forefront of 'the new domesticity', a cultural phenomenon which some commentators saw as a nostalgic reinvention of 1950s housewifey, which gained credibility from a perceived desire by numerous working women (especially mums) to return to full-time domesticity. For example, *The Times* announced that 'Home is a mother's preferred workplace' (16 May 2002). Critiques of Nigella's television series, books and personae as a nostalgic domesticity of a previous era miss the very tongue-in-cheek performivity of Nigella's domestic ideal which, like that of Fanny Craddock many years before, deconstructs the notion of the naturalness of domestic femininity. As Viv Groskop writing in the *New Statesman* pointed out:

> Her domestic goddess book was not supposed to be about one-upmanship, shackling yourself to the kitchen or going back to the 1950s. It was supposed to be about an attractive kitsch aesthetic that we would all love to buy into for a few moments of the day. The whole point was to give out an amusing illusion of being an old-fashioned lady while incurring absolutely none of the hassle and with your tongue planted firmly in your cheek (5 October 2005).

Nostalgia is certainly one response to the gap between lived experience of domesticity and its idealization, often drawing, as Hollows (2005) acknowledges, upon a familiar trope of domesticity, as a lost skill which needs relearning; previous housewives are mythically perceived to have happily and calmly coped with domestic tasks in a leisurely and competent fashion. Such a trope has a long history and was identifiable in the 1930s and even in the early nineteenth century in *Cobbett's Cottage Economy* (1822), although it does not go uncontested. Julie Burchill, for example, pointed out that 'If my mother had always been in the kitchen, or my father in the garden, I'd have thought there was something seriously wrong with their marriage' (*Guardian*, 4 November 2000), the wave of nostalgia for a previous domestic ideal was, as all nostalgia is, a critique of contemporary experience. Parkins has suggested that the urge for the resurgence of domestic skills such as knitting, and indeed baking, can be seen as 'a reaction to the speed and dislocation of postmodernity part of an attempt to live differently … to find meaning and identity in the practices of everyday life' (Parkins, 2004, p. 436, quoted in Hollows, 2008, p. 130).

The number of people normally working over 45 hours per week had been rising from winter 1992/93, although it peaked in autumn 1997; and continued on a fairly steady decline, despite a pause in this decline between early 1999 to mid-2001. Working hours were not necessarily compatible with childcare, given the increasing expectations upon families and parents in the later twentieth century. One explanation of the disquiet over domesticity can be seen in a survey by *Pregnancy and Birth Magazine* which suggested that many women had serious problems with childcare, the operation of maternity provision and limited opportunities for rewarding part-time work which could be combined with responsibility for children (*The Times*, 16 May 2002). Nevertheless, according to the National Office of Statistics, two-thirds of women with dependent children were in part-time or full-time work in 2008.

Nigella's 2007 television series and accompanying book entitled *Nigella Express* acknowledged the pressures on domestic women and for many the impossibility of achieving domestic ideals, when she announced:

> Most days, I approach cooking supper with less than absolute perkiness, … because at the end of long, working day and after I have wrestled with children's homework and other domestic

> demands and feel that I am nothing more than the sum of impatience and tetchy exhaustion I can't even think what there might be to cook.
>
> Actually cooking is the least of it ... planning, shopping, deciding these are the real drainers (2007, p. 3).

Nigella's lurch to fast food was quickly followed by Delia Smith's book *How to Cheat at Cooking* (2008) and Jamie's *30 Minute Meals* first broadcast in December 2009, the accompanying book led the best-seller charts the following year. The success of each of these suggests that 'tetchy exhaustion' rather than cooking as a leisure activity may have begun to strike a chord with the general public. Bonner suggests that: 'Ordinary television appeals to its audience not only by showing them themselves and their own mundane domestic activities, but also by asserting that there is a better, more exciting ordinary to be had by simple methods, and showing how this is to be achieved' (2003, p. 216). However, in each of these books and television series there is an acknowledgement that for most there is an incompatibility between the domestic reality that families face at meal times and the idealization that they consume through broadcast media. *Nigella Express* (2007) and its clones offered a solution to this incompatibility, discursively constructing the problem in terms of 'time', for many the freezer cabinet, the take-away and stores cupboards of tins may have offered more frequently used solutions.

COME DINE WITH ME: ETHICAL DEBATES AND COMPETING IDEALS OF DOMESTICITY

If Nigella's programmes produce a performance of ideal domesticity, *Come Dine With Me,* introduced by Channel 4 in January 2005, emphasizes that domesticity is a contested ideal that is always tantalizingly out of reach. The programme involves four or five domestic cooks hosting a dinner party for three or four other contestants in turn. As the evening draws to a close each guest reveals to the camera and viewers the score they have given the host for entertaining them. The winning host is presented with £1,000 in cash at the end of the week; bringing a competitive grading system, accountability, measurement and an increasing culture of performance into the domestic sphere. However, the show does not draw upon external experts, rather all contestants both partake in judging and being judged. The score is ultimately given for how close the evening is to participants' own subjective ideal of domestic entertaining. This is however dependent on a complex and contested matrix involving effort and attitude, caring but not too much controlling, and a circumnavigation of the treacherous terrain of cultural determinants which contribute to an individual's judgement of what is 'good taste' in food.

Dinner parties have been associated with a predominantly middle-aged and middle-class aesthetic and cultural capital, the social milieu, as Medhurst (1999) has pointed out, of the majority of lifestyle television. Thus at one level *Come Dine With Me* can be seen as an extension of the governance and 'norms of conduct', the operation of 'a regime of the self and the need for acquiring skills and making the choices to actualise oneself' (Rose, 1999, p. 87). This would be too simplistic; *Come Dine With Me* suggests a more complex picture, not about governance but contestation, ethical debate and judgement. Not all *Come Dine With Me* contestants are middle-class, nor are the middle-class a culturally uniform group. The clashes of taste and sensibilities within the text suggest that idealizations of domesticity are contested. That so many participants, inhabiting so many different domestic environments are confidently putting themselves and their homes forward for scrutiny suggests a broadening of the notions of domesticity, a new confidence in the multiplicity of domesticities that people experience and enact. Viewers look recipes up on the accompanying website or participate in their own untelevised versions of *Come Dine With Me:* 'At the end of each party, we give a mark out of 10 and then each of us donates £5. Then when the final dinner is over, we'll give the money to a charity of the winner's choice, It's a great way to get all the girls together for a meal and a chat' explained one reader of *Weightwatchers Magazine* in an article entitled 'We did it too! Here are two of the Weightwatchers members who've held their own *Come Dine With Me*-style dinner parties' (October 2010, p. 83). This endorses the programme's egalitarian and participatory impetus, the 'voice of god' narration by Dave Lamb provides a strong element or irony and sarcasm which, like the traditional sit-coms, punctures any signs of pretentiousness and begins the process of unravelling contestants 'presentation of the themselves' (Goffman, 1960).

The sense of seeing behind the social construed façade that hosts create is further enhanced to the viewers' prurient glee when, with a certain knowingness, the cameras provide the audience with a viewing of what is hidden behind the host's performance of domesticity. The viewer sees food scooped off the floor, handed in through the window from the local take-away or extracted from packets and passed off as the host's own. Hosting is a staged performance and viewers enjoy being privy to a backstage view, particularly if the kitchen is sinking into increasing levels of chaos and panic, which serve to deconstructs and acknowledge society's veneers of domestic harmony, order and control. A further insight behind the domestic stage is provided when, as the host finishes the food preparation, other contestants set off to voyeuristically snoop in other parts of the home, looking in bedrooms and bathrooms, cupboards and closets or studies and garden sheds. As they test beds, look in underwear drawers, make comments about knickknacks, bathrooms and photos, their critique and judgement is accompanied by caustic asides from the voiceover. The informality of the engagement with someone else's home invites engagement and comment from the audience who, for example, observe the bemused guests of a Stoke-on-rent vicar who has kitsch Christian artefacts and a church bell pull for a lightswitch in his downstairs loo. There is a delightful honestly and an element of subversiveness in these scenes, where the guests break social taboos and exhibit the reverse of bourgeois 'good taste' by invading private spaces. The inspection of the house also ensures that the show merges elements of the property programme with a foodie programme, as viewers are able to observe a lifestyle being presented by the host though food, dress and home. It is lifestyle television and its invasive voyeurism laid bare.

Women and gay men dominate the contestants and definitely the winners, and significantly the programme began broadcasting just a year after the introduction of civil partnerships in Britain in 2004. *Come Dine With Me*, more than any television programme before it, has made gay domesticity every day, introduced an ordinariness to it and brought it into the living rooms of the nation. In this programme gay men and their domestic spaces are not 'othered', that is the position frequently played by straight men whose involvement as solitary domestic 'hosts' suggests other changes in society. Food as a proportion of domestic expenditure has declined steadily throughout the twentieth century from 28–30 per cent during the first years of the century to 17 per cent in 1980 and 10 per cent at the end of the century; although as Benson argues, 'Women's power was weakened too because as income's rose, shopping became less burdensome and other family members began to take more of an interest in consumption, men took on an increasing role in shopping and consumption choices ... so that the so-called "new man," in so far as he existed has his roots in economic change as well as, if not more than, in ideological revelation' (2005, p. 40). *Come Dine With Me*, in following the contestants preparing their dinner party, enables both male and female contestants to display their expertise in purchasing food and wine.

Contestants submit their menu when they apply to take part in the show, before they have met the other contestants or know what they will be cooking, thus maximizing the already existing propensity for choices and responsibility in consumption to create anxiety (Bauman, 1988, quoted in Warde, 1997, p. 69). Furthermore, as Warde (1997, p. 70) suggests, four antinomies of taste, which carry four sets of contradictory messages can be seen in operation in food choice: novelty and tradition, health and indulgence, economy and extravagance, care and convenience. When host and dinner strongly lean towards different sides of these contradictory pairs, a low score is produced; food seen as too traditional is critiqued as not suitable for a dinner party, alternatively too much novelty may result in guests' unwillingness to even try food. The participants are, arguably, navigating their way between, through and around such contradictions, hence there is a surprising propensity to choose a similar range of foods which signify some novelty but which are not unfamiliar to those who eat in restaurants: scallops, goat cheese, monkfish, risotto, meringues, balsamic vinegar, chocolate fondants and panna cotta make frequent appearances, although any individual ingredient or dish's classification in relation to novelty and tradition or economy and extravagance, is structured by cultural, regional, ethnic and class specificities.

Participants make judgements and give scores, with careful ethical consideration of the host's circumstances, youngsters are looked upon sympathetically, especially if male. Conspicuous consumption by the wealthiest is not necessarily appreciated and other contestants often seem delighted when they can pick holes in the performance of wealthier contestants and score them badly. Parsimony is likewise not well regarded; the man with two houses who fed his guests Scotch broth and pigs' trotters was strongly critiqued. Furthermore, the selection of contestants foregrounds contradictions between care and convenience; there is usually one vegetarian, celiac or person who for religious reasons cannot eat certain foods and the degree of care that the hosts place upon ensuring that they are catered for is crucial to the grading they receive. Indeed debates over ethics lie at the heart of the programme. Contestants like to feel cared for, comments refer to the attention to their needs, tastes or wants. Empty wineglasses, being deserted for long periods of time while the host is in the kitchen and wine-buffs who lecture their guests incessantly produce low scores; alternatively one contestant enthused 'I'm going to give Jennifer 10 because her hospitality was fantastic' despite having had, by her own admission, a fairly mediocre meal.

Indeed Hill has argued that reality and factual programming with 'ordinary contestants is used within households to explore ethical models of caring for the private sphere which is' differentiated from competition and individualistic norms of social life' (2004, p. 57) hence the programme has a place within households who are 'negotiating issues of ethics and limits of care all the time' (Hill, 2004, p. 57). Arguably the winner frequently plays a maternal role, perhaps explaining why few straight men win, but it is a nurturing not a controlling maternal role. The demands by a religious woman from the USA that everyone take their shoes off as she had a 1-year-old who was crawling, and was consequently concerned about the cleanliness of the floor, led to another participant removing her boots as she muttered 'Damn I haven't shaved my legs'.

The hosts' struggle to control their own domestic environments is fundamental to the narrative tension of the programme, one struggle is for control over food which often goes wrong, another is over time, on occasions guests have waited hours to be fed or between courses as ovens go wrong or cooks struggle completely out of their depth in the kitchen. There are also struggles to control the conversation, atmosphere and mood. Attitudes to domesticity and precariousness of caring slipping into controlling produces social awkwardness and structures participants' responses to the entertainments provided. Demands that everyone gets in a hot tub, plays games, watches can-can dancers, respects strongly held views against alcohol, eats vegetarian food or tolerates a pet snake that defecates on the table illicit a predictably wide range of not necessarily favourable responses.

In the clash of varied versions of domesticity, attitudes to 'work' can surface as a key area of ethical debate. The work or effort put into the meal is valued; comments that accompany scoring often make a point of drawing attention to food that is too simple requiring limited time or skill. A bourgeois work ethic comes to the fore in the horror expressed at times when it is discovered some contestants have not cooked the food themselves or have had assistance. However on a number of occasions people have won while acknowledging they have not cooked a thing, particularly if there were indications that effort had been expended, shopping, designing a menu, arranging the flowers and hosting the evening. In one *Celebrity Come Dine With Me* – where the prize money was for charity – Christopher Biggins, won despite an uncharacteristically speedy dash to the local supermarket to buy ready-made trout mouse when his had failed to set. Asked in advance if he will confess he exclaimed, 'are you kidding I want to win'. His explanation of extracting the mousses from ramekins in response to Edwina Currie's careful questioning emphasized the performivity of culinary connoisseurship. His admission of not having cut the green beans and microwaved them, as he explained he 'couldn't be arsed', shocked Edwina Currie, while his retort of admission 'I can't tell a lie' led the voice-over to respond 'which is a lie / that's not true'. Arguably *Come Dine With Me* endorses the importance of effort and attitude in idealizations of domesticity, but here caring is placed centrally as the key element in defining the attitude that will construct ideal domesticity. Cooking and feeding people is ultimately valued as a manifestation of caring in this programme, thus endorsing the ideal of the home as haven and retreat from the stresses and strains of the risk culture and increasingly fast and cutthroat public sphere in which both men and women work in contemporary society.

The idealization of domesticity remains intact in the new millennium, displaced into the past, the future or another geographical space. A range of bridges or stepping stones towards the ideal are offered in broadcast media in the new millennium – consumerism and property ownership, the integration of work and home renovation, or personal input in terms of cooking, caring, DIY and home renovation. At one level this can be seen as symptomatic of new discourses of identity which lay emphasis on 'autonomous, self-regulating and enterprising individuals in the home as well as the workplace' (Hall and du Gay, 1991, p. 55) but all these programmes also acknowledge the impossibility of obtaining the ideal. Discursively, lack of time is constructed as a legitimate barrier to obtaining the ideal but the glimpses behind the scenes in *Come Dine With Me*, the armies of assistance brought in to sort out houses in *60 Second Make Over* and *How Clean is Your House?* affirm the viewer's awareness that the ideal is unattainable, just as *Come Dine With Me* affirms that domesticity is a contested ideal.

Afterword: an uncertain future for domesticity and broadcast media

It has been argued that broadcasting, radio and then television, have not merely entered the domestic space of the home but have been structured by that very domestic space, consequently domesticity has continually been a preoccupation of broadcasting. The origins of broadcasting's association with the domestic and with femininity were established in the 1930s and affirmed by the wireless' role on the wartime home front when it served as a link between fractured families. In the post-war period, with the rising popularity of television, increased broadcasting hours and commercialization, a steadily more complex and diverse array of domesticities entered the airwaves and the homes of broadcasting's audiences. Domesticity began to be seen as simultaneously in crisis and turmoil; it was the subject of political governance and increasingly took a place in political programming. The range of male spaces in the domestic sphere expanded from gardener and provider to include, designer, host and cook, while for women domesticity was an increasingly tongue-in-cheek performance epitomized in the popularity of 'Nigella'.

In the new millennium, Morley (2000) has suggested that domestic and national boundaries have been made more porous, less stable in the globalized postmodern contemporary world, although it does need to be pointed out that popular programming on television and radio remains predominantly national. Arguably, for the younger generation it is the web which both redefines and rejects the boundaries and meaning of domestic relationships and spaces, leaving broadcasting, with its domestic and feminine associations, an increasingly marginalized medium;

to some the future of broadcasting itself seems uncertain. There are certainly questions to be asked as to whether broadcast media can remain popular, financially viable or intrinsically intertwined with domesticity in an era beyond Web 2.0, with an emphasis on private individuals uploading and downloading: images, videos, music, contacts and content, contributing to discussion boards or social networking sites. In the 1930s there was consternation over the speed with which radio became a secondary medium: an accompaniment to housework or homework. In the new millennium television is also a secondary medium, the multitude of television hours provided by digital and satellite television and radio enable them to become merely background noises or images, accompanied by chatting, eating, music listening, mobile phone and internet interactions and communications via social networking sites. There are however continuities as well as changes in broadcasting's relationship with the domesticity in the new millennium.

Television and radio may have less significance but they are no longer restricted to the home. When Nella Last's husband in the 1950s had a car radio fitted to provide a mobile soundscape for their trips to the Lakes (Malcolmson and Malcolmson, 2008) it was an early example of the mobility of broadcast media, which was accelerated at the end of the twentieth century. Radio and television have taken their reassuring association with domesticity into a range of other areas well beyond the wartime factories or the late-twentieth-century shopping centres. Any space which pertains to an association with homeliness, comfort and privacy provides a television or access to a radio: caravans, hotels, student accommodation, hospital wards and even waiting rooms. McCarthy has drawn attention to the increasing use of television screens in public spaces from family restaurants to the sports bars, drawing on how they structure the patterns of 'time, duration and repetition' in hospitals, gyms, railway or airport waiting areas (2001, p. 196). The televisual screen also offers reassurance by its association with the domestic comfort of home. Thus the television screen in a bar or dentist's waiting room is both subject to a complex integration into the politics of it is new environment (McCarthy, 2001) and part of an attempt to make such a public space more private and comfortable – somewhere that people can ' feel at home' and be themselves.

Arguably, in the home and beyond, broadcast media continue to be integrated into a range of other activities and is embedded within new media technology. Audiences have always used broadcast media as a focus for discussion, within the home and with friends and family; these possibilities are now extended through the use of social networking sites and blogs. Audiences have always tended to listen or view at times that suited them rather than necessarily choose to engage with particular programmes; the streaming of broadcast media and digital availability has enabled audiences to more frequently view what they want, as well as when they want. The growing awareness of broadcasting producers that their audience is distracted and multi-tasking has perhaps exaggerated the construction of texts to facilitate this; much of the recent lifestyle television is geared to the glance, to providing momentary visual imagery that can be consumed without sound or undivided concentration.

Finally, it is worth pointing out that the future for domesticity also seems uncertain; both a reliance on the state to play a key role in the provision of housing and Thatcherism's property-owning democracy have been seriously undermined by the financial crisis of the new millennium. For many of the younger generation, a home of their own, a personal domestic space, is either unattainable, temporary or tenuous – no more achievable than it was for the heroine of *Cathy Come Home* (BBC, 1966) nearly 50 years ago. The increasing portability of television and radio, and the sounds and images they convey, for many provide a domestic 'ideal', or as close as they can get to this contested and unattainable ideal.

Bibliography

ARCHIVE, NEWSPAPER AND ORAL HISTORY SOURCES

Archive

BBC Written Archives (BBCWA) – including a range of programme files and files on individuals and scripts

British Film Institute Library, viewing and reading rooms and television resource files

Leisure Forecasts (1993)

Mass Observation Archives, University of Sussex (MOA) including:

Mass Observation Day Diaries 1937

Wartime Radio Report, Mass Observation reports on post-war broadcasting

National Office of Statistics material accessed at: http://www.statistics.gov.uk/cci/nugget.asp?id=2145

National Sound Archive

Nationwide Building Society notes for IFAs (2011)

Oral History Interviews carried out in 2002: at three nursing homes in West Sussex, (names have been changed for the interviewees) and individually with Mrs Lynch, Mrs Jones, Mr Eldred, Mr Edwards, Mrs Lordington, and Mrs Selsey

People's War Website (PWW) www.bbc.co.uk/ww2peopleswar/

Talk given by Jenni Murray at Lichfield Garrick (12 July 2010).

Newspapers and magazines including

Daily Herald

Daily Mail

Daily Sketch

Evening Standard

Guardian
Listener
New Statesman
Nurseryman and Seedsman
Picture Post
Radio Pictorial
Radio Times
Red Rag
South Wales Argus
Spare Rib
Sunday Telegraph
Sunday Mirror
Sunday Sun
The Times
Time Magazine
Weightwatcher's Magazine
Western Mail
Western Morning News
Women's Illustrated

REFERENCES

Abbott, M. (2003), *Family Affairs*. London: Routledge.

Adair, R. (trans.) (1948), *From Ease and Endurance*, by Boulestin, X. M. London: Home Van Thal.

Addison, P. (1975), *The Road to 1945: British Politics and the Second World War*. London: Jonathan Cape.

Anderson, B. (2006), *Imagine Communities: Reflections in the Origin and Spread of Nationalism*. London: Verso.

Andrews, M. (1997), *The Acceptable Face of Feminism: The Women's Institute Movement as a Social Movement*. London: Lawrence and Wishart.

—(2003), 'Nigella Bites the Naked Chef: the sexual and the sensual in television cookery programmes'. In Floyd, J. and Forster, L. (eds), *The Recipe Reader*. Basingstoke: Ashgate, pp. 39–48.

Andrews, M. and Carter, F. (2008), 'Who let the dogs out? Pets, parenting and ethics in lifestyle programming'. In Palmer, G. ed., *Exposing Lifestyle Television.* Basingstoke: Ashgate, pp. 187–204.

Arthurs, J. (2004), *Television and Sexuality: Regulation and the Politics of Taste.* Maidenhead: Open University Press.

Ashley, B., Hollows, J., Jones, S. and Taylor, B. (2004), *Food and Cultural Studies.* London: Routledge.

Attfield, J. (1990), The empty cocktail cabinet: display in the mid-century British domestic interior. In Putnam, T. and Newton, C. (eds), *Household Choices.* London: Futures Publications, pp. 55–61.

Ayers, P. and Lamberts, J. (1986), 'Marriage relations, money and domestic violence in working class Liverpool 1919–1939'. In Lewis, J. ed., *Labour and Love.* Oxford: Blackwell, pp. 182–8.

Bailey, M. (2009), *Narrating Media History.* London: Routledge.

Bakhtin, M. (1984 [1965]), *Rabelais and His World,* trans. H. Iswolsky, Bloomington: Indiana University Press.

Bauman, Z. (1988), *Freedom.* Maidenhead: Open University Press.

Beardsworth, A. and Keil, T. (1997), *Sociology of the Menu.* London: Routledge.

Beetham, M. (1996), *A Magazine of Her Own?: Domesticity and Desire in the Women's Magazine, 1800–1914.* Oxford: Routledge.

Benson, J. (1994), *The Rise of Consumer Society in Britain 1880–1990.* London: Longman.

—(2005), *Affluence and Authority: A Social History of* 20th *Century Britain.* London: Hodder Education Press.

Bentley, A. (1998) *Eating for Victory Food Rationing and the Politics of Domesticity.* Urbana, IL/Chicago, MA: University of Illinois Press.

Biressi, A. and Nunn, H. (2005), *Reality TV.* London: Wallflower Press.

—(eds) (2008), *The Tabloid Culture Reader.* Maidenhead: McGraw Hill and Open University Press.

Bocock, R. (1998), 'Choice and regulation sexual moralities.' In Thompson. K. ed., *Media and Cultural Regulation.* London: Sage, pp. 69–116.

Bonner, F. (2003), *Ordinary Television: Analysing Popular TV*. London: Sage.

Boyd-Orr, J. (1937), *Food Health and Income: Report on a Survey of Adequacy of Diet in Relation to Income*. London: Macmillan.

Boulestin, M. (1925a), *Simple French Cooking*. London: F. A. Stokes.

—(1925b), *Second Helpings*. London: W. Heinemann.

Bourdieu, P. (1984), *Distinction, A Social Critique of the Judgement of Taste*. London: Routledge Kegan and Paul.

Bourke, J. (1994), *Working Class Cultures in Britain 1890–1960*. Oxford: Routledge.

Bowers, A. ed. (2004), *Reel Food*. New York/Abingdon: Routledge.

Boyd Orr, J. (1937), *Food, Health and Income*. London: Macmillan.

Bramberg, J. (1989), 'Feed your head.' In Palmer, P. ed., *Domesticity and Dirt: Housewives and Domestic Servants in the United States 1920–1945*. Philadelphia, PA: Temple University Press, pp. 271–81.

Brand, G. and Scannell, P. (1991), 'Talk, identity and performance: the Tony Blackburn Show.' In Scannell, P. ed., *Broadcast Talk*. London: Sage, pp. 201–26.

Briggs, A. (1995), *History of the Broadcasting in Britain: Vol. 5 Competition*. Oxford: Oxford University Press.

Briggs, S. (1981), *Those Radio Times*. London: Weidenfeld & Nicolson.

Broad, R. and Fleming, S. (eds) (2006 [1986]), *Nella Last's War*. London: Profile Books.

Broddy, W. (1994), 'Archaeologies of electronic vision and the gendered spectator.' *Screen*, 35: 105–22.

Brown, M. E. (1994), *Soap Opera and Women's Talk*. London: Sage.

Browne, J. (2005), 'Decision in DIY women, home improvement and advertising in post-war Britain.' In Andrews, M. and Talbot, M. (eds), *All the World and Her Husband*. London: Cassell, pp. 130–45.

Brumberg, J. (1989), 'Beyond meat and potatoes: a review essay.' *Food and Foodways Explorations in the History and Culture of Human Nourishment*, 3(3): 271–81.

Brunsden, C. (2003), 'Lifestyling Britain.' *Journal of Cultural Studies*, 6(5): 5–24.

Bruzzi, S. (2007), *Seven Up*. London: BFI TV Classics.

Bullock, N. (2005), 'Re-assessing the post-war housing achievement: the impact of war-damage repairs on the New Housing Programme in London.' *Twentieth Century British History*,16(2): 256–82.

Butler, J. (1990), *Gender Trouble*. London/Oxford: Routledge.

Calder, A. (1969), *The People's War*. London: Cape.

—(1991), *The Myth of the Blitz*. London: Pimlico.

Callen, A. (1979), *Angel in the Studio*. London: Astragal.

Campbell, C. (2005), *The Romantic Ethic and the Spirit of Consumerism*. London: Writer Print Shop.

Cardiff, D. (1986), 'The serious and the popular: aspects of the evolution of style in radio talk 1928–1939.' In Collins, R. ed., *Media Culture and Identity: A Critical Reader*. London: Sage, pp. 228–41.

Carey, J. (1992), *The Intellectuals and the Masses*. London: Faber and Faber.

Chaney, D. (2002), *Cultural Change and Everyday Life*. Basingstoke: Palgrave.

Channel 4 (2011), http://www.channel4.com/4homes/on-tv/location-location-location/

Charles, N. and Kerr, M. (1998), *Women, Food and Families*. Manchester: Manchester University Press.

Cohen, S. (1972), *Folk Devils and Moral Panics: Creation of Mods and Rockers*. London: MacGibbon & Kee.

Constantine, G. (1981), 'Gardening and popular recreation in the 19th and 20th centuries.' *Journal of Social History*, 14(3): 387–406.

Couihan, C. (2004), 'Production, reproduction, food and women in Herbert Biberman's *Salt of the Earth* and Lourdes Portillo and Nina Serrano's *After the Earthquake*.' In Bowers, A. ed., *Reel Food*. New York/Abingdon: Routledge, pp. 167–80.

Craddock, F. (1966), The Adventurous Cook. London: BBC Publications.

Craddock, F. and Craddock, J. (1985), *The Ambitious Cook: A Lifetime in the Kitchen*. London: W. H. Allen.

Crisell, A. (1997), *An Introductory History of British Broadcasting*. London: Routledge.

—(2006), *A Study of Modern Television*. Basingstoke: Palgrave.

Curran, J. and Seaton, J. (2003), *Power Without Responsibility*. London: Routledge.

David, E. (1984), *Wine and Food*, Spring 1965. Reprinted in *An Omelette and a Glass of Wine*. London: Robert Hale, pp. 28–30.

Davin, A. (1978), 'Imperialism and motherhood.' *History Workshop Journal*, 5(1): 9–66.

Davis, J. (2001), 'Rents and race in 1960s London: new light on Rachaminsim.' *Twentieth Century Brit History*, 12(1): 69–92.

Dent, M. and Whitehead, S. (2002), *Managing Professional Identities: Knowledge, Perfomivity and the 'New' Professional*. London: Routledge.

Douglas, S. J. (2004 [1999]), *Listening: Radio and the American Imagination*, Minnesota, MN: University of Minneapolis Press.

Durham, M. (1991), *Sex and Politics: The Family, Morality and the Thatcher Years*. Basingstoke: Macmillan.

Dyer, R. (1981), *Coronation Street*. London: BFI.

—(1998), *Stars*. London: BFI.

Ellis, J. (2000), *Seeing Things*. London: I. B. Taurius.

Fairclough, N. (2000), *New Labour, New Discourse*. London: Routledge.

Feasey, R. (2008), *Masculinity and Popular Television*. Edinburgh: Edinburgh University Press.

Feiling, K. (1970), *The Life of Neville Chamberlain*. Basingstoke: Macmillan.

Feldman, S. (2000), '*Twin Peaks*: the staying power of BBC 4's *Woman's Hour*.' In Mitchell, C. ed., *Women and Radio Airing Difference*. London: Routledge, pp. 89–110.

Fink, J. (2005), 'The impact of the Cold War.' In Addison, P. and Jones. H. (eds), *A Companion to Contemporary Britain 1939–2000*. Oxford: Blackwell Publishing, pp. 263–80.

Forster, L. (2004), 'Futuristic foodways.' In Bowers, A. ed., *Reel Food*. New York/Abingdon: Routledge, pp. 147–68.

—(2008), 'Revealing the inner housewife.' In Palmer, G. ed., *Exposing Lifestyle Television*. Basingstoke: Ashgate, pp. 147–68.

Freeman, C. (1973), 'When is a wage not a wage?' *Red Rag*, 5: 178–214.

Friedan, B. (1992 [1963]), *The Feminine Mystique*. Harmondsworth: Penguin.

Frith, S. (1983), 'The pleasures of the hearth: the making of the BBC light entertainment.' In Formations Collective ed., *Formations of Pleasure*, pp. 101–23. London, Routledge Kegan and Paul.

Gardiner, J. (2004), *Wartime Britain 1939–1945*. London: Headline Book Publishing.

—(2010), *The Thirties an Intimate History*. London: HarperCollins.

Gay, P. ed. (1995), *The Freud Reader*, London: Vintage Classics.

Giddens, A. (1992), *Transformation of Intimacy in Everyday Life*. Cambridge: Polity Press.

Giles, J. (2004), *The Parlour and the Suburb: Domestic Identities, Class, Femininity and Modernity*. London: Berg.

Goffman, E. (1960), *The Presentation of Self in Everyday Life*. Harmondsworth: Penguin Books.

Goldstein, C. M. (1997), 'From service to home economics in light and power 1920–1940.' *Technology and Culture*, 38(1): 121–52.

Hall, C. and Davidoff, L. (1987), *Family Fortunes: Men and Women of the English Middle Classes*. London: Routledge.

Hall, S. (1981), 'Notes in deconstructing the popular.' In Samuel, R. ed., *People's History and Socialist Theory*. London: Routledge, pp. 88–101.

—ed. (1997), *Representation and Signifying Practice*. London: Sage.

Hall, S. and du Gay, P. (1996), *Questions of Cultural Identity*. London: Sage.

Hartley, J. (1999), *The Uses of Television*. London: Routledge.

Hendy, D. (2007), *Life on Air: A History of Radio Four*. Oxford: Oxford University Press.

Hermes, J. (1995), *Reading Women's Magazines: An Analysis of Everyday Media Use*. Cambridge: Polity Press.
Higonnet, P. and Higonnet, L. R. (1993 [1989]), *Behind the Lines: Gender and the Two World Wars*. New York: Yale University Press.
Higson, A. (2003), *English Heritage, English Cinemas: Costumer Drama Since 1980*. Oxford: Oxford University Press.
Hill, A. (2004), *Reality TV Audiences and Popular Factual Television*. London: Routledge.
Hill, J. (1986), *Television and the Home 1926–1986*. London: BFI.
Hilmes, M. (2006), 'Front line family: women's culture comes to the BBC. *Media, Culture and Society*, 29(1): 5–29.
Hinton, J. (2010), *Nine Wartime Lives*. Oxford: Oxford University Press.
Hobson, D. (2003), *Soap Opera*. Cambridge: Polity.
Hoggart, R. (1957), *Uses of Literacy*. Harmondsworth: Penguin.
—(2008), *Domestic Cultures*. Maidenhead: Open University Press.
Holmes, S. (2007), 'The BBC and television fame in the 1950s: living with the Grove Family (1954–7) and going Face to Face (1959–62) with television.' *European Journal of Cultural Studies*, 10: 427–45.
—(2008a), 'Riveting the real – a family in the raw: (Re)visiting the Family (1974) after reality TV. *International Journal of Cultural Studies*, 11: 193–207.
—(2008b), 'An … unmarried mother sat in a wing-backed chair on TV last night …' *Television, New Media*, 9: 175–210.
Hoskins, L. (2004), *Fiftiestyle*. Barnet: Museum of Domestic Design and Architecture.
Howes, K. (1993), *Broadcasting It*. London: Cassell.
Howkins, A. (1987), 'The discovery of rural England.' In Dodd, P. and Colls, R. (eds), *Englishness: Politics and Culture 1880–1920*. London: Croom Helm, pp. 78–92.
—(2003), *The Death of Rural England*. Oxford, London.
Hughes, G. and Fergusson, R. (2004), *Ordering Lives: Family Work and Welfare*. London: Routledge.
Humble, N. (2004), *The Feminine Middlebrow Novel 1920s to 1950s Class Domesticity and Bohemianism*. Oxford: Oxford University Press.

Huyssen, A. (1986), *After the Great Divide Modernism Mass Culture Post Modernism.* Bloomington, IN: Indiana University Press.
Izod, J., Kilborn, R. and Hibberd, M. (2000), *From Griers on to the Docusoap: Breaking the Boundaries.* Luton: University of Luton Press.
Jackson, P., Stevenson, N. and Brooks, K. (2001), *Making Sense of Men's Magazines.* Cambridge: Polity Press.
Jameson, F. (1991), *Postmodernism, or the Cultural Logic of Late Capitalism.* London: Verso.
Jefferies, S. (2001), *Mrs Slocombe's Pussy.* London: Flamingo.
Jenks, C. ed. (1995), *Visual Culture.* London: Routledge.
Jennings, H. and Gill, W. (1939), *Broadcasting in Everyday Life A Survey of the Social Effects of the Coming of Broadcasting.* London: BBC Publications.
Lacey, K. (1996), *Feminine Frequencies Gender German Radio and the Public Sphere 1923–1945.* Ann Arbor, MI: University of Michigan Press.
—(2002), 'Radio in the Great Depression.' In Hilmes, M. and Lovigilio, J. (eds), *Radio Reader.* London/New York: Routledge, pp. 21–40.
Laing, S. (1986), *Representations of Working Class Life.* Basingstoke: Palgrave.
Lambert, R. S. (1938), *Ariel and all its Quality.* London: Victor Gollanz.
Langhamer, C. (2005), 'The meaning of home in post-war Britain.' *Journal of Contemporary History*, 40: 341–63.
Lawson, N. (2007), *Nigella Express.* London: Chatto and Windus.
Laybourn, K. (1999), *Modern Britain Since 1906: A Reader.* London: I. B. Tauris.
Leisure in the Home Consultants (1993), *Leisure Forecasts 1993–1997.* Sudbury: Leisure in the Home Consultants.
Longhurst, B. and Savage, M. (1996), 'Social class and consumption and the influence of Bourdieu, some critical issues.' In Edgell, S., Hetherington, K. and Warde, A. (eds), *Consumption Matters.* Oxford: Blackwell, pp. 274–301.

McCarthy, A. (2001), Ambient Television. Durham, NH/London: Duke University Press.

McCracken, G. (1988), Culture and Consumption: New Approaches to the Symbolic Character of Consumer Goods and Activities. Minneapolis, MN: Indiana University Press.

Macfarlane, L. J. (1981), *Issues in British Politics*. Harlow: Longman.

MacMurraugh-Kavanagh, M. (2002), 'The BBC and the birth of the *Wednesday Play*, 1962–66: institutional containment versus "agitational comtemporaneity".' In Thumin. J. ed., *Small Screens Big Ideas: Television in the 1950s*. London: I. B. Tauris, pp. 98–110.

McRobbie, A. (2004), 'Notes on what not to wear and post-feminist symbolic violence.' *The Sociological Review*, 52(Supplement): 97–109.

Maine, B. (1939), *The BBC and its Audience*. London: Thomas Nelson and Sons.

Malcolmson, P. and Malcolmson, R. (eds) (2008), *Nella Last's Peace*. London: Pimlico Books.

Mann, J. (2005), *Out of Harm's Way*. London, Hodder Headline.

Marshall, P. D. (1997), *Celebrity and Power: Fame in Contemporarily Society*, South Minneapolis, MN: University of Minnesota Press.

Marwick, A. (1996), *British Society Since 1945*. London: Penguin.

—(1999), *The Sixties: Social and Cultural Transformation in Britain, France, Italy and the USA*. Oxford: Oxford Paperbacks.

Mass Observation (1943), *An Inquiry into People's Homes*, London: John Murray.

Matheson, H. (1933), *Broadcasting*. London: Thornton Butterworth.

Mattelart, M. (1997), 'Everyday life.' In D'Arci, J. and Spigel, L. (eds), *Feminist Television Criticism*. Oxford: Blackwell, pp. 23–35.

Medhurst, A. (1999), 'Day for night.' *Sight and Sound*, 9(6): 26–7.

—(2007), *National Joke: Popular Comedy and English National Identity*. Oxford, Routledge.

Medhurst, J. (2008), 'Minorities with a message.' The Beveridge Report on Broadcasting (1949–51). *Twentieth Century British History*, 19(2): 217–23.

Mellencamp, P. (1997), 'Situation comedy, feminism and Freud discourses of Gracie and Lucy.' In D'Arci, J. and Spigel, L. (eds), *Feminist Television Criticism*. Oxford: Blackwell, pp. 253–72.

Meller, H. (2002), 'Housing and town planning 1900–1939.' In Wrigley, C. ed., *A Companion to Early Twentieth Century British History*. Oxford: Blackwell, pp. 388–404.

Mennell, S. (1996), *All Manners of Food: Eating and Taste in England and France from the Middle Ages to the Present.* , IL: University of Illinois Press.

Meyrowitz, J. (1985), *No Sense of Place*. New York: Oxford University Press.

Mitchell, C. (2001), *Women and Radio*. London: Radio.

Monk, C. and Sargeant, A. (2002), *British Historical Cinema*. London: Routledge.

Montgomery, M. (1986), 'DJ talk.' *Media, Culture and Society*, 8(4): 421–40.

Moores, S. (1988a), '"The box on the dresser". Memoirs of early radio and everyday life.' *Media Culture and Society*, 10(1): 23–40; reprinted in Mitchell, C. ed. (2000), *Women and Radio Airing Difference*. London: Routledge, pp. 116–25.

—(1998b), 'Broadcasting and its audiences.' In McKay, H. ed., *Consumption and Everyday Life*. London: Sage.

—(2000), *Media and Everyday Life in Modern Society*. Edinburgh: Edinburgh University Press.

Morley, D. (1986), *Family Television: Cultural Power and Domestic Leisure*. London: Routledge.

—(1995), 'Television not so much a visual medium, more a visual object.' In Jenks, C. ed., *Visual Culture*. London: Routledge, pp. 170–89.

Mosley, R. (2000), 'Makeover takeover on British television.' *Screen*, 41(3): 299–314.

Murdoch, G. (1999), 'Rights and representations: public discourse and cultural citizenship.' In Gripsrud, J. ed., *Television and Common Knowledge*. London: Routledge, pp. 7–17.

Murray, S. and Oullette, L. (2004), *Reality TV Remaking Television Culture.* New York/London: New York University Press.

National Office of Statistics (2009), http://www.statistics.gov.uk/cci/nugget.asp?id=1654

Nationwide Building Society (2011), Briefing Notes for IFAs 2011.

Nettleton, S., Burrows, R., England, J. and Seavers, J. (1999), *The Social Consequences of Mortgage Repossession for Parents and their Children.* London: Joseph Rowntree Foundation.

Nicholas, S. (1996), *The Echo of War.* Manchester: Manchester University Press.

Nolan, M. (1990), 'Housework made easy: the Tailorised housewife in Weimar, Germany's rationalised economy.' *Feminist Studies,* 16(3): 549–77.

Oakley, A. (1976 [1974]), *Housewife.* Harmondsworth: Penguin Books.

—(1985 [1974]), *Sociology of Housework.* Oxford: Blackwell.

Oliver, J. (2010). *30 Minute Meals: A Revolutionary Approach to Cooking Good Food Fast.* London: Michael Joseph.

Ouellete, L. and Hay, J. (2008), *Better Living through Reality TV.* Oxford: Blackwell.

Paget, D. (1998), *No Other Way to Tell it: Dramadoc. Docudrama on Television.* Manchester: Manchester University Press.

Partington, A. (1989), 'The designer housewife in the 1950s.' In Attfield, J. and Kirkham, P. (eds), *A View from the Interior.* London: Women's Press, pp. 67–81.

Plummer, K. (1995), *Telling Sexual Stories: Power, Change and Social Worlds.* London: Routledge.

Priestley, J. B. (1977 [1934]), *English Journey: Being a Rambling but Truthful Account of What One Man Saw and Heard and Thought during a Journey the Autumn of the Year 1933.* Harmondsworth: Penguin.

Pullar, P. (2001), *Consuming Passions: A History of English Food and Appetite.* Harmondsworth: Penguin.

Purcell, J. (2010), *Domestic Soldiers.* London: Constable and Robinson.

Putnam, T. (1992), 'Regimes of closure: the representation of cultural process in domestic consumption.' In Silverstone, R. and Hirsch E. (eds), *Consuming Technologies*. London: Routledge, pp. 109–15.

Rappaport, E. (2001), *Shopping for Pleasure: Women in the Making of London's West End*, Princeton, NJ: Princeton University Press.

Ravetz, A. (1995), *The Place of the Home: English Domestic Environments 1914–2000*. London: Routledge.

Roberts, E. (1984), *A Woman's Place: An Oral History of Working Class Women 1890–1940*.Oxford: Blackwell.

—(1995), *Women and Families*. Oxford: Wiley-Blackwell.

Rose, N. (1999), *Governing the Soul: Shaping of the Private Self*. London: Free Association Books.

Ross, E. S. (2007), *Travelers, Ladies and London Poverty 1860–1920.* , CA: University of California Press.

Rowntree, B. S. (1938), *Condition of the People*. London: Liberal Publication Department.

Rutherford, J. W. (2000), 'A foot in each sphere: Christine Frederick and early C20 advertising.' *The Historian*, 22 September: 67–86.

Ryan, D. (1995), The Daily Mail Ideal Home Exhibition and Suburban Modernity 1908–1951, University of London Doctoral Thesis.

Samuel, R. (1996), *Theatres of Memory: Past and Present in Contemporary Culture*. London: Verso.

Savage, M., Watt, P. and Arber, S. (1990), *Housing Mobility and Social Stratification*. University of Surrey Department of Sociology.

Scannell, P. (1980), 'Public service broadcasting and modern public life.' *Media, Culture and Identity*, 11: 135–66.

Scannell, P. and Brand, G. (1991), *Broadcast Talk*. London: Sage.

Scannell, P. and Cardiff, D. (1991), *A Social History of British Broadcasting 1922–1939*. Oxford: Wiley-Blackwell.

Schaffer, T. (2010 [2003]), 'The importance of being greedy: connoisseurship and domesticity in the writing of Elizabeth Robins Pennell.' In Floyd, J. and Forster, L. (eds), *The Recipe Reader*. London: University of Nebraska Press, pp. 105–26.

Sendall, B. (1982), *Independent Television in Britain*. London: Macmillan.

Shapley, O. (1996), *Broadcasting a Life*. London: Scarlett Press; reprinted in Mitchell, C. (2000) ed. *Women and Radio Airing Difference*. London: Routledge, pp. 29–41.

Shingler, M. and Wieringa, C. (1998), *On Air: Methods and Meanings of Radio*. London: Bloomsbury.

Shuttac, J. (1997), *The Talking Cure: TV Shows and Women*. London: Routledge.

Sieveking, L. (1934), *The Stuff of Radio*. London: Cassell.

Silverstone, R., Hisch, E. and Morley, D. (1992), 'Information and communication technologies and the moral economy of the household.' In Silverstone, R. ed., *Television and Everyday Life*. London: Routledge, pp. 9-17.

Sinfield, A. (1997), *Literature, Politics and Culture in Postwar Britain*. London. Continuum.

Skeggs, B. (2004), *Class, Self, Culture*. London: Routledge.

Smith, D. (2008), *How to Cheat at Cooking*. London: Ebury Press.

Sokooloff, S. (1999), 'How are they at home? Community, state and servicemen's wives in England, 1939–1945.' *Women's History Review*, 8(1): 27–52.

Solier de, I. (2008), 'Foodie makeovers: public service television and lifestyle guidance.' In Palmer, G. ed., *Exposing Lifestyle Television*. Basingstoke: Ashgate, pp. 65–72.

Sparke, P. (1995), *As Long as it's Pink: The Sexual Politics of Taste*. London: Pandora.

Sparks, C. and Dahlgren, P. (1993), *Communication and Citizenship: Journalism and the Public Sphere*. London: Routledge.

Spigel, L. (1997), 'The suburban home companion: television and the neighbourhood ideal in post-war America.' In D'Arci, J. and Spigel, L. (eds), *Feminist Television Criticism*. Oxford: Blackwell, pp. 211–34.

—(2003), 'The suburban home companion: television and the neighbourhood ideal in post-war America.' In Jones, A. ed., *The Feminism and Visual Culture Reader*. Oxford: Routledge, pp. 329–37.

Spigel, L. and Olsson, J. (eds) (2004), *Television after TV*. Durham, NH/London: Duke University Press.

Stacey, J. (1994), *Star Gazing: Hollywood Cinema and Female Spectatorship*. London: Routledge.

Stanley, L. (1995), *Sex Surveyed, 1949–94: From Mass Observation's Little Kinsey to the National Survey and the Hite Reports*. Basingstoke: Taylor & Francis.

Steedman, C. (1998), *Landscape for a Good Woman*. London: Virago.

Stewart, A. and Burridge, R. (1989), 'Housing tales of law and space.' In Gambel, A. and Wells, C. (eds), *Thatcher's Law*. Oxford: Blackwell, pp. 77–91.

Strange, N. (1998), 'Perform, educate and entertain: ingredients of the cookery genre.' In Lusted, D. and Geraghty, C. (eds), *The Television Studies Book*. London: Edward Arnold.

Street, S. (2006), *Crossing the Ether*. Eastleigh: John Libbey Press.

Sturken, M. (2008), *Tourists of History: Memory, Kitch and Consumerism from Oklahaoma City Bombing to Ground Zero*. New York: Duke University Press.

Summerfield, P. (1986), *Women Workers in the Second World War: Production and Patriarchy in Conflict*. London: Croom Helm.

—(2000), 'Women in the firing line: the Home Guard and the defence of gender boundaries in Britain in the Second World War.' *Women's History Review*, 9(2): 231–55.

Tacchi, J. (1998), 'Radio textures: between self and others.' In Miller, D. (ed.), *Material Cultures*. London: University of London Press, pp. XXX–XX.

—(2000), 'Gender, fantasy and radio consumption: an ethnographic case study.' In Mitchell, C. ed., *Women and Radio*. London: Routledge, pp. 25–47.

Taylor, F. (2003 [1911]), *The Principles of Scientific Management*. Dover: Dover Publications.

Taylor, L. (2008), *A Taste for Gardening: Classed and Gender Practices*. Aldershot: Ashgate.

Tebbutt, M. (1995), *Women's Talk? A Social History of 'Gossip' in Working Class Neighbourhoods, 1880–1960*. Aldershot: Scholar Press.

Thane, P. (1978), *The Origins of British Social Policy*. London: Croom Helm.
—(2010), *Women and Citizenship in Britain and Ireland in the 20th Century: What Difference Did the Vote Make?* London: Continuum.
Thumin, J. (2004), *Inventing Television Culture: Men Women and the Box*. Oxford, Oxford University Press.
—ed. (2002), *Small Screen Big Ideas*. London: I. B. Tauris.
Tolson, A. (2006), *Media Talk Spoken Discourse on TV and Radio*. Edinburgh: Edinburgh University Press.
Turner, G. (2010), *Ordinary People and the Media*. London: Sage.
Turnock. R. (2007), *Television and Consumer Culture*. London: I. B. Tauris.
Van Zoonen, L. (2001), 'Desire and resistance: big brother and the recognition of everyday life.' *Media, Culture and Society*, 23: 669–77.
Wagg, S. (1998), *Because I Tell a Joke or Two*. London: Routledge.
Warde, A. (1997), *Consumption, Food and Taste*. London: Sage.
Webb, Mrs A. (1939), *Wartime Cookery*. London: J. M Dentt and Sons.
Webster, W. (1998), *Imagining Home: Gender, Race and National Identity 1945–64*. Oxford: Routledge
Wernick, A. (1991), *Promotional Culture*. London: Sage.
Wheeler, W. (1994), 'Nostalgia isn't nasty.' In Perryman, M. ed., *Altered States: Postmodernism, Politics and Culture*. London: Lawrence and Wishart, pp. 94–112.
White, M. (1992), *Tele-advertising: Therapeutic Discourse in American Television*. Durham, NC: The University of North Carolina Press.
Wilkins, M. (1975), *Family Affair*. London: M. Joseph.
Williams, R. (1976), *Keywords*. London: Fontana.
Willis, J. ed. (2000), 'Breaking the boundaries.' In Izod, J., Kilborn, R. and Hibberd, M. (eds), *From Grierson to the Docusoap*. Luton: University of Luton Press.
Wilson, T. (2004), *The Playful Audience: From Talk Show Viewers to Internet Users*. :Hampton Press.
Winship, J. (1987) *Inside Women's Magazines*. London: Pandora Press.

—(1992). 'The impossibility of best: enterprise meets domesticity in practical women's magazines of the 1980s.' In Strinati, D. and Wagg, S. (eds), *Come on Down? Popular Media Culture in Post-war Britain*. London: Routledge, pp. 44–60

Wood, H. (2007), 'Television is happening: methodological considerations for capturing digital television reception.' *European Journal of Cultural Studies*, 10: 485–502.

Woodward, K. (1998), *Identity and Difference*. London: Sage.

Wylie, P. (1996 [1955]), *Generation of Vipers*, Dalkey, Co. Dublin: Dalkey Archive Press.

Žižek, S. (2000), *The Ticklish Subject: The Absent Centre of Political Ontology*. London: Verso.

Zweiniger-Bargielowska, I. (2005), 'Living standards and consumption.' In Addison, P. and Jones, H. (eds), *A Companion to Contemporary Britain 1939–2000*. Oxford: Blackwell, pp. 226–44.

FURTHER READING

Abercrombie, N. and Longhurst, B. (1998), *Audiences and Sociological Theory and Performance and imagination*. London: Sage.

Addison, P. and Jones, H. (eds) (2005), *A Companion to Contemporary Britain 1939–2000*. Oxford: Blackwell Publishing.

Aldridge, M. (2001), 'Confessional culture, masculinity and emotional work.' *Journalism*, 2: 91–XXX.

Allan, G. and Crow, G. (2001), *Families, Households and Society*. Basingstoke: Palgrave.

Beck, U. (1992), *Risk Society: Towards a New Modernity*. London: Sage.

Bell, D. and Hollows, J. (2005), *Ordinary Lifestyles*. Maidenhead: Open University Press.

Bell-Williams, M. (2007), 'Gender and modernity in post-war British cinema: a case study of young wives tales.' *Women's History Review*, 16(2): 227–43.

Breitenbach, E. and Thane, P. (2010), *Woman and Citizenship in Britain and Ireland in the Twentieth Century*. London: Continuum.

Brunsdan, C. and Morley, D. (1978), *Everyday Television: Nationwide*. London: BFI.
Cameron, D. (1997), 'Performing gender identity: young men's talk and the construction of masculinity.' In Johnson, S. ed., *Language and Masculinity*. Oxford: Blackwell, pp. 47–64.
Coates, J. (1986), *Women, Men and Language*. London: Longman.
Cobbett, W. (2000 [1822]), *Cottage Economy*. London: Verey & Von Kanitz Publishing.
Corner, J. (2004), 'Adworlds.' In Allen, R. C. and Hill, A. (eds), *The Television Studies Reader*. London: Routledge, pp. 226–41.
Coutts, J. (1931), *All About Gardening*. London: Ward, Lock & Co.
Currie, T. (2001), *The Radio Times Story*. Tiverton: Kelly Publications.
D'Arci, J. and Spigel, L. (eds) (1997), *Feminist Television Criticism*. Oxford: Blackwell.
Day, S. (1998), 'The forgotten "matey's" women workers in Portsmouth Dockyard, England 1939–45.' *Women's History Review*, 7(3): 361–82.
Ellis, C. (2007), *Fabulous Fanny Craddock*. Stroud: Sutton Publishing.
Evans, J. and Hessmondhalgh, D. (eds) (2005), *Understanding Media Celebrity*. Maidenhead: Open University Press.
Floyd, J. and Forster, L. (2010 [2003]), *The Recipe Reader*. London: University of Nebraska Press.
Fredrick, C. (1920), *Scientific Management in the House Household Management*. London: George Routledge and Sons.
Freeman, C. (1973), 'When is a wage not a wage?' *Red Rag*, 5. Reproduced in Malos, E. ed. (1980), *The Politics of Housework*. London: Allison and Busby, pp. 88–112.
Geraghy, C. (1991), *Woman and Soap Opera a Study of Primetimes Soaps*. Cambridge, Polity.
Giddens, A. (1991), *Modernity and Self Identity: Self and Society in Late Modern Age*. Cambridge: Polity Press.
Gillis, S. and Hollows, J. (2009), *Feminism, Domesticity and Popular Culture*. Oxford: Routledge.

Griffen-Foley, B. (2004), 'From *Tit-Bits* to *Big Brother*: a century of audience participation in the media.' *Media Culture and Society*, 26(4): 533–48.

Hermes, J. (1999), 'Media figures in identity construction.' In Alasuutari, P. ed., *Rethinking the Media Audience*. London: Sage, pp. 69–85.

Hilmes, M. (1997), *Radio Voices*. Minneapolis, MN/London: University of Minnesota Press.

—(2003), 'British quality, American chaos: historical dualisms and what they leave out.' *Radio Journal*, Intellect 1(1): 13–27.

Hollows, J. (2003), 'Feeling like a domestic goddess: post-feminism and cooking.' *European Journal of Cultural Studies*, 6(2): 179–202.

Holmes, S. (2006), '(Re)visiting the Grove Family – "Neighbours to the Nation" (1954–57).' *New Review of Film and Television Studies*, 4(3): 287–310.

Klein, J. (1970 [1965]), *Samples from English Culture*. London: Routledge Kegan and Paul.

Letwin, S. R. (1992), *The Anatomy of Thatcherism*. London: Fontana.

McKay, A. (1988), 'Speaking up: voice amplification and women's struggle for public expression.' In Mitchell, C. ed., *Woman and Radio*. London: Routledge, pp. 15–28.

McRobbie, A. (2009), *The Aftermath of Feminism*. London: Sage.

Majima, S. (2008), 'Affluence and the dynamics of spending in Britain 1961–2004.' *Contemporary British History*, 22(4): 573–97.

Medhurst, A. (1994), 'Negotiating the gnome zone: visions of suburbia in British popular culture.' In Silverstone, V. R. ed., *Television and Everyday Life*, London: Routledge, pp. 240–68.

Moran, J. (2004), 'Housing memory and everyday life in contemporary Britain.' *Cultural Studies*, 18(4): 607–27.

Murray, J. (1996), *The* Woman' Hour*: 50 Years of Women in Britain*. London: BBC Books.

O'Sullivan, T. (2005), 'From television lifestyle to lifestyle television.' In Bell, D. and Hollows, J. (eds), *Ordinary Lifestyles*. Maidenhead: Open University Press, pp. 21–34.

Palmer, G. (ed.) (2008), *Exposing Lifestyle Television*. Basingstoke: Ashgate.

Parkins, W. (2004), 'Out of time: fast subjects and slow living.' *Time Society*, 13(2–3): 363–82.

Rowe, K. K. (1997), 'Roseanne: unruly women as domestic goddess.' In D'Arci, J. and Spigel, L. (eds), *Feminist Television Criticism*. Oxford: Blackwell, pp. XXX–XX.

Rutherford, J. W. (2003), *Selling Mrs Consumer: Christine Federick and the Rise of Household Efficiency*. Athens, GA: University of Georgia Press.

Sheridan, D. ed. (2000 [1990]), *Wartime Women*. London: Orien Books.

Taylor, F. (2002), 'From life to lifestyle: the ordinarisation of British gardening lifestyle television.' *European Journal of Communication*, 17(4): 479–94.

Tims, B. (1976), *Food in Vogue: Sixty Decades of Cooking and Entertaining*. London: Harrap.

Turner, G. (2004), *Understanding Celebrity*. London: Sage.

Vickery, A. (1993), 'Golden age to separate spheres? A review of the categories and chronology of English women's history. The Historical Journal, 36: 383–414.

Waters, E. and Waters, D. (1940), *Gert and Daisy's Wartime Cookery Book*. Manchester: Withy Grove Press.

Winship, J. (2000), 'New disciplines for women and the rise of the chain store in the 1930s.' In Andrews, M. and Talbot, M. (eds), *All the World and Her Husband*. London: Continuum, pp. 44–60.

Index